LIFE HISTORIES
AND PSYCHOBIOGRAPHY

Explorations in
Theory and Method

William McKinley Runyan

University of California, Berkeley

D0963498

New York   Oxford
OXFORD UNIVERSITY PRESS
1984

Library of Congress Cataloging in Publication Data

Runyan, William McKinley.
Life histories and psychobiography.

Bibliography: p.
Includes index.
1. Psychology—Methodology. 2. Psychohistory.
3. Personality. 4. Biography (as a literary form)
I. Title.
BF38.5.R86   155   82–6458
ISBN 0-19-503189-X
ISBN 0-19-503486-4 pbk.

Printing (last digit): 9 8 7 6 5 4 3 2 1
Printed in the United States of America

"A major contribution to personality theory and research. This volume is among the most significant contributions to the study of lives since Henry Murray's *Explorations in Personality,* and provides the foundation for a life-course approach to the study of the single-case which is theoretically elegant and methodologically rigourous."

BERTRAM J. COHLER, Professor, Departments of
Behavioral Science, Education, and Psychiatry,
University of Chicago

"Over the past few years Runyan has established his credentials as one of the foremost experts in psychohistorical methodology. . . . If a library has only one book on psychohistory, this should be it."   *Choice*

"The present book, by an author who has spent his academic career examining the value of qualitative, narrative, and introspective methods for the study of lives and draws on wide and catholic reading does much to make the investigation of individual life history respectable once more for academicians."

Science

"The most useful, informative, judicious, and clearly written study of its kind, a book that will do duty in a wide variety of university courses in history, political science, psychology, sociology and the humanities."

ROBERT C. TUCKER, Professor of Politics,
Princeton University, author of *Stalin as Revolutionary*

"A remarkable and pathmaking accomplishment. In a brilliantly integrative and critical review, Runyan shows how we can bring both rigor and insight to the study of individual lives."

ZICK RUBIN, Professor of Social Psychology,
Brandeis University

"It contributes more to the study of lives than any book since Erik Erikson's *Young Man Luther.*"

The Psychohistory Review

"It will serve as a reference, the best available, for a survey and evaluation of the various approaches and controversies concerned with the study of life histories and psychobiography."

The American Political Science Review

For My Mother and Father
Who Gave Without Measure

Preface

This book examines a number of basic methodological and conceptual problems encountered in the study of life histories and in the field of psychobiography. It explores problems in the description and explanation of individual lives, conceptualization of the life course, and the critical examination of case study, idiographic, and psychobiographical methods.

The seed from which this project grew was a one-page outline for a project of applying the scientific method to the study of life histories, sketched in the fall of 1969, my first year in graduate school, in preparation for a first meeting with Erik Erikson. The proposal was, I suspect, too scientistic in his eyes, but on the other hand, not scientific enough in the view of many of the other graduate faculty. Over the intervening years, my conception of what is involved in the scientific method and in the study of life histories has undergone considerable change. My views have both softened, in feeling more optimistic about the value of qualitative, narrative, and interpretive methods in this particular area, and hardened, in the sense of believing that there are criteria and procedures which can and should be used in making these "soft" methods more rigorous and useful. The present volume focuses on descriptive, conceptual, and interpretive issues in the study of individual lives, both because these are the areas of my greatest interest and because, as many would agree, there is significant room for methodological improvements in just these areas.

The process of developing this project into a book has been a long and difficult one. I have, however, been fortunate in having a number of sympathetic teachers, colleagues, and students over the last dozen years who have helped it and me grow. Their influence is gratefully acknowledged. To recognize several of these debts in particular, I felt, as an undergraduate at Oberlin College, that the precise and powerful thinking of J. Milton Yinger was helping to prepare me for some as-yet-undefined project of my own. As a graduate student in Clinical Psychology and Public Practice at Harvard University, the project became more clearly defined, and I profited greatly, both personally and professionally, from the intellectual support and encouragement of my dissertation committee: Edwin N. Barker, Lawrence Kohlberg, Alexander H. Leighton, David F. Ricks, and Zick Rubin. The journey through graduate school was enlivened by the zestful company of fellow-explorer Eric Olson. Professors Ricks and Rubin have also been particularly helpful in subsequent years in the process of turning my initial thoughts in this area into publishable form.

Robert W. White has long been a source of thoughtful criticism and much-valued support, even though we differed somewhat in strategies for advancing the study of lives. I eventually came to follow his advice of turning more to the concrete study of individual lives. I will always be grateful to Henry A. Murray, who responded positively to glimmers of promise in early sketches of this project, when so many indicated that it was not a legitimate kind of topic for a young psychologist to be involved with. His intellectual vision, contagious enthusiasm, and general encouragement have been a continuing source of inspiration.

Since coming to Berkeley in the fall of 1975, discussions with Kenneth H. Craik, Ravenna Helson, Gerald Mendelsohn, Alan C. Elms, Carol D. Ryff, Lonnie Snowden, Jerome C. Wakefield, and Diana Watts have helped to develop my thinking about these topics. Visiting Professor Carl G. Hempel provided an inspiring model of intellectual integrity, fairness to opposing points of view, and personal warmth. His style of combining abstract general principles with vivid substantive examples influenced the writing of the present work.

Unfortunately, it has not all been so pleasant. A number of people reacted to these efforts at understanding life histories with responses ranging from indifference to contempt. At times this was depressing, but at other times it stimulated greater efforts.

For their useful critical comments on one or more chapters of the manuscript, I would like to thank Kenneth H. Craik, Carl G. Hempel, Daniel J. Ozer, David F. Ricks, Carol D. Ryff, and Robert W. White. Alan C. Elms provided richly detailed and constructive comments on the entire manuscript. At Oxford University Press, Marcus Boggs has been a most conscientious and helpful editor, with unusual insight into the author's experience. Leona Capeless has shepherded an unruly manuscript into print with both skill and patience.

Work on this project has been facilitated over the years by a variety of forms of institutional and financial support, including a postdoctoral fellowship in the Personality and Social Structure Training Program, University of California, Berkeley, supported in part by National Institute of Mental Health Grant MH 08268, and directed by John A. Clausen and Guy E. Swanson; the use of facilities at the Institute of Human Development, University of California, Berkeley, courtesy of its Director at the time, Paul Mussen; several Committee on Research Grants and a Junior Faculty Summer Research Grant from the Regents of the University of California; a fellowship to the Summer Institute on "Life-Span Human Development: Interdisciplinary Prespectives," directed by Paul B. Baltes and David L. Featherman, at the Center for Advanced Study in the Behavioral Sciences, Stanford; and finally, the climate and congenial institutional environment provided by the School of Social Welfare, and its Dean, Harry Specht, and the Institute of Personality Assessment and Research, directed by Harrison G. Gough, both at the University of California, Berkeley. I count myself fortunate for this support, and am most grateful to these individuals and institutions.

For help in searching the literature, I would like to thank Sonya Kaufman and Charles Martell of the Education-Psychology Library and Peter Pomerantz and the staff of the BAKER library service. For aid in typing and re-typing successive versions of these materials, my gratitude goes to Margery Selby and Sharon Ikami. Toni Sweet, Ruth Mundy, and Kay Yates also provided valuable help in the final stages of the project.

As a draft of each chapter was completed, parts of it were sometimes submitted as journal articles, with reviewers' comments often leading to revisions and improvements in the original chapter. I would like to thank these publishers for permission to reprint revised or adapted versions of the following materials: Runyan, W. M. "The life course as a theoretical orientation: Sequences of person-situation interaction," *Journal of Personality*, 1978, *46*, 569–593, © 1978 Duke University Press; Runyan, W. M. "Alternative accounts of lives: An argument for epistemological relativism," *Biography: An Interdisciplinary Quarterly*, 1980, *3*(3), 209–224, © 1980 by the Biographical Research Center; Runyan, W. M. "A stage-state analysis of the life course," *Journal of Personality and Social Psychology*, 1980, *38*, 951–962, © 1980 by the American Psychological Association; Runyan, W. M. "Why did Van Gogh cut off his ear? The problem of alternative explanations in psychobiography," *Journal of Personality and Social Psychology*, 1981, *40*, 1070–1077, © 1981 by the American Psychological Association; Runyan, W. M. "In defense of the case study method," *American Journal of Orthopsychiatry*, 1982, *52*, 440–446, © 1982 by the American Orthopsychiatric Association, Inc.; and Runyan, W. M. "The psychobiography debate: An analytical review," in L. Wheeler, ed., *Review of Personality and Social Psychology: 3*, © 1982, Sage Publications, Inc.

Berkeley, California   W.M.R.
May 1982

Contents

PART II   CONCEPTUALIZATIONS OF THE LIFE COURSE

PART III   THEORY AND METHOD IN THE STUDY OF INDIVIDUAL LIVES

LIFE HISTORIES
AND PSYCHOBIOGRAPHY

I

Introduction

There are few things more fascinating or informative than learning about the experience of other conscious beings as they make their way through the world. Accounts of their lives have a power to move us deeply, to help us imagine what it must have been like to live in different social and historical circumstances, to provide insights into the workings of lives, and perhaps, to provide a frame of reference for reassessing our own experience, own fortunes, own possibilities of existence.

In spite of the great popular or intuitive appeal of biographical studies, life history studies have long occupied a controversial position within the social sciences. Adherents of the study of lives argue that it has unusually great theoretical and practical importance. For example, "We are safe in saying that personal life-records, as complete as possible, constitute the *perfect* type of sociological material" (Thomas and Znaniecki, 1927, Vol. II, p. 1833). Or, the study of personality "is most perfectly represented in the study of lives in all their individuality" (White, 1972, p. 2). "As I reflect on my own experience, the life history is the most impressive kind of data, whether one is making decisions or engaging in therapy" (Dailey, 1971, p. xii). Or finally, "The life history is, after all, the basic criterion against which all other methods should be tested" (Allport, 1961, p. 410).

Critics, on the other hand, argue that the study of individual life histories is often based on retrospective and introspective data of uncertain validity, is only the first step in the scientific method in that it is useful for generating hypotheses but not for testing them, has low "internal validity" in that alternative causal explanations can usually be found for observed patterns of events, and finally, has low "external validity" in that it is unsafe to generalize from a study of the individual case (e.g., Campbell and Stanley, 1966; Carlsmith, Ellsworth, and Aronson, 1976; Kratochwill, 1978). There is, in short, a tension in the social sciences between conflicting beliefs about the value of the study of individual life histories and about the nature and seriousness of the methodological and conceptual difficulties believed to be associated with the enterprise.

Objectives

The aims of this work are to explore principles and procedures in the study of life histories, with the intent of providing more secure methodological and conceptual foundations for the study of lives. This requires a careful critical analysis of the arguments of both adherents and critics. An attempt will be made to distinguish exaggerated from legitimate claims for the study of lives as well as to sort out valid from confused or unwarranted criticisms of the study of individual lives. More specifically, the objectives of this book are

1. to provide a rationale for the study of individual life histories within psychology and the social sciences,
2. to examine methodological problems that arise in describing and interpreting the course of events in individual lives,
3. to suggest several ways of conceptualizing the causal and probabilistic structure of the life course, and
4. to critically examine those methods used in the in-depth study of individual life histories, namely, the case study, idiographic and psychobiographical methods.

Studies of individual life histories, whether in the form of clinical case studies or psychobiographies, are faced with a common set of problems in representing the course of experience in a life, in drawing upon background knowledge from the social sciences in interpreting that experience, and finally, in evaluating the adequacy of particular accounts and interpretations. The present work is organized around an examination of these basic problems in describing and interpreting individual life histories and in developing criteria and procedures for critically evaluating such studies.

This effort to explore the relationships between the study of individual life histories and the social sciences is in line with the work of a substantial number of earlier investigators in psychology, sociology, and anthropology, from the initial contributions of Allport (1937, 1942), Murray (1938, 1948), Dollard (1935), and Kluckhohn (1945), to the more recent work of Bertaux (1981), Bromley (1977), Dailey (1971), Denzin (1978), Langness and Frank (1981), Levinson et al. (1978), and White (1952, 1963, 1972). It is hoped that the present investigation may be of interest to all those involved with the intensive study of individual life histories, whether in personality and developmental psychology, sociology, anthropology, psychobiography and psychohistory, or in the clinical professions of psychiatry, social work, and clinical psychology.

Intellectual and Historical Background

A Confusion Between Method and Subject Matter

Controversy about the value of the study of life histories stems in part from a lack of clarity about whether life histories are to be considered as a method of data collection or as a subject matter which can be investigated with an array of different methods. The term "life history" has sometimes been used to mean the story of a person's life told in his or her own words (e.g., Denzin, 1970). According to this conceptualization, it makes sense to talk of a "life history method," referring to the procedure of eliciting and recording personal stories in the subject's own words. As a source of data in the social sciences, this "life history method" has been subject to a variety of criticisms, such as gaps in topical coverage, lack of representativeness of informants, and reliance on possibly inaccurate retrospective reports. For purposes such as studying correlations among variables or testing general causal theories, the collection of life histories was seen as a method of only limited utility. This led to the unfortunate and unnecessary consequence that anything associated with "life histories" came to be viewed with disfavor by a sizable segment of the social scientific community.

In order to understand the approach to life histories taken in this book, it is necessary to distinguish between the life history as a *method* for having a respondent recount the story of his or her life, and the life history as a *subject matter*, namely, the sequence of events and experiences in a life from birth until death. In this latter sense, it should be clear that there is no single life history method, any more than there is a single personality research method, and that life histories may be studied through phenomenological self-reports, archival research, prospective longitudinal research, and experimental research. This book is primarily concerned not with the "life history method" of people telling their own story, but rather with life histories as a subject matter and with problems in analyzing and interpreting the course of experience in individual lives.

Three Levels of Generality in the Study of Lives

The study of individual life histories as a subject matter is often met with skepticism in the social sciences, even in personality psychology where the study of lives has historically received some of its strongest support from the Allport-Murray-White tradition. How, critics ask, can the study of individual lives possibly contribute to a science of psychology? Isn't the detailed study of individual lives more properly the concern of the biographer, novelist, or historian? Put more bluntly, "If you can't generalize from these studies of individual lives, what's the point of doing them?"

According to the classic nomothetic view, the primary goal of psychology is "the development of generalizations of ever increasing scope, so that greater and greater varieties of phenomena may be explained by them, larger and larger numbers of questions answered by them, and broader and broader reaching predictions and decisions based upon them" (Levy, 1970, p. 5). According to this view, progress should be sought through the development of generalizations as wide in scope as possible, which can then be applied in a deductive-nomological fashion (Hempel, 1965) to explain and predict particular behaviors.

There is, however, an alternative picture of the internal structure or organization of the field of personality psychology, a pic-

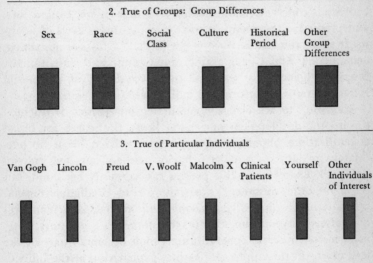

Figure 1.1   Three levels of generality in the study of lives.

ture based in part on Kluckhohn and Murray's classic dictum, "Every man is in certain respects (a) like all other men, (b) like some other men, (c) like no other man" (1953, p. 53). This statement suggests the ways in which persons are or are not similar to other persons. The structure of our knowledge about persons can be seen as occurring on three relatively distinctive levels or tiers (Fig. 1.1).

According to this view, the goals of personality psychology are threefold. They are to discover:

1. What is true of all human beings,
2. What is true of groups of human beings (distinguished by sex, race, social class, culture, historical period, occupation, and combinations of these and other characteristics), and
3. What is true of individual human beings (such as particular

public or historical figures, clinical patients, ourselves, or others of interest).

According to this view, there is order or regularity in the world at each of these three levels, and there is a need to develop universal generalizations, group-specific generalizations, and generalizations applying to specific individuals. The field of psychology is concerned with making true descriptive, explanatory, and predictive statements at each of these three levels of analysis. In short, the field is concerned with the five tasks of describing, generalizing about, explaining, predicting, and intentionally changing behavior at each of the three levels of persons-in-general, groups of persons, and individual human beings.

According to the classic nomothetic view (which is oriented toward the development of general laws), the search for broad generalizations about all human beings will enable us to adequately explain and predict behavior at the group and individual level. Examples of this process can certainly be found, but in many other instances, explanation and prediction depend crucially upon knowledge available only at that particular level of analysis. Anyone who attempts to interpret a life history solely in terms of universal generalizations soon becomes aware of the limitations of this approach. Rather, explanation at the individual level often occurs, not through the deductive application of universal generalizations, but rather through processes such as searching for the individual's reasons for acting in a particular way, through collecting as much information as possible about the individual and looking for idiographic patterns within it, and through organizing information about the case into an intelligible narrative (Dray, 1971; Gallie, 1964).

This is not to argue that these three levels of analysis are completely independent. There can be both trickle down and ripple up effects. Psychobiography proceeds at least in part through the use of general theories in explaining individual lives. For example, discovery of the metabolic defect porphyria in the 1930's made it possible to explain the mental disorders of King George III, which had puzzled investigators for more than 150 years (Macalpine and Hunter, 1969). As an example of ripple up effects, Stolorow and Atwood (1979) argue that the theories of Freud, Jung, Otto Rank, and Wilhelm Reich were based in important ways on interpretations of themselves, which were then put forward as more general theories of human personality. Dukes (1965) surveys a number of examples in the history of psychology where studies of single cases were influential in the development of more general theories, such as Ebbinghaus' studies of himself in developing theories of memory.

The position being advocated here is that the three levels of inquiry are at least *semi-independent*. The solution of problems at one level of analysis will not necessarily solve problems at the other levels. It is widely recognized that generalizations about individuals cannot be assumed to be true at the group or universal level (e.g., Campbell and Stanley, 1966). Conversely, broad generalizations can be applied only with great caution to particular individuals (Chassan, 1979), as the relationship between variables in a group study may be very different from the relationship of these variables within a single individual. Learning what is true about persons-in-general often has substantial limitations in enabling us to understand and predict the behavior of individuals.

As progress within the universal, group, and individual levels of analysis is partially independent of progress at the other levels, our investigative resources should be devoted not exclusively to the study of universal generalizations and group differences but also to the study of individual lives. The present book examines a number of the methodological and conceptual problems encountered at this individual level of analysis. To indicate the background for this work, the next section briefly reviews the history of life history studies in the social sciences.

Historical Background
The historical background for the study of life histories is a complex one, as life histories have been studied with waxing and waning enthusiasm by psychologists, sociologists, anthropologists, and a number of political scientists throughout the twentieth century.[1] While the present discussion focuses on the study of life histories in the social sciences, there is also a substantial tradition of work on the study of individual lives in biography and autobiography,[2] as well as more practically oriented experience with case studies of individuals in medicine and the clinical professions.[3]

Within the social sciences, it is possible to identify roughly three periods in the study of life histories. From approximately 1920 through World War II, there was a substantial and growing interest in the study of life histories, much of it associated with the "life history method," and the study of personal documents (i.e., autobiographies, diaries, and letters). Within sociology, the single most influential study was Thomas and Znaniecki's *The Polish Peasant in Europe and America* (1918–1920). Volume III of their five-volume work consisted of the edited autobiography of Vladek, a Polish immigrant to America. Other significant sociological contributions to the critical use of life history material were associated with the Chicago symbolic interactionist tradition, including Shaw's *The Jack Roller: A Delinquent Boy's Own Story* (1930), *The Natural History of a Delinquent Career* (1931), and *Brothers in Crime* (1938). More general methodological discussions of life history studies included Blumer's (1939) critique of Thomas and Znaniecki's *The Polish Peasant,* Dollard's *Criteria for the Life History* (1935), and a review of the field by Angell (1945).

Within psychology, there had long been an interest in clinical case studies, but within academic psychology, a major boost to the study of lives came from the personology of Murray (1938) and his students (cf. White, 1963). Murray argued that "the life cycle of a single individual should be taken as a unit, the *long unit* for psychology. . . . The history of the organism *is* the organism. This proposition calls for biographical studies" (Murray, 1938, p. 39). Allport (1937) and his students (e.g., Baldwin, 1942; Polansky, 1941) were also influential during this period with their interests in idiographic methods, personal documents, and the question of "How shall a psychological life history be written?" (Allport, 1967, p. 3). The Social Science Research Council commissioned a review of *The Use of Personal Documents in Psychological Science* by Allport (1942), as well as Blumer's (1939) critique of *The Polish Peasant,* and a review of *The Use of Personal Documents in History, Anthropology and Sociology* (Gottschalk, Kluckhohn, and Angell, 1945). Other significant psychological contributions during this period were those by Bühler (1933) and Dollard (1935).

In anthropology, the use of life histories began with a great number of informal life stories of American Indians in the nineteenth century, with a turn to more methodologically sophisticated studies beginning with Radin's *Crashing Thunder: The Autobiography of an American Indian* (1926). Other notable examples were Dyk's *Son of Old Man Hat: A Navaho Autobiography Recorded by Walter Dyk* (1938), Simmon's *Sun Chief: The Autobiography of a Hopi Indian* (1942), and DuBois' *The People of Alor* (1944).

The second period, lasting approximately from World War II through the mid-1960's, witnessed a significant decline in interest in the study of individual life histories. In psychology, the interest in experimental and quantitative methods far outran interest in the study of life histories. In anthropology, interest seemed to peak between 1925 and 1945, and diminish from 1945 to the mid-1960's (Langness, 1965). In sociology, Bertaux (1981) observes that with regard to the question of what can be done with life stories, the answers "have shifted from enthusiasm in the twenties to utter rejection in the fifties; from the strongly positive opinion of Thomas and Znaniecki . . . to the strongest form of critique: silence" (p. 1). The decline of life history studies in sociology during this period is attributed by Becker (1966) to factors such as a greater concern with abstract theory, a greater interest in social structural variables, a greater interest in hypothesis-testing forms of research, and the "customs, traditions, and organizational practices" of institutional sociology which demanded clear-cut (i.e., statistically significant?) "findings" in dissertations, or the promise of such findings in grant proposals.

Work on the study of life histories did not, though, totally cease during this period, as a number of significant works continued to be produced (e.g., Leighton and Leighton, 1949; White, 1952; Erikson, 1958; Lewis, 1961). The study of individual life histories was, however, distinctly less mainstream, received less methodological attention, and was relatively less influential than more popular experimental and quantitative methods.

During the third period, beginning approximately in the mid-1960's and continuing to the present, there has been an enormous amount of work in the social sciences related to the study of lives, much of it associated with aggregate studies of the life course. Important contributions have been made in fields such as studies of normal adult personality development (e.g., Block,

1971; Levinson et al., 1978; Lowenthal, Thurnher, and Chiriboga, 1975; Vaillant, 1977; and White, 1966, 1972), life history research in psychopathology (e.g., Roff and Ricks, 1970; Mednick and Baert, 1981), and life-span human development (e.g., Baltes, Reese and Lipsitt, 1980; Brim and Kagan, 1980).[4] Another stream of contemporary work has focused more on sociological, demographic, and historical approaches to the life course (e.g., Clausen, 1972; Elder, 1974, 1981b; Hareven, 1978), including work in areas such as the sociology of aging and age stratification, social mobility research, socialization research, social-psychological research on archival biographical data, history of the family and of the life course, and demographic studies of the life course.[5] These areas share a common concern for studying how life paths are shaped by an interaction of individuals with their social and historical worlds over time.

Contributions dealing more specifically with studies of individual life histories are to be found in the field of oral history and life stories (Thompson, 1978; Bertaux, 1981), psychobiography and psychohistory (see Chapter 10), and anthropology, which has experienced a renewed interest in life history studies (Langness, 1965; Langness and Frank, 1981).[6] There is, in short, an enormously rich and diverse tradition to draw upon in the study of lives, with much work in recent years examining how the life course is influenced by social structural, demographic, and historical conditions.

This book is intended, however, to contribute to an aspect of the study of lives which is still relatively underdeveloped, that of the study of individual life histories. In many of the fields listed above, life histories have been treated as adjuncts or supplements to another area of inquiry within psychology, sociology, or history. Life histories have been used as vehicles for learning about personality development, psychopathology, socialization processes, culture and personality, history of the family, and so on. The present work, however, is based on the belief that there are benefits in shifting figure and ground, and making individual life histories themselves the focus of inquiry—benefits such as identifying common methodological problems involved in the understanding of individual lives, and directing our attention to a set of questions and puzzles about understanding individual lives which are of both theoretical and practical importance.

The focus of this book is on the understanding of individual life histories as they are encountered in a variety of contexts, ranging from clinical case histories to psychobiographical studies of historical figures. Thus, its intellectual roots are closest to those of personology in personality psychology, to the concern for individuals in the clinical professions, and to the interpretation of individual lives in psychobiography. Other literatures have been drawn from on occasion, as they seemed necessary or helpful for illuminating questions under investigation.

No claim or effort is made to survey all those issues associated with study of the life course. The emphasis is primarily on methodological and conceptual issues involved in the study of individual life histories. From the perspective of a sociologist, a demographer, or even of many psychologists, a focus on the individual is sometimes seen as a sign of simple-mindedness or methodological naïveté, not really adequate for the rigorous testing of scientific hypotheses. For the specific purpose of testing *general* hypotheses, this may be correct, but this is *not* the only goal of the human sciences. The in-depth understanding of particular individuals is also a legitimate objective of intellectual inquiry and one of the fundamental levels of analysis. The study of life histories has much to contribute to the social sciences, both in its own right and as a complement to other forms of research.

The social sciences have made enormous strides in this century in developing experimental, quasi-experimental, and quantitative methods for studying group phenomena. Far less progress has been made in the equally important task of developing our ability to understand individual lives. This book is intended as a contribution to that endeavor.

Preview

A few words about the organization of this volume may help the reader, like a house guest, to find his or her way around the structure. Each chapter deals with a different aspect or facet of the study of life histories, linked by a common concern for clarifying methodological and conceptual issues which arise in the study of lives.

The chapters can be seen as relatively independent pieces and thus can be read selectively in response to a variety of interests and purposes. Although each chapter approaches the study of lives from a somewhat different perspective, they can usefully be grouped into three sections covering, respectively, issues in the description and explanation of life histories, conceptualizations of the life course, and methods used in the study of individual lives.

Two themes appear recurrently in different forms, providing a connecting thread between a number of different chapters. One is the search for appropriately rigorous criteria and procedures for evaluating and improving our understanding of individual life histories, whether in assessing alternative biographical accounts, evaluating competing explanations of the same life event, or deciding among alternative case history formulations. A second recurrent theme is the interplay of rational and intellectual considerations with social and political factors in the process of generating and critically evaluating explanatory accounts of lives, whether in clinical case formulations or psychobiographical studies.

To indicate briefly the topics covered, Part I is concerned with issues in the description and explanation of individual life histories. Chapter 2 examines alternative accounts which have been given of the lives of Jesus, Shakespeare, and Lincoln and explores the possibility and desirability of reconciling these diverse accounts. The issue of alternative biographical accounts is discussed in relation to the notion of the "reliability" of the biographical method and in relation to issues of epistemological relativism.

Chapter 3 examines more than a dozen different explanations of why Van Gogh cut off his ear and gave it to a prostitute. This example is used to explore the logic of critically evaluating alternative explanations of events in individual lives.

While Chapter 3 is primarily on the logical and rational considerations involved in explaining events in individual lives, Chapter 4 discusses some of the social and political processes which, in conjunction with intellectual considerations, influence the initiation, course, and outcome of explanatory endeavors. These processes are illustrated by a psychiatric profile of Daniel Ellsberg written for the CIA and by the inquiry into the death in prison of South African Black Consciousness leader Stephen Biko.

Life histories are most often described and interpreted through biographical narratives, which combine a variety of descriptive, generalizing, interpretive, explanatory, and evaluative statements. The texture or structure of life history narrative is examined in a preliminary way in Chapter 5, with examples from biographies of Woodrow Wilson, Virginia Woolf, and Samuel Johnson.

Part II presents two different approaches to conceptualizing the course of lives, which can be used for analyzing groups of lives, and also drawn upon in the study of individual life histories. Chapter 6 discusses the life course as a theoretical orientation, with an emphasis on sequences of person-situation interaction, or sequences of behavior-determining, person-determining, and situation-determining processes throughout the life course. The implications of this sequential interactionist perspective for the prediction of behavior are briefly explored.

Chapter 7 outlines a stage-state analysis of the life course which is an approach for studying individual differences in the causal and probabilistic structure of the course of experience. A stage-state approach can be used to identify types of life courses and their relative frequency, to estimate the likelihood of following particular state sequences, and to analyze the routes or processes connecting initial states (or initial person-situation configurations) with a variety of potential outcomes.

Part III, the heart of the book, is concerned with theory and method in the study of individual lives. Chapter 8 reviews and responds to a number of common criticisms of the case study method and distinguishes debate over the case study method from debates over retrospection, introspective reports, and quantification. Criteria and procedures for making the case study method more rigorous are proposed. The process of critically evaluating and reformulating case studies is illustrated through studies of King George III and two of Freud's cases, those of Little Hans and the psychotic Dr. Schreber.

Chapter 9 attempts to clarify the conceptualization of idiographic methods, or those methods designed to study individuality, and their relationship to nomothetic or generalization-seeking methods. The discussion takes account of a number of criticisms of idiographic methods and surveys recent developments in idiographic methods.

Chapter 10 reviews in some detail the methodological and theoretical debate in psychobiography as this debate raises fundamental issues of evidence and interpretation in the study of lives. The chapter begins with three sample psychobiographical interpretations drawn from studies of Woodrow Wilson, Emily Dickinson, and Wilhelm Reich, and then critically examines a number of controversial issues in the psychobiographical enterprise. These include the issues of inadequate evidence, reductionism, historical reconstruction, the influence of childhood experience, the trans-historical and cross-cultural generality of psychological theory, the adequacy of psychoanalytic theory as a foundation for psychobiography, examples of nonpsychoanalytic approaches (drawn from studies of Benjamin Franklin, B. F. Skinner, and Malcolm X), and finally, issues in the disciplinary backgrounds of psychobiographers, and the ethical dilemmas involved in studies of living political figures. The concluding chapter reviews a number of common themes in earlier chapters and identifies directions in which progress in the study of life histories has been made and can continue to be made.

NOTES

1. The history of life history studies in psychology is reviewed by Allport (1942) and Murray (1955), with a history of life-span developmental psychology by Reinert (1979); in sociology by Angell (1945), Becker (1966), and Bertaux (1981); in anthropology by Kluckhohn (1945), Langness (1965), and Langness and Frank (1981); and in political science by Glad (1973) and Greenstein (1975a). A two-volume history (in German) on the use of personal documents in anthropology, sociology, and psychology is provided by Paul (1979).

2. The history of autobiography is reviewed by Pascal (1960), Morris (1966), Butterfield (1974), and Cooley (1976). Momigliano (1971) traces the development of Greek biography, and Delehaye (1907) reviews the history of hagiography, or the writing of saints' lives. The history of biographical writing in English is reviewed by Altick (1965), Garraty (1957), Johnson (1937), Kendall (1965), Nicolson (1928), and O'Neill (1935). Critical studies of the goals and methods of biographers are contained in Bowen (1969), Clifford (1962, 1970), Edel (1959), Garraty

(1957), Gittings (1978), and Pachter (1979). One early work which proposed a systematic study of biography was Stanfield's *An Essay on the Study and Composition of Biography* (1813). A useful review of early literature on biography and autobiography is provided by Garraty's (1957) 28-page essay on sources in the field.

Historical accounts of the use of psychoanalytic theory in biography are provided by Mack (1971), Bergmann (1973), and Coles (1975), while methodological issues in psychobiography are discussed in J. Anderson (1981a, 1981b), T. Anderson (1978), Crosby and Crosby (1981), Gedo (1972), Greenstein (1975a, 1975b), Hofling (1976), Runyan (1981, 1982b), Stannard (1980), Tetlock, Crosby and Crosby (1981), and Chapter 10 of the present work.

3. In medicine, clinical histories have been recorded at least since the time of Hippocrates in the fifth and fourth centuries B.C. The use of clinical histories in medical practice is briefly discussed in Calder (1958), Marti-Ibanez (1958), and Sigerist (1958). "The most revealing historical document on the medical progress of an epoch is not a list of its foremost figures or discoveries, but any clinical *case history* made by a conscientious physician at his patient's bedside" (Marti-Ibanez, 1958). Clinical case histories with an emphasis on psychological and social factors have also become established parts of practice in psychiatry, clinical psychology, and social work. In the treatment professions, case histories have been used for research, for administrative purposes, as teaching devices, and as aids for prediction and decision making. Examples and discussions of clinical case histories are contained in Burton and Harris (1955), Dailey (1971), Eysenck (1976), Freud (1963b), Greenwald (1959), Hersen and Barlow (1976), Horowitz (1979), Leon (1977), Lindner (1954), Kanzer and Glenn (1980), Runyan (1982a), Tallent (1976), Ullmann and Krasner (1965), and Wedding and Corsini (1979).

4. Several additional significant works within studies of normal adult development are those by Bühler and Massarik (1968), Maas and Kuypers (1974), Birren and Schaie (1977), Sarason (1977), Gould (1978), and Smelser and Erikson (1980); in life history research in psychopathology by Roff, Robins, and Pollack (1972), and Ricks, Thomas, and Roff (1974); and in life-span human development by Goulet and Baltes (1970), Nesselroade and Reese (1973), Baltes and Schaie (1973), Datan and Ginsberg (1975), Baltes (1978), and Baltes and Brim (1979).

5. A sample of contributions to each of these lines of work includes, in the sociology of the life course, Riley (1979), and Back (1980); the sociology of aging and age stratification, Neugarten (1968), Elder (1975), Riley, Johnson, and Foner (1972); in social mobility research, Blau and Duncan (1967) and Featherman and Hauser (1978); in socialization research, Brim and Wheeler (1966), Clausen (1968), and Mortimer and

Simmons (1978); in social-psychological research on archival biographical data, Simonton (1975, 1976, 1977, 1981); in history of the family and the life course, Shorter (1975), Gordon (1978), Hareven (1978), Elder (1981a); and in demographic approaches to the life course, Vinovskis (1977), Hogan (1978, 1981), and Easterlin (1980).

6. Additional recent work on life histories in anthropology has been done by Frank (1979), Mandelbaum (1973), Lewis, Lewis, and Rigdon (1977a, 1977b), Freeman (1979), Rosaldo (1976, 1980), Shaw (1980), Watson (1976), and LeVine (1980).

PART I

Description and Explanation

2

Alternative Accounts of Lives

One of the problematic issues in the biographical enterprise is the diversity of accounts that are often given of individual lives. For example, Adolf Eichmann has been described as a man with a dangerous, perverted personality, obsessed with a desire to kill, and as "a cold-blooded scheming plotter, one of the gang of hardened Nazis set upon clambering over pyramids of corpses to the pinnacle of world conquest" (Hausner, 1966, p. 4). Alternatively, he has been described as a man whose "whole psychological outlook, his attitude toward his wife and children, mother and father, brothers, sisters, and friends, was 'not only normal but most desirable,'" (Arendt, 1964, pp. 25–26) and as a man whose actions in World War II were merely those of a conscientious and unremarkable civil servant following assigned orders (Hausner, 1966).

A more detailed example of divergence in biographical accounts is provided by the life of Lenin. One view is that Lenin was "the son of a poor schoolmaster who proclaimed himself a revolutionary at a very early age and was thrown into jail and sentenced to the living death of hard labor in Siberia. Then he escaped from Russia and led the life of an impoverished exile in Europe until in 1917 he returned to Petrograd and led the workers in an armed uprising against the Tsar. Thereafter, living calmly and modestly, a detached scholar with no vices, he ruled over Russia as the acknowledged dictator until his death of a

cerebral hemorrhage in 1924" (Payne, 1964, pp. 13–14). An
alternative account is that Lenin

> was the son not of a poor schoolmaster, but of the superinten-
> dent of education over an entire province, a landowner and
> hereditary nobleman who was addressed as "Your Excellency."
> Arrested and sent to Siberia, Lenin lived there comfortably,
> quietly, in the seclusion necessary for his work; he was never
> physically assaulted, and he was permitted to carry a gun. In
> Europe, too, he lived comfortably in middle-class comfort: at
> least three immense fortunes passed at various times through
> his hands. Like other men, he had mistresses, and he was not
> always the detached scholar. When he returned to Petrograd
> he conquered the city with the help of Trotsky and the armed
> forces, the sailors of the Baltic fleet and the local garrisons. The
> Tsar had been dethroned long before . . . and he died of poi-
> son administered at the order of Stalin (Payne, 1964, p. 14).

What are we to make of all this? Is the biographical enterprise
essentially unreliable? Is "objectivity" in the description and
interpretation of lives unattainable? Finally, what implications
does this diversity of accounts have for our understanding of the
biographical endeavor?

This chapter illustrates the variety of accounts that can be
given of individual lives and attempts to identify several of the
conditions and processes leading to such diversity. The discussion
will be organized around three lives that have received some of
the most extensive biographical attention, those of Jesus, Shakespeare, and Lincoln. No single individual can be an expert on
the extensive scholarship associated with all three of these lives,
but it is still possible to draw examples from these literatures
for present purposes. It will be argued that the existence of
substantial diversity in accounts of lives is not the same as
chaos and does not mean that the biographical enterprise is
hopelessly arbitrary. There are major critical standards for biographical inquiry that need to be respected, and it is necessary
to develop a point of view that distinguishes between diversity
resulting from inadequate scholarship and diversity resulting
from different yet supplementary perspectives on the same central figure.

Alternative Accounts of the Life of Jesus

Questions about the life of Jesus from an historical perspective did not receive substantial critical attention until the second half of the eighteenth century. Prior to that time, the picture of Jesus painted by the Catholic and Protestant churches was widely accepted. Within the last two centuries, it has been estimated that more than 60,000 biographies of Jesus have been written (Anderson, 1967). The ironic consequence is that this deluge of scholarship has reduced rather than increased our store of accepted knowledge. It is now generally believed that we know almost nothing about the first thirty years of Jesus' life, and that the established facts of his life occupy no more than a few paragraphs.

Albert Schweitzer's *The Quest of the Historical Jesus* (1910) is a classic history and critique of endeavors to write biographies of Jesus. More recent histories of these efforts have been written by Hugh Anderson (1967) and Charles Anderson (1969), which are also used as sources in the following discussion. Significantly different accounts of Jesus are also found in the Gnostic Gospels (Pagels, 1979), but the present discussion focuses on New Testament scholarship.

One of the earliest lives of Jesus was written by Samuel Reimarus (1694–1768), and published posthumously in 1778. Reimarus, a professor of Oriental languages at Hamburg, wrote a controversial biography aimed at discrediting ecclesiastical Christianity. He argued that Jesus was not attempting to start a new religion, but rather to establish an independent Jewish state. Reimarus selected and interpreted material in the Gospels in order to support this picture of a political Messiah rather than a metaphysical one. According to this interpretation, Jesus' frequent references to the coming kingdom of God refer not so much to a new spiritual kingdom as to a new political state.

In the subsequent history of lives of Jesus, writers have placed different amounts of confidence in the available materials. From Reimarus onward, most Jesus scholars have placed greater reliance upon the Gospels of Matthew, Mark, and Luke than upon John. In the early nineteenth century, the priority of the Gospel of Mark was established. Before that time, Mark was seen as an abbreviated account of Matthew and Luke, while since then,

Matthew and Luke have been viewed as later elaborations of Mark.

Questions about the historical value of the Gospels were taken to one extreme by Bruno Bauer in the mid-nineteenth century, who believed, that "Everything that is known about Jesus is a product of the imagination of the early Christian community, and as a consequence the conception that developed had no connection with any concrete personality called Jesus in the history of the world. Or to put it more succinctly, the historical Jesus never existed" (C. Anderson, 1969, p. 22). Scholarly arguments that Jesus was a mythical figure persisted through the 1920's, but were less frequent after persuasive rebuttals in the 1930's (H. Anderson, 1967).

Within the multitude of approaches taken toward the life of Jesus, it is not surprising that individual events in his life have received a variety of interpretations. For example, three stages have been identified in the description and interpretation of Jesus' movements from Galilee to Jerusalem. Originally, people thought that Jesus had left Galilee because of the hostility of Herod. Soon, however, the Church became dissatisfied with this account, feeling that something as important as going to Jerusalem could not have been determined by external threats. They then concluded that Jesus went to Jerusalem either in order to preach to a larger audience or to present himself in a triumphal entrance to the city as the Messiah, or as the One who "cometh in the Name of the Lord." At the third stage, it was reasoned that Jesus could not have been unaware of what was going to happen in Jerusalem. "Thus he left Galilee knowing that he would meet the Cross in the Holy City, and in consequence that in going up to Judea he would fulfill the divine purpose. The triumphal march was then transformed into a march to execution" (H. Anderson, 1967, p. 72). At the same time details in the story indicating that Jesus was fleeing Herod or that he hoped to spread his message in Jerusalem were not entirely removed from the record.

The place of miracles in the life of Jesus has also received numerous interpretations. Within rationalistic lives of Jesus, three different treatments of the miracles can be identified. In the early period, there was no attempt to eliminate the idea of miracles, although some of the miracles were given naturalistic causes. In the second period, there was a complete rejection of the miraculous, and with this, an attempt to explain apparent miracles in terms of natural causes. In the final period, there was a lessening in the effort to account for all of the miracles through naturalistic explanations (C. Anderson, 1969, pp. 13–14).

As an example from the first period, Johann Hess accepted miracles such as the virgin birth or the resurrection of Lazarus, but gave a naturalistic explanation of the Gadarene demoniacs. Hess said that the demoniacs themselves, rather than the demons, ran into the herd of swine and caused them to go over the cliff. A representative of the second period, Heinrich Paulus, argued that *all* the miracles in the Gospels, with the single exception of the virgin birth, could be given naturalistic explanations. For example, the people supposedly raised from the dead were actually raised from comas. As an example of the third period, Karl Hase provided a naturalistic explanation for some of the miracles, but suggested that other events, such as Jesus' resurrection, could be attributed either to natural causes such as recovery from a trance or to supernatural causes.

The purposes of writers about the life of Jesus have varied over time, ranging from concern with enhancing faith, to ascertaining historical facts, to criticizing the established Church. The nineteenth century liberal lives of Jesus were partly shaped by a desire to make Jesus sympathetic and relevant to contemporaries. A criticism of this movement is that "the portraits of Jesus were in fact highly subjective and fanciful modernizations, in which in turn the idealist, rationalist, socialist, or romanticist created his hero in conformity with his own aspirations" (H. Anderson, 1967, p. 17). Schweitzer (1910) tried to counter this trend by drawing a picture of Jesus more faithful to his historical context, even though emphasis on themes such as Jesus' preoccupation with the imminent coming of the kingdom of God are not easily assimilated by the modern mind.

Several writers have argued that Jesus was psychopathological and have described his life in these terms. A number of such studies are reviewed and criticized by Schweitzer (1913). William Hirsch, for example, argued that Jesus presents a classical case of paranoia. In support of this diagnosis, Hirsch presented the following picture. As a boy, Jesus had unusual mental talents, but was predisposed to psychological disturbance. His excessive

reading of Holy Scripture contributed to his illness. Jesus' paranoid ideas crystallized when he heard about John the Baptist,
the "forerunner of the Messiah." The following forty days in
the wilderness, filled with hallucinations about conversations
with God, marked the transition from latent to active paranoia.
Jesus' ministry was characterized by marked megalomania and
constant use of the word *I*. In believing that the predictions of
the prophets applied to him, Jesus was displaying the paranoid's
typical ideas of reference (Hirsch, 1912). Schweitzer (1913) is
sharply critical of this psychiatric study of Jesus, as well as of
the others examined. His criticisms are that the authors are un-
familiar with Jesus' historical setting and that the material consistent with these hypotheses is largely unhistorical.

In a few pages, it is possible only to touch upon the mass of
material dealing with the life of Jesus. The selections made
here indicate how alternative accounts of the life of Jesus have
been shaped by different sources (different opinions about the
priority of the Gospels), different conceptual frameworks (a
rationalistic or supernatural approach to the miracles), different
principles of selection (selecting data to portray a picture of
psychopathology), and different purposes (writing a life of Jesus
for religious, anticlerical, or historical purposes).

The Life of Shakespeare

What can we learn from Shakespearean scholarship about the
process and problems of producing reliable accounts of lives?
The following discussion is based upon material available in
Bentley (1961), who provides a modern summary of facts about
Shakespeare's life, and in Schoenbaum (1970), who traces, in a
volume of more than 800 pages, the history of efforts to write
biographies of Shakespeare. He covers the search for documents,
the forgeries, the legends, anti-Stratfordians, and the search for
autobiographical elements of Shakespeare's work, as well as the
continuing stream of full-fledged biographies.

A first lesson is that the facts about many past lives are no
longer accessible and seem to be beyond recovery. In spite of
untold years of labor, our knowledge of Shakespeare's life is
meager. Because of the low status of the theater, no contemporary biographies of Shakespeare, or of other dramatists of

his time, were written. Shakespeare's first biography was not published until 1709, ninety-three years after his death. The sources for a description of Shakespeare's life, and particularly his personal life, are severely limited. "Letters to or from or about William Shakespeare have all disappeared except for a few referring to business transactions; diaries or accounts of his friends are gone" (Bentley, 1961, p. 4). A description of Shakespeare's life must be constructed almost solely "from the impersonal records set down with no thought of recording the personality of an individual but intended merely to keep straight property transfers, or to preserve evidence of births, deaths, and marriages, or to keep account of public expenditures of money. Through the efforts of several generations of searchers, one hundred or more records of the activities of the dramatist have been unearthed" (Bentley, 1961, p. 5).

The great interest in Shakespeare, combined with the shortage of information about his life, has led to the creation of numerous legends. With the absence of established knowledge about his personal life, "the temptations to amplify, to embroider, in fact to create an appealing and interesting figure, have been too strong for many of Shakespeare's admirers" (Bentley, 1961, pp. 4–5).

One story is that Shakespeare, as a boy, would make a speech while killing a calf for his father. A second legend is that the young Shakespeare used to hold horses for theater-goers and take care of them during the play. According to another legend, Queen Elizabeth once dropped her glove upon the stage, and Shakespeare picked it up and returned it to her. One other story is that Shakespeare left Stratford for London because he had been caught poaching deer. The truth behind the deer-poaching legend is uncertain, while the other legends are seen by Shakespeare scholars as highly unlikely, if not actually impossible.

The amount of energy and time devoted to the search for information about Shakespeare's life has been enormous. Scholars such as Edmund Malone, James Halliwell-Phillips, and Edmund Chambers spent large portions of their professional lives in search of facts about his life. The intensity of the search can be illustrated by the work of Charles and Hulda Wallace. In 1914, Wallace gave up his salary at the University of Nebraska in order to remain in London searching for Shakespearan documents. For the team of Dr. and Mrs. Wallace, "tedium hardly existed. They worked fifteen to eighteen hours a day. They looked at millions of documents that held nothing for them; eventually, Wallace claimed, they examined over five million records" (Schoenbaum, 1970, p. 648).

Their researches at the Public Record Office in London uncovered a sixth authenticated signature, documents dealing with Shakespeare's legal claim to the Blackfriar's gatehouse, and his testimony in the Mountjoy-Belott case about his part in arranging their marriage. These small pieces of information about Shakespeare's participation in two legal cases have been hailed as the most important factual contribution of the twentieth century to our knowledge of Shakespeare. The excitement surrounding these discoveries indicates the value attached to *any* factual information about Shakespeare's life.

The lust for information about Shakespeare has contributed to the forgery of Shakespearean documents. John Payne Collier, a leading Shakespeare scholar, was found to have inflated his own already substantial reputation by producing a stream of Shakespearean forgeries and advertising them as discoveries. Some of the more pathetic forgery efforts were made by the young William Ireland in an effort to gain the attention and respect of his father, who had a passion for Shakespearean relics. The crudities of the Ireland productions and the flaws of the Collier documents were both exposed, with damaging personal consequences for both men. Ireland's father thought him a dolt and died believing that his son could not have produced the forgeries. At age ninety-three, the nearly-blind John Payne Collier wrote, "I am bitterly sad and most sincerely grieved that in every way I am such a despicable offender. I am ashamed of almost every act of my life" (Schoenbaum, 1970, p. 361).

Some of the problems in interpreting a specific biographical fact can be illustrated by Shakespeare's will, in which he leaves his "second-best bed" to his wife. The meaning of this bequest has often been debated. The opinion of Edmund Malone is that in leaving his second-best bed, Shakespeare "had recollected her, —but so recollected her, as more strongly to mark how little he esteemed her" (Schoenbaum, 1970, p. 174). Other scholars have found similar bequests in other wills of the period, and have suggested that willing the second-best bed was a common way of expressing affection. The second-best bed may have had sentimental associations that the first bed, perhaps reserved for guests, did not have.

One of Schoenbaum's (1970) themes in reviewing the history of lives of Shakespeare is that "biography tends toward oblique self-portraiture" (p. ix). The tendency of writers to perceive, select, and imagine facts about Shakespeare's life that resemble the facts of their own lives can be illustrated by different attempts to account for the "lost years" in Shakespeare's life, from approximately ages twenty-one through twenty-eight, where there is a gap in the biographical record. A former soldier (in a book titled *Sergeant Shakespeare*) argued that Shakespeare enlisted and served in the army during this time. Lawyers have argued that Shakespeare was a member of the legal profession. An authority on canoeing argued that Shakespeare was a sailor during these years and had earlier sailed with Sir Francis Drake on the *Golden Hind*.

A number of amateur scholars have proposed that Shakespeare did not write the plays attributed to him. It has been argued that the plays were written by Francis Bacon, or by Walter Raleigh, or Christopher Marlowe, or the Earl of Oxford, the Earl of Rutland, the Earl of Salisbury, Queen Elizabeth, or Mary, Queen of Scots. Other proposed candidates include a nun named Anne Whately, an Italian, Michele Agnolo Florio, a Frenchman, Jacques Pierre, and an Irishman, Patrick O'Toole (Bentley, 1961, pp. 16–17).

Many anti-Stratfordians argue that the known facts about Shakespeare's life make it difficult to believe he could have written the plays. Their argument, and their account of his life, illustrate again how a point of view may color a biographical portrait:

> This Shakespeare was reared in bookless surroundings by illiterate and poverty-haunted parents who could do no better than educate their offspring at the local free school (if indeed he even attended that). In youth he poached deer and made an unappetizing marriage with a wilting village enchantress. To escape prosecution after having incensed the local magistrate with a scurrilous ballad exhibiting not a glint of poetical power, he absconded to the capital where he found mean employment in playhouses no better than barns. First he held

horses, then he botched up old plays. Someone in a position to know charged him with plagiarism. But he prospered, getting and spending, and ended his days a stout Warwickshire burgher laid low by a drinking bout. Could this most ordinary of men have written *Romeo and Juliet, Hamlet,* and *The Tempest?* . . . Perhaps, rather, this Shakespeare was just such a myth as contemporary—highly respectable—Homeric scholarship was showing the bard of *The Iliad* to be [Schoenbaum, 1970, pp. 555–556].

Although standing as a tribute to the powers of human imagination, arguments for alternative authors of Shakespeare's work typically ignore the bulk of evidence that is inconsistent with their conclusions and indicate the crying need for standards of critical biographical inquiry.

The Life of Lincoln

With the life of Abraham Lincoln, we begin to encounter some of the problems of contemporary biography. Alternative accounts of his life are made possible not so much by the shortage of information, as with Jesus or Shakespeare, as by the quantities of available data. In addition to masses of primary sources, and hundreds of biographies ranging from one to ten volumes, whole books have been written on facets of Lincoln's life such as his paternity, his education, his reading matter, his work as a surveyor, his legal career, the women in his life, his personal finances, his religious beliefs, his political career, his military leadership, his speech at Gettysburg, and his assassination.

Curiosity about Lincoln extended in all directions. An antiquarian interest in his life developed, in which any fact or memento, no matter how inconsequential, became prized. One of Lincoln's biographers, Jesse Weik, received inquiries such as the following: "Did he sweat easily?" "Was he good at chess?" "Did he have piles or hemorrhoids?" (Thomas, 1947, p. 208).

The quantity of descriptive detail available about Lincoln is suggested by the three volumes of *Lincoln Day by Day: A Chronology,* which contain a documented record of his daily activities (Miers, 1960). For example, on February 24, 1844, "Lincoln has trunk rack of his buggy repaired ($1) at carriage shop." On March 5, 1845, "Lincoln buys half pound of gun-powder tea, 75¢." This day-by-day record consists largely of legal activities, financial transactions, and political activities. As such, the entries fail to describe the inner life of the man. The loss of Ann Rutledge, believed by many to be the main love of his life, is described as follows, for August 25, 1835: "Ann Rutledge, ill six weeks, dies at Rutledge farm seven miles north-west of New Salem."

Lincoln's relationship with Ann Rutledge illustrates some of the problems in reaching consensus about a single biographical event. According to the legend, Lincoln and Ann had been engaged, and when she died in 1835, Lincoln was so upset that his friends were afraid he might kill himself. Ann was supposed to have been the only woman that Lincoln ever really loved, and her loss has been proposed as a cause of his life-long melancholy.

To what extent will the nature of this relationship, and its effects upon Lincoln, ever be known? A report of the relationship was first widely circulated in a lecture in 1866 by Herndon, Lincoln's former law partner. Herndon had interviewed the residents of New Salem, and some "remembered that Lincoln and Ann had been deeply in love and that her death had driven him to the edge of derangement; others could recall nothing of the kind" (Angle, 1947, p. 120).

The Herndon account was attacked as improbable by William Barton in 1927. He noted that John McNamar, the New Salem resident from whom Herndon got most of his story, was out of town from the fall of 1832 until several weeks after Ann's death in 1835, just the time when the affair would have occurred. How-ever, Herndon's account was strengthened by the discovery in 1941 of a newspaper story from 1862 that described Lincoln's love for Ann Rutledge and his nearly insane grief when she died. This article made Herndon's story seem more likely, but it was not entirely an independent piece of evidence, in that the article was found among Herndon's notes and may have led him to interview New Salem residents about the affair (Thomas, 1947). The established facts are that Ann Rutledge died in 1835, that Lincoln took her death unusually hard, and that he often visited her family after her death. Testimony from equally competent witnesses conflicts about the depth of their relationship and the extent of its effects upon Lincoln. Thus, the meaning and effects of this romance in Lincoln's life may, unless new evidence emerges, remain forever unknown.

Fraud and forgery have not been as notable in Lincoln biography as in Shakespearean scholarship. One of the few known forgeries has to do with Lincoln's "Lost Speech" at the formation of the Republican Party at the Bloomington Convention on May 29, 1856. The speech was supposed to have thrilled the crowd, but there was no known record of it until Henry Whitney, who claimed he had taken notes on the speech, sold a copy of it to *McClure's Magazine* in 1896. Several Lincoln experts doubted the veracity of this report, and in 1930, when a contemporary account of the speech was found in an obscure 1856 newspaper, Whitney's report was revealed as a fraud.

In the history of biographies of Lincoln, there has been a tension between idealistic and realistic portrayals of the President. The idealists tended to remove imperfections and magnify his virtues, while realists tried to portray Lincoln as he was, with faults and flaws as well as notable virtues. One of the earliest biographies, written by Josiah Holland in 1866, followed the idealist mold and "depicted Lincoln as a model youth, rising through sheer merit and the force of high ideals to the highest office his admirers could bestow (Thomas, 1947, p. 208). This approach was highly popular and was rewarded with book sales of more than 100,000.

In contrast, Herndon and Weik (1889), who wrote one of the early realistic biographies, had to contend not only with lower sales but with public reactions such as the following:

> It is one of the most infamous books ever written and printed in the garb of a historical work to a great and illustrious man. It vilely distorts the image of an ideal statesman, patriot and martyr. It clothes him in vulgarity and grossness. . . . It brings out all that should have been hidden. . . . It is not fit for family reading. Its salacious narrative and implications, and its elaborate calumnies not only of Lincoln himself but of his mother, and in regard to morals generally of his mother's side of the family are simply outrageous. . . . Equally shameful is the discussion of Lincoln's unripened religious, or rather irreligious, beliefs, which he abandoned when he came to feel and know

that an overwhelming Providence was his guide. In all its parts and aspects—if we are a judge, and we think we are, of the proprieties of literature and of human life—we declare that this book is so bad it could hardly have been worse [*Chicago Evening Tribune*, 1889, quoted in Thomas, 1947, pp. 150–151].

While idealists dominated the earlier decades of Lincoln biography, realistic biographers became more influential and publicly accepted by the twentieth century.

Lincoln's life has been a quarry, mined for a multitude of purposes, with different authors pursuing a variety of themes and issues. These diverse accounts illustrate how biographical treatments of a single life may reflect the changing values and concerns of a society. "Earlier Lincoln books—those written during his presidency or shortly afterwards—tended to stress the poverty to fame motif. Then came the theme of the Great Emancipator, followed by that of a saviour of the Union" (Thomas, 1947, p. 307). With World War I, Lincoln came to be seen as a protector of democracy and its ideals. And use of the Lincoln legend continues, as President Nixon, while refusing to release information about Watergate, characterized Lincoln as a man who followed his conscience without giving in to public pressure and attack.

Lincoln was a complex man, and the panorama of Lincoln biography suggests the value of multiple perspectives on the same figure. Different biographers drew upon, and were limited by, their own experience in understanding Lincoln. Religious authors emphasized his spiritual characteristics, while unorthodox biographers were more attentive to his religious doubts. Political colleagues were more aware of his political growth and achievements. Academic scholars helped to get the facts straight, while poets and literary figures helped to reveal the spirit of the man. Lincoln developed significantly in moral and personal stature between his days as a young lawyer, his time in the Illinois legislature, and his days in the Presidency, and different biographers, who knew him at the different stages of his career, have contributed valuable material to our understanding of the full life.

The value of these multiple perspectives is reflected in *A Shelf of Lincoln Books* (Angle, 1947), which contains the work of fifty-eight biographers. "Here are many Lincolns, contrasting yet not incongruous; the same man seen in different points of time and from diverse vantage points; one man in many aspects" (Thomas, 1947, p. 307). Our final portrait of Lincoln is a composite, being "the joint product of several different draftsmen whose combined efforts have given us an essentially faithful portrayal of a subject so difficult to comprehend that no artist could have done the job alone" (Thomas, p. 302).

Interpreting the Diversity of Accounts

How are we to interpret these alternative accounts of Jesus, Shakespeare, and Lincoln? What does it mean to discover that so many different accounts of individual lives can and have been produced? One possible response is to feel that the biographical enterprise is hopelessly arbitrary, and is, perhaps, closer to imaginative fiction than is commonly acknowledged. A second possible response is to think that this diversity of accounts is a result of inadequate scholarship, and that more extensive research would resolve areas of disagreement and lead to greater convergence among biographies. Undoubtedly, there are sources of variety in accounts of lives, such as the forgery of Shakespeare documents or unwarranted interpretations of Jesus as pathological or the deliberate omission of unflattering material in idealized portraits of Lincoln, that are unacceptable, and that ought to be eliminated. However, even after this excess and unjustifiable diversity has been eliminated, there still remains a fundamental core of diversity in biographical accounts that is, I suspect, irreducible, resulting from factors such as differences between authors in theoretical perspective, purpose, relationship to the subject, and available source materials.

This diversity leads to a third possible response, which is to develop or to draw upon an epistemological relativism that is capable of coming to terms with the diversity of accounts. This stance is based upon a sense of the multiple perspectives held by human beings located at different places in the social and historical world toward objects of knowledge, and in this case, toward other lives. As suggested by Alfred Schutz (1962), individual inquirers can be seen as central coordinates in their own subjective frames of reference. According to this view, there are strong contextual influences on the perception, comprehension, and representation of any single life, which may lead to differences between individuals and groups in their perception of a given life and to changes in these perspectives over time.

To use a physical analogy, observers may be compared to constantly moving particles in a gas, which are continually changing their position in relationship to any stable object. Similarly, different investigators will have different angles or perspectives on the same life, and over time will periodically revise or reconstruct their understandings of particular events and lives in light of changes in theoretical perspective, present purposes, personal experience, social and historical context, additional data, and so on. Considered from this viewpoint, it is not surprising that different authors offer different accounts of the same life, or that understandings of a life may vary across individuals, groups, and historical periods.

Does epistemological relativism, or perspectivism, mean that anything goes, that objectivity and critical standards are lost, that Shakespeare can reasonably be seen as a sergeant or seaman, and that any biographical account—no matter how speculative or distorted—is as good as any other? Definitely not. Relativism (or at least the version advocated here) need not conflict with rigorous critical thought. It is necessary to correct "the vulgar idea of historical relativism" (Raymond Aron, 1959, p. 160) and to identify its boundaries and limitations. (For criticism of some of the untenable arguments for historical relativism, see Danto (1965), Mandelbaum (1977) and Nagel (1961).) Relativism (or perspectivism) is frequently contrasted with objectivity, but this can be a misleading dichotomy. A more illuminating comparison is between multiple perspectives or a single perspective, between diversity or uniformity of viewpoint. Just because analyses and accounts of lives are embedded in and relative to particular personal, social, intellectual, and historical conditions, does not mean that they cannot be objective or cannot be rigorously examined. Relativism does not mean that one ignores evidence or throws out procedures of critical inquiry, but rather that empirical evidence and logical inference are employed within the context of a particular perspective.

A statue can be viewed from many different angles, and sketches from different angles supplement rather than conflict with each other. Within any given perspective, however, there are certainly standards for judging a drawing; there can be more or less faithful portraits from the front, from the back, or from the side. A biography is a portrait painted by a specific author from a particular perspective, using a range of conceptual tools and available data. Within this context, the biography can be critically evaluated for its use and interpretation of empirical data, its theoretical persuasiveness, and its literary style. (There is, incidentally, usually no such thing as a "definitive" biography, but rather the best that can be constructed at a particular time with the available materials, which will frequently be replaced at a later time by another "definitive" biography.)

If one grants that lives are exceedingly complex and thinks of different biographical accounts offering different "perspectival views" of that life, then "the advantages of multiplying the perspectives from which one views that object become obvious" (Mandelbaum, 1977, p. 154). "The object of thought becomes progressively clearer with [the] accumulation of different perspectives on it" (Berger and Luckman, 1966, p. 10). As noted earlier in the case of Abraham Lincoln, "Different biographies of the same person—though starting with varying interests, and stressing different aspects of that person's character and career—will, when taken together, yield a more trustworthy interpretation than will any single biography that seeks to interpret his achievement and failures solely with reference to one of many alternative points of view" (Mandelbaum, 1977, p. 167). The optimal biography will often be an integrative or synthetic one, which recognizes and takes into account a variety of more particular perspectives, weaving them into a more comprehensive and multifaceted representation of the life.

Conclusion

It should be abundantly clear that the facts of a life do not uniquely determine any single biographical account.[1] The position argued for here is that alternative biographical accounts are not necessarily indications of inadequate scholarship, but may reflect different yet supplementary perspectives on the same central figure, and that rigorous critical standards can and should be employed within any given perspective. Due to changes in theoretical perspective, available evidence, authors' purposes, and the characteristics of audiences, a continuing diversity in biographical accounts seems inevitable. This should not be misinterpreted to mean that any biographical account is as good as any other one. Most people would agree that, other things being equal, those accounts based on the most extensive body of evidence, best incorporating the variety of relevant perspectives, and most effectively organized and interpreted, are to be preferred.

Even though agreement on such general evaluative criteria may be relatively easy to reach, it can be complicated applying them in specific instances. The next chapter explores in greater detail the problem of critically evaluating the range of interpretations of a single life event.

NOTES

1. Further illustrations of this point are provided by the history of alternative biographies of Jefferson (Peterson, 1960), Rimbaud (Etiemble, 1961), and Freud (Sulloway, 1979).

3

Why Did Van Gogh Cut off His Ear? The Problem of Alternative Explanations in Psychobiography

Late Sunday evening December 23, 1888, Vincent Van Gogh, then thirty-five years old, cut off the lower half of his left ear and took it to a brothel, where he asked for a prostitute named Rachel and handed the ear to her, requesting that she "keep this object carefully."

How is this extraordinary event to be accounted for? Over the years a variety of explanations have been proposed, and more than a dozen of them will be sketched below. Is one of these explanations uniquely true, are all of them true in some way, or perhaps, are none of them true? What criteria and procedures are there for critically evaluating and deciding among these alternative interpretations? This incident is examined in order to explore the problem of alternative explanations in the study of individual lives, a problem of central importance in psychobiography (Anderson, 1981a; Crosby, 1979), in personality psychology (Allport, 1961; Hogan, 1976; Murray, 1938), and in the clinical professions (Horowitz, 1979; Spence, 1976).

A Variety of Explanations

1. One explanation of Van Gogh's behavior is that he was frustrated by two recent events: the engagement of his brother Theo, to whom he was very attached, and the failure of an attempt to establish a working and living relationship with Paul Gauguin.

The aggressive impulses aroused by these frustrations were first directed at Gauguin, but then were turned against himself (Lubin, 1972).

2. A second interpretation is that the self-mutilation resulted from a conflict over homosexual impulses aroused by the presence of Gauguin. According to this account, the ear was a phallic symbol (the Dutch slang word for penis, *lul,* resembled the Dutch word for ear, *lel*), and the act was a symbolic self-castration (Lubin, 1972; Westerman Holstijn, 1951).

3. A third explanation is in terms of Oedipal themes. Van Gogh was sharing a house with Gauguin, and Gauguin reported that on the day before the ear mutilation Van Gogh had threatened him with a razor but, under Gauguin's powerful gaze, had then run away. According to this interpretation, Gauguin represented Van Gogh's hated father and that, failing in his initial threat, Van Gogh "finally gratified his extraordinary resentment and hate for his father by deflecting the hatred onto his own person. In so doing Van Gogh committed, in phantasy, an act of violence on his father with whom he identified himself and at the same time he punished himself for committing the act" (Schnier, 1950, p. 153). Then "in depositing his symbolic organ at the brothel he also fulfilled his wish to have his mother" (pp. 153–154).

4. Another interpretation is that Van Gogh was influenced by bullfights he had seen in Arles. In such events the matador is given the ear of the bull as an award, displays his prize to the crowd, and then gives it to the lady of his choice. The proponent of this interpretation, J. Olivier (in Lubin, 1972), says: "I am absolutely convinced that Van Gogh was deeply impressed by this practice. . . . Van Gogh cut off the ear, his own ear, as if he were at the same time the vanquished bull and the victorious matador. A confusion in the mind of one person between the vanquished and the vanquisher" (p. 158). Then, like the matador, Van Gogh presented the ear to a lady of his choice. (The following explanations, unless otherwise noted, are also from Lubin's (1972) comprehensive analysis.)

5. In the months preceding Van Gogh's self-mutilation, there were fifteen articles in the local paper about Jack the Ripper, who mutilated the bodies of prostitutes, sometimes cutting off their ears. "These crimes gave rise to emulators, and Vincent

may have been one of them. As a masochist instead of a sadist, however, it is conceivable that he would reverse Jack's act by mutilating himself and bringing the ear to a prostitute" (Lubin, 1972, p. 159).

6. Van Gogh was emotionally and financially dependent on his brother Theo, and usually spent the Christmas holidays with him. This year, however, Vincent learned that Theo would spend the holiday with his new fiancée and her family. One interpretation suggests that Van Gogh's self-mutilation was an unconscious strategy for holding on to his brother's attention, and a way of getting Theo to come and care for him rather than spending the holidays with his fiancée.

7. Van Gogh had recently been painting a picture of a woman rocking a cradle, using Madame Roulins as his model. He felt great affection for the Roulins family and may have envied the love and attention their children received. In mutilating himself, Van Gogh may have been attempting to obtain care and love from these substitute parents. The immediate response of Madame Roulins is not known, but Monsieur Roulins came to Van Gogh's aid on the night of the injury and helped to care for him afterward.

8. Van Gogh had a great sympathy for prostitutes and identified with their status as social outcasts. One suggestion is that his self-mutilation was a reflection of this identification. "In June, just a few months before butchering his ear, he had written that 'the whore is like meat in a butcher shop': when he treated his own body as 'meat in a butcher's shop,' he reversed their roles, identified himself with the whore, and showed his sympathy for her" (Lubin, 1972, p. 169).

9. Vincent felt that his mother saw him as too rough and as a bad boy. During the psychotic state surrounding this incident, primitive symbolic thought processes may have led Van Gogh to cut off his ear from a desire to be perceived more positively by his mother. "Because the unconscious mind tends to regard protuberances as masculine and aggressive, removing the protuberant part of the ear may have been to inform the prostitute, a substitute for his mother, that he was not an aggressive, hurtful male—the 'rough' boy whom his mother disliked—but helpless, penetrable, the victim of a hurt" (Lubin, 1972, p. 173).

10. It is likely that Van Gogh experienced frightening audi-

tory hallucinations during his psychotic attack similar to those he experienced in other attacks. Afterward, while in the sanatorium, he wrote that other patients heard strange sounds and voices as he had and speculated in one case that this was probably due to a disease of nerves in the ear. Thus, in a psychotic state, Van Gogh could have felt that his own ear was diseased and cut it off to silence the disturbing sounds.

11. In the Garden of Gethsemane scene in the Bible, Simon Peter cut off the ear of Malchus, a servant of the high priest, who had come to seize Christ. This scene had been on Van Gogh's mind. He attempted to paint it in the summer of 1888, and also mentioned it in a letter to his sister in October. In his delirium, Van Gogh may have acted out the scene at Gethsemane, carrying out the roles of both victim and aggressor.

12. Another explanation is that Vincent identified with the crucified Jesus and that the Virgin Mary lamenting over the dead body of Christ represented Vincent's mother. "In giving the mother surrogate, Rachel, a dead segment of his body, Vincent symbolically repeated the scene on Calvary" (Lubin, 1972, p. 179).

13. Vincent Van Gogh lived in the shadow of a dead brother, also named Vincent, who died at birth exactly one year before Vincent the painter was born. It is suggested that Vincent had the feeling he was unloved by a mother who continued to grieve over an idealized lost son. Killing part of himself may have been an attempt to win his mother's love. Vincent's self-mutilation "represented a symbolic death, exhibiting Vincent in the image of his dead brother, the first Vincent—someone mother adored. As a gift, the severed ear was specifically the gift of a baby, a dead baby. Thus it was both a reliving of wishes to unite him with mother and a bitter mockery of his mother's attachment to her dead son" (Lubin, 1972, pp. 182–183.)

What To Make of These Alternative Explanations?

Here are thirteen different psychodynamic explanations for why Van Gogh cut off his ear and gave it to a prostitute, and additional interpretations have been proposed (Lubin, 1972; Nagera, 1967; Schneider, 1950; Schnier, 1950; Untermeyer, 1955; Westerman Holstijn, 1951). There is a substantial list of explanations for Van Gogh's disturbances which also consider biological factors (Monroe, 1978; Tralbaut, 1969). How should we interpret these alternative explanations? Are all of them true, are some true and some false, or, perhaps, are none of them true? Do the various explanations conflict, so that if one is chosen then one or more of the others must be rejected, or do a number of them supplement each other? Is there, perhaps, some other explanation that would replace all of these possibilities? Do we end up with a feeling that we understand Van Gogh's behavior, that we know why he acted as he did?

Individuals may vary widely in their responses to this material. From one point of view, it is a richly woven tapestry connecting a single event to many themes, conflicts, symbols, and unconscious wishes and processes in Van Gogh's life. According to the principle of "overdetermination," which suggests that actions typically have multiple causes and meanings, this material can be seen as a rich set of complementary explanations for Van Gogh's behavior. Lubin (1972) for example, after discussing a number of possible explanations, suggests that "there may be truth in all of these suggestions. One's motivations include the superficial factors that are well known to oneself as well as deep, troubling factors that one would vehemently deny when confronted with them. Man carries his conflicts from one period of life to the next, and each stage of development puts its mark on the next" (p. 163). From the standpoint of overdetermination, it would be surprising to find a single explanation for any human action, and events can be expected to have more than one cause, more than one meaning. At other points, Lubin states that "various aspects of Vincent's life converged in this single episode" (p. 155) and that what we have is a set of "interrelated" explanations (p. 182).

A second way of making sense of these multiple explanations is to note that several of the different explanations are concerned with different aspects or features of the larger episode. For example, the choice of an ear may have been related to Van Gogh's observation of bullfights, the fact that it happened at Christmastime may have been associated with the presentation of the ear as a gift, and his choice of a prostitute as the recipient may have been related to recent publicized accounts of Jack the Ripper. A substantial number of interpretations, however, are concerned with similar aspects of the event. His choice of the ear has been related to his observation of bullfights, the newspaper accounts of Jack the Ripper, the ear as a phallic symbol, a belief that auditory hallucinations may have come from diseased nerves in the ear, and his concern with the Gethsemane scene.

A third approach is to work from the assumption that several of these explanations may be valid while the others are not, and that procedures for critically evaluating alternative explanations are needed in order to assess their relative credibility. The doctrine of overdetermination may be correct in that psychological events often have multiple causes and meanings, but to assume that all possible interpretations "are ultimately members of one happy family is to abandon critical thinking altogether" (Hirsch, 1967, p. 164). For therapeutic purposes, it may be useful to explore as many meanings as possible for a single event, but for scientific or explanatory purposes, it is necessary both to critically assess the plausibility of alternative explanations and then to examine the extent to which the remaining explanations supplement or conflict with one another.

A fourth possible response is to think that all of this symbolic interpretation is somewhat arbitrary, perhaps even hopelessly arbitrary. If interpretations can be generated merely by noting similarities between the event in question and earlier events and experiences, then connections "are embarrassingly easy to find" and "the number of possible (and plausible) explanations is infinite" (Spence, 1976, pp. 377, 379). It can be argued that the process of interpretation is so loose and flexible that it can be used to explain anything, and its opposite, not only once but in many different ways. A milder version of this criticism is that the process of psychodynamic interpretation is perfectly legitimate but that it has been used with insufficient constraint in this particular example.

The Critical Evaluation of Explanatory Conjectures

This incident forcefully raises several basic questions about the logic of explanation in psychobiography. What procedures exist, or can be developed, for critically evaluating alternative explanations of life events? How can we know whether we do or do not have a "good" explanation of a particular event or set of events in a life history? The Van Gogh example is useful in that it pushes the explanatory endeavor further than usual by suggesting a wide range of possible interpretations, with supporting evidence for each. In doing so, it raises with unusual clarity questions about the generation of explanatory hypotheses, about the critical evaluation of such hypotheses, and about the choice among, or integration of, a variety of explanatory possibilities.

It seems helpful, following Popper (1962), to distinguish between the processes of conjecture and refutation and to make a distinction between the processes of generating and critically evaluating explanatory conjectures. The literature on Van Gogh provides an excellent example of the processes of explanatory conjecture, and can also be used to illustrate the process of critically evaluating such conjectures. Consider, for example, the hypothesis that Van Gogh may have been influenced by contemporary newspaper accounts of Jack the Ripper. This particular explanation depends on the assumption that Van Gogh read these stories in the local paper, that he noticed the ear-cutting detail mentioned in two of the fifteen stories, that it made a lasting impression on him, and that it influenced him the night he mutilated his own ear. This explanation depends on a chain of assumptions, none of which has direct empirical support, which leaves this particular conjecture relatively unsubstantiated.

In comparison, the probability that he was influenced in his actions by visions of a matador and bull may be somewhat higher (although still perhaps low on an absolute basis) in that his letters indicate that he had attended bullfights in Arles. There is evidence that he had at least witnessed this scene, and that it had made an impression on him, whereas we can only presume that he may have read about Jack the Ripper and his cutting of ears.

Consider also the theory that he identified with a prostitute by treating his own body like meat in a butcher shop. The phrase "the whore is like meat in a butcher's shop" occurred in a letter in June of 1888, six months before the ear-cutting incident. Without further supporting evidence that this image occurred to Van Gogh nearer in time to the ear-cutting incident, there is little reason to believe that it played a significant part in his self-mutilation.

Part of the evidence supporting an Oedipal interpretation of the incident also seems open to question. Gauguin did not report that Van Gogh threatened him with a razor until fifteen years after the incident; indeed, in Gauguin's account to a friend four days after the event, this was not mentioned. Gauguin left Arles for Paris immediately after Van Gogh's self-mutilation. It has been suggested by Rewald (1956) that Gauguin was concerned about the propriety of his conduct, and may have invented the threat story later as a justification for having abandoned Van Gogh in a moment of crisis.

In yet another explanation, Untermeyer (1955) suggested that Van Gogh "had cut off an ear and sent it to one of the prostitutes he and Gauguin had visited. It was a Christmas present, a return for being teased about his over-sized ears" (p. 235). There are several reasons for being suspicious of this particular explanation. As far as I have been able to determine, there is no evidence that Van Gogh was teased by the prostitute about the size of his ears. This highly relevant circumstance is not mentioned in such primary sources as Van Gogh's letters or Gauguin's memoirs or in far more extensive biographies of Van Gogh, such as Tralbaut's (1969) or Lubin's (1972), which contain detailed analyses of the ear-cutting episode. Furthermore, the same paragraph containing this assertion has at least two other factual errors in its description of the incident. Instead of supposing that Untermeyer's book of ninety-two biographical sketches has access to information unavailable to scholars such as Tralbaut, who has spent more than fifty years studying and writing about Van Gogh, it seems more reasonable to conclude that there is no reliable evidence supporting this explanatory conjecture and that the evidence was fabricated in order to produce a plausible account. Similar criticisms may be made of Meier-Graeffe's (1933) story that the prostitute had earlier asked Van Gogh for a five-franc piece, he had refused, and that she then said that "if he could not give her a five-franc piece he might at least honour her with one of his large lop-ears for a Christmas present" (p. 163).

An explanation not based on such unreliable evidence rests on Van Gogh's report several months later in the sanatorium that other patients heard words and voices, just as he had, probably because of diseased nerves of the ear. Such beliefs may have played a part in the ear-mutilation episode.

The evidence presented must, in addition to being reliable in itself, be shown to have explanatory relevance or explanatory force in relation to the events in question. This explanatory relevance may, according to various construals, be obtained through deductive use of a theory or law relating the available evidence to the event to be explained (Hempel, 1965), through identifying reasons that the agent had for acting as he or she did (Dray, 1957), or through constructing a coherent narrative linking the evidence to the event to be explained (Sherwood, 1969). Consider, for example, the explanation which suggests that Van Gogh identified with the crucified Jesus, and that in giving the mother surrogate, Rachel, a dead segment of his body, he symbolically repeated the scene on Calvary. In his presentation of the ear, Van Gogh hoped that his mother would adore him as Mary adored the crucified Jesus (Lubin, 1972, p. 180). This explanation is based on a set of symbolic equivalencies, with Vincent representing Jesus, the severed ear representing the dead body, and Rachel representing the Virgin Mary. The events of his ear-mutilation can be translated into these terms, but what is the explanatory force of such a translation? It is not sufficient to suggest such possible symbolic equivalences; it is also necessary to provide reasons for believing that such representations were causally relevant to the actual course of events, in other words, that Van Gogh, either consciously or unconsciously, made such symbolic connections and that they influenced his actions. At various times in his life, such as in his struggles to be a minister and in his compassion for the downtrodden, Van Gogh did indicate an identification with Jesus; but that the severed ear represented to him the dead body of Christ, that Rachel represented the Virgin Mary, or that images of the Calvary scene influenced his self-destructive actions that night remains to be demonstrated.

Perhaps the single most strongly supported explanatory factor in Vincent's breakdown was the perceived loss of his brother's care. Specifically, the ear-cutting incident and two later mental breakdowns coincided with learning of Theo's engagement, his marriage, and the birth of his first child. In each case, Vincent was threatened by the prospect of losing his main source of emotional and financial support, as it seemed that Theo might redirect his love and money toward his new family (Tralbaut, 1969).

A masochistic response under situations of rejection or loss of love was not alien to Van Gogh. In 1881, he had visited the parents of Kee Voss, a woman he loved but who was avoiding him.

When he heard that Kee had left the house in order to avoid seeing him, Van Gogh "put his hand in the flame of the lamp and said, 'Let me see her for as long as I can keep my hand in the flame' " (Tralbaut, 1969, p. 79). They blew out the lamp and said that he could not see her. These other incidents make it seem more likely that Van Gogh's self-mutilation was influenced by a perceived loss of love from his brother.

It is no easy task to winnow through a range of explanatory hypotheses, and given limitations in the accessible evidence about historical events, it is sometimes impossible to directly test every explanatory conjecture. However, substantial progress can still be made in identifying faulty explanations and in gathering corroborative evidence in support of others. Explanations and interpretations can be evaluated in light of criteria such as (1) their logical soundness, (2) their comprehensiveness in accounting for a number of puzzling aspects of the events in question, (3) their survival of tests of attempted falsification, such as tests of derived predictions or retrodictions, (4) their consistency with the full range of available relevant evidence, (5) their support from above, or their consistency with more general knowledge about human functioning or about the person in question, and (6) their credibility relative to other explanatory hypotheses (Bromley, 1977, chap. 8; Cheshire, 1975; Crosby, 1979; Hempel, 1965, 1966; Sherwood, 1969).

For each explanatory problem we can imagine a tree of explanatory inquiries, with the trunk representing the initial question or puzzle, each limb representing an explanatory conjecture, and smaller branches off the limb representing tests of that particular hypothesis or conjecture. Any single explanatory hypothesis can be submitted to a variety of tests, with each test providing partial, although not definitive, corroboration or disconfirmation of the hypothesis.

The least developed inquiries would consist of a trunk with a single bare limb, representing a single explanatory conjecture that has received little or no critical examination. A comprehensive explanatory inquiry would resemble a well-developed tree, filled out with limbs and branches, representing a great variety of explanatory conjectures, with extensive testing of each explanatory hypothesis. This picture of an ideal tree, or of a fully rational explanatory inquiry, provides a framework for assessing the progress of particular explanatory inquiries and for visualizing what has been done in relation to what could be done.

The Search for Single Explanations

Psychobiographical studies of individual lives are often criticized for being open to a variety of explanations. For instance, it is claimed that Freud's case studies "suffer from the critical flaw of being open to many interpretations" (Liebert and Spiegler, 1978, p. 50). Popper (1962) states: "Every conceivable case could be interpreted in the light of Adler's theory, or equally of Freud's. . . . I could not think of any human behavior which could not be interpreted in terms of either theory. It was precisely this fact—that they always fitted, that they were always confirmed—which in the eyes of their admirers constituted the strongest argument in favour of these theories. It began to dawn on me that this apparent strength was in fact their weakness" (p. 35). Similarly, Gergen (1977) says: "The events of most people's lives are sufficiently variegated and multifarious that virtually any theoretical template can be validated. The case study simply allows the investigator freedom to locate the facts lending support to his or her preformulated convictions" (p. 142).

These criticisms are, I believe, overstated and apply most readily to poorly developed explanatory inquiries. It may be possible to interpret any life with any theory, but often only at the cost of distortion or selective presentation of the evidence. Any explanatory conjecture *can* be made, but not all of them stand up under critical examination. In legal proceedings, self-serving explanations of the course of events by a guilty defendant often crumble under rigorous cross-examination. Similarly, explanations of a life history using a particular theory sometimes fail to stand up under critical examination. For example, the disorders of George III had widely been seen as manic-depressive psychosis until Macalpine and Hunter (1969) persuasively reinterpreted them as symptoms of porphyria, a hereditary metabolic disturbance. Even if some evidence can be found in a life history that is consistent with a wide variety of theories, this does not mean that all of these theories provide an adequate interpretation of the events in question.

Critical testing of the claims and implications of various explanations can lead to the elimination of many of them as implausible or highly unlikely. Ideally, this process will lead to a single well-supported explanation. In some cases, though, even after a great number of unsatisfactory conjectures are eliminated, more than one explanation that is consistent with the available evidence may remain. We are sometimes faced with "many possible explanations, all of which may be equally valid theoretically and which the facts equally fit, and when this happens there is no way we can say which explanation is the most correct" (Pye, 1979, p. 53).

This problem may not be frequently encountered in everyday practice, where minimal resources are available for inquiry, where investigation ceases once a single plausible explanation is reached, or where inquiry stops once an interpretation consistent with a prevailing theoretical orthodoxy is produced. However, if an explanatory problem is extensively investigated, if it is approached from a variety of theoretical perspectives, or if it touches on conflicting social and political interests, it becomes more likely that a variety of alternative explanations will be generated.

Conclusion

It is sometimes suggested that the interpretation of single cases is little more than an arbitrary application of one's theoretical preferences. No doubt this happens at times, but *any* method can be poorly used. Effective use of the case study method requires not only the formulation of explanations consistent with some of the evidence but also that preferred explanations be critically examined in light of all available evidence, and that they be compared in plausibility with alternative explanations. After the implausible alternatives have been eliminated, more than one explanation consistent with the available evidence may remain, but this is far different from saying that the facts can be adequately explained in terms of any theoretical conjecture.

When faced with a puzzling historical or clinical phenomenon, investigators are sometimes too ready to accept the first psychodynamic interpretation that makes previously mysterious events appear comprehensible. The case of Van Gogh's ear illustrates the dangers of this approach, as further inquiry often yields a variety of other apparently plausible explanations. When this happens, it is not sufficient to suggest that all of the explanations may be simultaneously true; rather, the situation requires that the alternative explanatory conjectures be critically evaluated and compared in terms of their relative plausibility.

The likelihood that alternative explanatory conjectures will be formulated, or that existing explanatory hypotheses will be critically scrutinized, depends not solely upon rational considerations but also upon the social and political interests of those involved in the inquiry. The following chapter examines the influence of such social factors upon the initiation, course, and outcome of explanatory endeavors.

4

Social Influences on
the Course of Explanatory Endeavors

The actual course of explanatory endeavors often diverges substantially from the rational ideal of generating and critically evaluating a comprehensive range of explanatory hypotheses. This is due at times to the influence of social and political interests which bias investigators toward proposing certain congenial hypotheses while neglecting others, and toward being differentially critical of the range of hypotheses considered. The influence of social and political processes upon the course of explanatory inquiries will be illustrated with a study of Daniel Ellsberg by the Central Intelligence Agency (C.I.A.) and with a more extensive discussion of the controversy surrounding the death of Stephen Biko, the founder of Black Consciousness in South Africa. It will not be argued that social and political interests inevitably override rational considerations or even that the two are necessarily in conflict, but rather that social interests do, at least some of the time, have a powerful influence upon the course of explanatory inquiries, and that our understanding of explanatory endeavors is often enriched by a consideration of the social and political interests of those involved.

Daniel Ellsberg

After Daniel Ellsberg leaked the Pentagon papers, which conveyed politically embarrassing historical details of United States involvement with Vietnam, the White House asked the C.I.A. to prepare a psychiatric profile of Ellsberg. The C.I.A. profile concluded that "Ellsberg probably leaked the Pentagon papers out of a need for recognition as well as what 'he deemed to be a higher order of patriotism' " (*Time*, Aug. 12, 1974, p. 41). "The first profile, which turned out to be reasonably favorable, was judged unsatisfactory by the White House, and the C.I.A. was sent back to crank out another" (*Time*, Aug. 12, 1974, p. 41).

This second report, published in the *New York Times* (July 15, 1974, p. 16), says that there is "no available evidence to indicate that he is emotionally disturbed in a psychotic or gross manner." He is described as a very intelligent man "with very strong although fluctuant emotional attachments." These "fluctuant emotional attachments" are traced back to an automobile accident in which Ellsberg's father was driving and his mother and sister were killed. According to the C.I.A. account, this led to feelings of anger and jealousy toward his father. "Such feelings of jealousy toward his father (or latter-day versions of it) are the outgrowth of the male child's intensive unsettled rivalry with his father for the mother. Whether this intense anger toward his father arose out of resentment toward him for taking the mother from him by death, or whether out of resentment at the father for not accepting him in her place and for marrying another woman, cannot be discerned from the material available."

It is later explained that to an important degree the leaking of the Pentagon papers was "an act of aggression at his analyst, as well as at the President and his father" for not receiving the attention and recognition he desired. His efforts to interest Senator Fulbright, Senator McGovern, Henry Kissinger, and others in the Pentagon papers are interpreted as part of a "continuing search for a senior official who would appreciate his gifts." His activities in antiwar appearances "provide some small, cold measure of what he seeks," which is the appreciation of a senior personage. "Personally his pursuit is doomed to failure, for what he seeks is a close, intimate relation of a boy to his father, and that he can no longer have." The report also claims (in November 1971) that Ellsberg "has been essentially unsuccessful in gaining his vengeful primary objective—diluting the power of 'the executive.' Rather, Vietnam is fading somewhat as the foreign affairs focus of the country shift[s] to the President's upcoming trips to Moscow and Peking."

Alternative possible explanations of Ellsberg's behavior, such as that he may have been morally outraged at the war in Vietnam, that he went to different senior officials in an effort to influence government policy, or that he wanted to inform the public about United States involvement in Vietnam, are not explicitly considered. Nor are the proffered explanations critically examined. In short, a politically congenial interpretation of Ellsberg's behavior, attributing it to unresolved psychological conflicts, is put forward without critical examination, and alternative explanations based on his conscious motives and reasons are not considered. This C.I.A. report provides a clear example of a biased and incomplete assessment of explanatory alternatives and indicates how political interests may influence the course of explanatory endeavors.

Stephen Biko

A more detailed illustration of the ways in which conflicting social and political interests can influence explanatory endeavors is provided by the inquiry into the death of South African Black activist, Stephen Biko. Biko was born in King William's Town, South Africa, on December 18, 1946. He entered medical school in 1966, but then turned his attention to politics and helped to found two Black organizations, the South African Student Organization in 1970 and the Black People's Convention in 1972. By his late twenties, Biko was recognized as a founder and leader of the Black Consciousness movement in South Africa, which was committed to attaining psychological and political emancipation through the development of Black pride and solidarity through an all-Black political movement. In 1973, Stephen Biko was "banned" or restricted to King William's Town. A banning order in South Africa prevents a person from traveling freely, from addressing an audience, from being in the presence of more than one other person (except for family members), and from being quoted by the media.

On August 8, 1977, Biko was arrested at a roadblock outside of King William's Town and held for traveling outside his hometown in defiance of his banning order and on suspicion of traveling in order to distribute inflammatory pamphlets. He was detained under Section 6 of South Africa's Terrorism Act, which authorizes indefinite detention for anyone suspected of broadly

defined activities such as challenging law and order, furthering
hostility between the races, or doing anything to embarrass the
administration or the state. Under the act, suspects are held in-
communicado and are outside the protection of the law, as
courts are not allowed to order the release of detainees or to
prosecute the police for actions taken under this section. This
veil of secrecy makes it more difficult to ascertain precisely what
happened, but an inquest, which was made possible under South
African law by the fact that Biko died, did bring certain facts to
light.

Biko was in good health when arrested on August 18, but died
on September 12, 1977, after three and one-half weeks in the
custody of the Security Police. How can his death be explained?
On September 13, Minister of Justice James T. Kruger issued a
public statement saying that "Mr. Biko refused his meals and
threatened a hunger strike. But he was, however, regularly sup-
plied with meals and water which he refused to partake of" (Arnold, 1978, p. 343). While in detention, Biko was examined several times by physicians, who reported nothing wrong with him.
Minister Kruger later commented that the death of Mr. Biko
"leaves me cold," and agreed with a member of his National
Party who applauded him "for allowing the black leader his
'democratic right' to 'starve himself to death'" (Arnold, 1978,
p. 344).

The pathologists' reports, however, indicated that Biko died
of a brain injury resulting from a blow to the left forehead,
which also led to blood clotting and acute kidney failure. On
October 7, an investigation by the *Rand Daily Mail* reported
that at the time of his death Mr. Biko was overweight and
showed no signs of a hunger strike. The government demanded
disciplinary action against the paper. On October 19, the government banned eighteen protest groups, including all those af-
filiated with the Black Consciousness movement, arrested more
than fifty Black leaders and closed two leading Black newspapers. In an interview with the *New York Times* on October 21,
Mr. Kruger conceded that brain damage was the primary cause
of death, but claimed that there was no evidence of wrongdoing
by the police and that the injury may have come from a struggle over handcuffs. On October 27, the government suggested to
newspapers that the head injuries were probably self-inflicted

(*New York Times,* Nov. 14, 1977). An inquest began on November 14 and continued through December 2, 1977, in order to determine the cause or likely cause of death and to determine if the death could be attributed to any criminal act or omission on the part of the police. The details of the thirteen days of the trial are reported in Woods (1978).

According to the police officers, around 7:15 A.M. on the morning of September 7, 1977, Mr. Biko's leg irons and handcuffs were removed and then he got a wild look in his eyes and threw a chair at one of the officers. After a struggle or "scuffle" which lasted for several minutes, the officers restrained him and put back the leg irons and handcuffs. At 7:30 A.M., their superior, Colonel P. J. Goosen, head of the Security Police in Fort Elizabeth, was called in. Biko was reported to be talking incoherently and in a slurred manner, and would not respond to questions. A physician was summoned, and at 10:10 A.M. that morning issued a certificate saying that he could find nothing physically wrong with the detainee.

Several of the police officers suggested that Mr. Biko was shamming illness in order to avoid further interrogation. Examination by another physician on September 8 indicated that Biko suffered from echolalia, in which a person repeats words or sentences addressed to him, and also displayed an extensor plantar reflex, a reflex movement of the toes which indicates brain damage and which cannot be faked. On September 9, a lumbar puncture was taken which found blood in the cerebral spinal fluid, another sign of brain damage. The physicians were convinced that there had been a head injury and brain damage, but did not convey this in their reports at the time. By September 11, Stephen Biko was lying naked on the cement floor, breathing irregularly with glazed eyes and froth on his mouth, was not responsive to questions, and had not urinated for days. At the inquest, Colonel Goosen stated, "Everything possible was done by me to ensure the comfort and health of Mr. Biko while in detention" (Woods, 1978, p. 301). On the evening of September 11, Biko, now in a semicoma, was placed naked with a blanket in the back of a Land Rover, and driven not to a local hospital, but 700 miles to the central prison in Pretoria, where he died on September 12.

The inquest established that the fatal injury was suffered on either the evening of September 6 or the morning of September 7. The police officers reported that in the scuffle on September 7 Biko fell and may have hit his head. There are, though, several problems with this explanation, as none of the officers reported seeing him hit his forehead, where the main injury was received. Also, pathologists indicate that a blow of this severity would almost certainly lead to unconsciousness, and none of the officers reported a period of unconsciousness.

Mr. Kentridge, attorney for the Biko family, rejected this "scuffle theory" and argued that "the verdict which we submit is the only one reasonably open to this court is one finding that the death of Mr. Biko was due to a criminal assault upon him by one or more of the eight members of the security police in whose custody he was . . . on the 6th or 7th of September, 1977" (Arnold, 1978, p. 13). Or, as summarized more graphically by Donald Woods (1978, p. 13), "On Tuesday, September 6, 1977, a close friend of mine named Bantu Stephen Biko was taken by South African political police to Room 619 of the Sanlam Building in Strand Street, Port Elizabeth, Cape Province, where he was handcuffed, put into leg irons, chained to a grille and subjected to twenty-two hours of interrogation in the course of which he was tortured and beaten, sustaining several blows to the head which damaged his brain fatally, causing him to lapse into a coma and die six days later."

It is worth noting that between 1963 and 1977, forty-four other South Africans died while in custody of the Security Police with causes of death alleged by the police as "suicide by hanging," "natural causes," "fell against chair during scuffle," "slipped in shower," and "fell downstairs," with none of the deaths attributable to actions by the police.

The inquest in the Biko case was conducted not as a jury trial but before a single magistrate, who concluded that brain injury was the likely cause of death, but that no wrongdoing could be attributed to the police. A criticism of the verdict by Louis H. Pollack, dean of the University of Pennsylvania School of Law, who attended parts of the trial, is that "the crucial difficulty with the verdict is, of course, that it announced the magistrate's findings without explaining them" (Arnold, 1978, p. 355). It accepts the scuffle theory, but "it does not purport to clear away the weighty evidence undercutting the theory. Nor does it offer a syllable of justification for rejecting the opposed Kentridge analyses" (p. 355), which argued that death was due to a criminal assault.

The primary purpose of discussing this example is not to politicize (although it may have that effect), but rather to illustrate how social and political interests can influence the course of explanatory endeavors. The original explanation given by Minister Kruger implied that Biko died of a hunger strike. If there had been no public outcry, no pressing of the issue by Donald Woods and other journalists, there might have been no inquest and no opportunity for learning more of the details about what happened. Biko's prominence and support made it impossible for the Security Police to report a death with no explanation given, as happened with eight other deaths earlier in 1977. The public inquest made it possible to critically examine the explanations claiming that Biko died from a hunger strike, from hitting his head during a scuffle, or from a self-inflicted brain injury.

Even after the inquest, social and political forces continued to affect the course of the inquiry. On July 28, 1979, as a result of a civil suit, it was announced that the South African government would pay $78,000 to Steve Biko's family. Minister of Police Louis Le Grange "insisted the payment was not a concession of responsibility. 'The file on the Biko affair is now closed' " (*New York Times*, July 29, 1979, p. 6). Mr. Biko's widow, Nontsikelolo Biko, said that the out-of-court settlement of her suit blocked an open inquiry into causes of the death. She "denounced the offer as 'blood money' and said she would continue to press the Government to disclose how her husband died" (*New York Times*, July 29, 1979, p. 6).

The course of this explanatory endeavor has depended not just upon issues of evidence and logic but also in important ways upon the social and political interests surrounding the collection and interpretation of evidence and the critical examination of alternative explanatory hypotheses. Often in a less dramatic way, the course of inquiry in biography, in clinical case studies, and in psychobiography also depends not solely upon rational and logical considerations but also upon a range of social and historical influences. In the case of biography, the influence of various political interests have been reflected in the varying biographical accounts of the lives of Jesus, Shakespeare, and Lincoln discussed in Chapter 2. In clinical case studies, the course of inquiry is often significantly affected by extrarational interests and concerns. To take one example which will be discussed in detail in Chapter 8, Freud's case study of Little Hans (1909) was used as a foil by Wolpe and Rachman (1960) to critique the evidential and inferential foundations of psychoanalytic theory and to argue for the superiority of learning theory formulations. In psychobiographical interpretation, a graphic example of the influence of external or political considerations upon psychological interpretation (to be discussed in Chapter 10) is provided by the *Fact* magazine article (1964) which surveyed psychiatrists on the question of whether they thought Barry Goldwater was "psychologically fit" to serve as President of the United States. This question was used by many of the more than 2,000 responding psychiatrists as a forum to vent their political views, either to declare that Goldwater was insane and a menace to society, similar in psychological makeup to Hitler or Stalin, or a very mature person, a "psychological 'superman'," who compared favorably with other past presidents and presidential candidates.

The Empirical Course of Explanatory Endeavors

The actual course of explanatory endeavors is influenced not solely by social and political forces but also by individual psychological forces and processes; both affective and cognitive, the latter due to limitations or biases in the mind's information-processing capacities. For example, a common cognitive bias is "the fundamental attribution error," in which observers typically overestimate the importance of dispositional relative to situational factors in interpreting the behavior of others (Ross, 1977). In other words, there seems to be a systematic tendency to underestimate the extent to which the behavior of others is affected by situational forces and to overestimate the extent to which it expresses enduring personal characteristics.

A second kind of common psychological error is to start with a limited number of explanatory hypotheses and then to interpret additional information (even if it is irrelevant) as corroborating existing hypotheses, rather than remembering the information separately or using it to generate new and more appropriate hypotheses (Elstein, Shulman, and Sprafka, 1978). The mind has a limited capacity for processing information and tends to sim-plify the world by organizing new evidence around a few ex-planatory hypotheses developed early in the course of inquiry.

Further examples of these psychological influences upon ex-planatory processes may be found in the literatures on person perception, attribution theory, clinical judgment, cognitive heu-ristics, and problem solving and decision making (e.g., Elstein, Shulman, and Sprafka, 1978; Jones et al., 1971; Nisbett and Ross, 1980; Ross, 1977; Schneider, Hastorf, and Ellsworth, 1979; Slovic and Lichtenstein, 1971; Tversky and Kahneman, 1974). This is not the place to review the literature on studies of psychological processes which influence attributional and explanatory pro-cesses, but rather to suggest that such research and theory needs to be taken into account in developing a comprehensive analysis of the actual course of explanatory endeavors.

A complete analysis of the course of explanatory endeavors would need to consider their psychological, sociological, politi-cal, historical, and economic aspects, as well as their logical and rational features. These social conditions determine whether the logical and empirical machinery of investigation is employed and influence the amount of time, energy, and money invested in the inquiry. The extent of an explanatory inquiry may vary from casual analysis by an individual, to systematic pursuit by a trained investigator (as with a detective, scientist, or historian pursuing a specific question), to organized debate by competing parties (as in legal debates or scientific quarrels), to massive investigations which occupy widespread public attention for years (as in the stream of books on the Sacco and Vanzetti case or the Hiss-Chambers affair). A recent example is the controversy over the assassinations of John F. Kennedy and Martin Luther King, in which the Select Committee on Assassinations of the U.S. House of Representatives spent $5.5 million investigating an array of conspiracy theories (U.S. House of Representatives, 1979).

Conclusion

Personal and social factors are involved in the origin, course, and outcome of explanatory endeavors. They may affect the ques-tions selected for investigation, the generation of explanatory hypotheses, the collection and interpretation of evidence, the resources invested in attempting to support or refute a particular hypothesis, the point at which inquiry is terminated, and the conclusions reached. Comparable analyses of the joint rational and social determinants of inquiry may also be made of the course of predictive endeavors and of the course of evaluative, descriptive, and policy endeavors, as well as of explanatory endeavors.

This emphasis upon the personal and social factors in explanatory inquiries does *not* mean that the process of explanation is necessarily arbitrary or irrational. Awareness of relevant personal and social forces does not lessen the need for assessing the logical or rational persuasiveness of particular explanatory hypotheses, both in relation to the evidence and to other plausible alternatives. At any point in time, one can examine independently (1) the logical status of explanatory arguments, and (2) the personal and social conditions related to the inquiry. Awareness of relevant personal and social processes may, in fact, alert us to potential biases and limitations in an explanatory argument and aid in the formulation of more logically persuasive explanations. With complex explanatory problems, the range of explanatory conjectures which could be examined is enormous. Given limited investigatory resources, only a few of the potential lines of inquiry will be pursued, and an understanding of the relevant personal and social processes may help in perceiving the extent to which the range of logical possibilities has or has not been explored, and in perceiving plausible alternative explanations which may have been neglected.

In summary, this chapter has argued that understanding of the explanatory process can be deepened by considering not only the logic of explanation but also the interaction of rational processes with personal and social processes in the course of explanatory endeavors. This conception of the course of explanatory endeavors can, I believe, be useful for thinking about the current status of our understanding of individual lives, the historical development of that understanding, and the ways in which it might be advanced.

5

The Structure of Biographical Narrative

Within the social sciences, and particularly within psychology, life history narrative is not typically seen as one of the basic tools of the trade. Methodology textbooks have sections on measurement, observation, questionnaire design, interviewing, experimental design, and quantitative data analysis, but usually without any accompanying discussion of narrative as a method. The objectives of this chapter are to explore several of the logical and empirical features of biographical narrative and to indicate the utility of narrative methods for the study of lives.

Narrative is useful, if not indispensable, for indicating how people thought and felt, what they said and did, what situations they were in, the subjective meanings of events, how their words and actions were interpreted by others, and the processes by which they interacted with their worlds over time. Many of these tasks are not handled easily, if at all, by more standard social scientific methods such as measurement, quantitative analysis, or experimentation. In light of the importance of these tasks, it is unfortunate that life history narrative has, with few exceptions (e.g., Bromley, 1977; Cohler, 1982; Sherwood, 1969), received so little methodological attention in the social sciences.

This chapter does not claim to provide a comprehensive analysis of literary narrative (e.g., Chatman, 1978; Scholes and Kellogg, 1966; Toliver, 1974); rather, it focuses on aspects of the theoretical and empirical foundations of biographical narrative. Narrative accounts of lives can be examined in terms of issues such as the conceptual framework used, the kinds of information selected for inclusion, the use of generalizations versus particularistic descriptions, the types of explicit or implicit explanations embedded in the narrative, and the extent to which social scientific concepts, theories, and findings are drawn upon in analyzing the life.

Before discussing these more general issues, several samples of biographical narrative will be presented in order to illustrate how these more abstract issues are encountered in actual biographical practice. Examples are drawn from biographies of Woodrow Wilson, Virginia Woolf, and Samuel Johnson. The following section presents a list of basic questions about biographical narrative, intended to generalize issues raised in the earlier examples and to outline a more systematic set of questions about the foundations of biographical narrative. Three issues are then selected from this list for more extensive discussion: (1) the problem of selection, (2) the causal structure of narrative accounts, and (3) statements about the historical influence of lives.

Woodrow Wilson

The following examples are drawn predominantly from Chapter 1 of *Woodrow Wilson and Colonel House* by Alexander and Juliette George (1964).

1. Chapter 1 opens with a quotation from Wilson as an epigraph: "A boy never gets over his boyhood, and never can change those subtle influences which have become a part of him, that were bred in him when he was a child" (p. 3).

This statement is consistent with the Georges' theoretical perspective, which draws substantially upon psychoanalytic theory and emphasizes the importance of childhood experience in the formation of adult personality. It is to Wilson's early years "that we must look for the origins of his superb strength and of his truly classical tragic weakness" (p. 3).

2. Wilson was not familiar with the alphabet until age nine, and did not learn to read readily until he was eleven. In a family where intellectual skills were revered, how can this striking fact be explained? "One wonders whether Tommy's capacity to learn was not reduced by his father's perfectionist demands. . . . Per-

haps, too, failing—*refusing*—to learn was the one way in which the boy dared to express his resentment against his father" (p. 7).

This is provided as a possible explanation, and appears plausible. Potential alternative explanations are neither explicitly considered nor ruled out, which seems to be a common procedure in biographical writing. A single explanation is proposed and accompanied by consistent evidence. There may, however, often be unstated evidence inconsistent with a particular hypothesis, or other bodies of evidence consistent with an alternative interpretation.

3. "Wilson's own recollections of his youth furnish ample indication of his early fears that he was stupid, ugly, worthless and unlovable. . . . It is perhaps to this core feeling of inadequacy, of a fundamental worthlessness which must ever be disproved, that the unappeasable quality of his need for affection, power and achievement, and the compulsive quality of his striving for perfection, may be traced" (p. 8). A central hypothesis of the book is that "power was for him a compensatory value, a means of restoring the self-esteem damaged in childhood" (p. 320).

This explanation is presented as an hypothesis, a "perhaps." Substantial evidence is presented which is consistent with this argument, and little that conflicts with it. In light of the material presented, this analysis feels persuasive in many ways. As the authors note, the biographer's "view of his subject gradually achieves an internal consistency as he works and reworks the material" (p. xi). However, as was argued in Chapter 2, alternative consistent accounts drawing upon other evidence, alternative theoretical frameworks, and other points of view might also be constructed. (For a debate over conflicting interpretations of Wilson, see Weinstein, Anderson and Link, 1978; George and George, 1981.)

4. "Tommy was always obedient and respectful. He delighted in doing chores for his father. As a young man, he cheerfully helped his father with the dull task of writing the minutes of the General Assembly of the Church. Even in successful maturity, he retained a feeling of incompetence in his father's presence. He once said the most difficult speech he ever had to make was one during which he suddenly espied his father in the audience" (p. 9).

The generalization that Wilson delighted in doing chores for his father is followed by an illustrative example, as is the claim that he felt incompetent in his father's presence even in maturity. Along with the sequential ordering of events, the making of descriptive generalizations followed by corroborative detail and illustration seems to be one of the central organizing principles of biographical narrative.

5. Wilson was troubled repeatedly throughout his career from president of Princeton to President of the United States by an unwillingness to compromise, demonstrated most dramatically by his self-defeating refusal to compromise with Senator Lodge over the Versailles Treaty and the League of Nations. Wilson felt that *"His* will must prevail, if he wished it to. . . . He bristled at the slightest challenge to his authority. Such a characteristic might well have represented a rebellion against the domination of his father, whose authority he had never dared openly to challenge. Throughout his life his relationships with others seemed shaped by an inner command never again to bend his will to another man's" (p. 11).

This is an example of an idiographic generalization, derived from the perception of a pattern of similar events throughout Wilson's career. Biographical narrative seems to rely in important ways not just upon general theory but also upon idiographic generalizations derived from detailed study of the individual person.

Virginia Woolf

The next set of examples are from the opening chapters of Quentin Bell's *Virginia Woolf: A Biography* (1972), a literary work in both style and subject.

1. The second chapter covers Virginia Woolf's life from birth until age thirteen. The narrative account is informative, entertaining, and exquisitely written. If the reader has no questions, the narrative feels full and satisfying. Temporal gaps are not obvious and are not explicitly stated. However, if the same narrative is approached from a particular theoretical orientation, it may appear seriously incomplete. A psychoanalyst would look in vain for information about weaning, toilet training, or early sexual experiences. A developmental psychologist would be frustrated in trying to learn about age of sitting, walking, or stages of cognitive development, though the late advent of speech is

mentioned. The narrative form is unstructured enough so that a highly selective account may feel satisfactorily complete, but gaps and omissions become apparent if the account is approached with specific questions in mind, or for the purpose of tracing a particular line of development.

2. Virginia's parents, Mr. and Mrs. Leslie Stephen, belonged to "the lower division of the upper middle class" (p. 20). This statement is elaborated to indicate that "They kept seven maid-servants but no man-servant. They might sometimes travel in a cab but kept no carriage; when they went by rail they travelled third class. The ladies had their clothes made by a reasonably good dressmaker. Leslie was a member of the Athenaeum and of course of the Alpine Club. . . . Their house was in a respectable part of town. It was taken for granted that the boys would go to public schools and then to Cambridge. As for the girls, they would, in a decorous way, become accomplished and then marry" (pp. 20–21).

The meaning of social class in their particular social and historical context is sketched in some detail, through providing information about household economy, travel, dress, education, and social expectations. This illustrates a common organizing principle of biographical narrative, which is to have an interplay between general or summary statements and a wealth of detailed particulars, thus working simultaneously at several different levels of abstraction.

3. Bell's biography raises the question of aesthetic expression and communication, and its relationship to more historical and scientific modes of communication. For example, the Stephen children collected butterflies and moths, described by Bell as follows: "As blood sports go, the killing of lepidoptera has a good deal to recommend it; it can offend only the most squeamish of humanitarians; it involves all the passion and skill of the naturalist, the charm of summer excursions and sudden exhilarating pursuits, the satisfaction of filling gaps in the collection, the careful study of text books, and, above all, the mysterious pleasure of staying up late, and walking softly through the night to where a rag, soaked in rum and treacle, has attracted dozens of slugs, crawly-bobs and, perhaps, some great lamp-eyed, tipsy, extravagantly gaudy moth" (p. 33).

How is the truth and meaning of this activity best communicated? In comparison to this imaginative literary portrayal, how effective would a straight historical description of a bug-hunting trip be in communicating this experience? Bell's narrative conveys a feel for the experience; we feel we know something about what it must have been like. Although the present chapter focuses on philosophical and scientific aspects of biographical narrative, these issues do not exhaust the complexities of narrative style. The writing in Bell's biography contains a vividness and charm, not to say insight, that is missing from much social science. Part of the appeal and promise of biography is that, at its best, it can combine historical, scientific, and literary approaches to human experience.

4. One final passage illustrates again something of the power of narrative for conveying the subtleties of a relationship, the discrepancies between public appearance and inner reality, and in short, the meaning of an experience.

Virginia is thirteen, and her mother has just died. One of the few apparent supports of the family is her half-brother, George Duckworth.

> He was now twenty-seven, very handsome, comfortably well-off, pleasant, urbane and generous. His devotion to his half-sisters was exemplary. He made them presents, he took endless trouble to arrange treats, parties, excursions; he would even go off butterfly-hunting with them, and this for a fashionable young man represents a considerable sacrifice.
>
> After their mother's death his kindness knew no bounds; his was an emotional, a demonstrative nature; his shoulder was there for them to weep on; his arms were open for their relief.
>
> At what point his comfortable fraternal embrace developed into something which to George no doubt seemed even more comfortable although not nearly so fraternal, it would be hard to say. Vanessa came to believe that George himself was more than half aware of the fact that what had started with pure sympathy ended by becoming a nasty erotic skirmish. . . .
>
> To the sisters it simply appeared that their loving brother was transformed before their eyes into a monster, a tyrant against whom they had no defence, for how could they speak out or take any action against a treachery so covert that it was half unknown even to the traitor? Trained as they were to preserve a condition of ignorant purity they must at first have been unaware that affection was turning to concupiscence, and were

> warned only by their growing sense of disgust. . . . It would
> have been hard for his half-sisters to know at what point to draw
> a line, to voice objections, to risk evoking a painful and em-
> barrassing scandal; harder still to find someone to whom they
> could speak all. Stella, Leslie, the aunts—all would have been
> bewildered, horrified, indignant and incredulous [pp. 42–43].

It is difficult to imagine how the nature of this relationship
or the meaning of this experience could be conveyed in quantitative, mathematical, or other nonnarrative terms. If the social
sciences are to deal with life histories, and with the meaning of
individual human experiences, it seems that, in spite of their
limitations, narrative methods may *have* to be used.

Samuel Johnson

1. In addition to direct accounts of a life, biographies often contain a range of other narrative material, one example of which
is statements about the subject's historical significance or relationship to our own experience. One unusually effective example, which also conveys something of the value of biography in
general, is provided by the opening pages of Walter Jackson
Bate's *Samuel Johnson* (1977).

> Samuel Johnson has fascinated more people than any other
> writer except Shakespeare. Statesmen, lawyers, and physicians
> quote him, as do writers and scientists, philosophers and farm-
> ers, manufacturers and leaders of labor unions. . . . The rea-
> son why Johnson has always fascinated so many people of dif-
> ferent kinds is not simply that Johnson is so vividly picturesque
> and quotable, though these are the qualities that first catch our
> attention. The deeper secret of his hypnotic attraction, especi-
> ally during our own generation, lies in the immense reassurance
> he gives to human nature, which needs—and quickly begins to
> value—every friend it can get. . . .
> His honesty to human experience cuts through the "cant,"
> the loose talk and pretense, with which all of us get seduced
> into needlessly complicating life for both ourselves and other
> people. We laugh also at the unpredictability and novelty of
> Johnson's way of putting things. Consequently, as he expresses
> himself, we have the sense of a living originality—of the genuine
> personality of an experiencing nature—operating upon all the
> facts of life. . . .

To no one since Shakespeare could we more truthfully apply what the ancient Greek epigram said of Plato: "In whatever direction we go, we meet him on his way back." . . . Whatever we experience, we find Johnson has been there before us, and is meeting and returning home with us [pp. 3–5].

2. A crucial dimension of the story of a life, which can be effectively expressed through narrative (and perhaps only through narrative), is the relationship between intentions and actions, and often, the discrepancy between intentions and results.

Shortly after his birth, Johnson's aging parents decided to employ a wet nurse, to ensure that he would be adequately nourished. "What the Johnsons could not know was that the milk of the wet nurse was tubercular." The baby's eyes became infected, and "as his condition grew worse and sores appeared, it was realized that he had the tubercular infection of the lymph glands known as scrofula or the 'King's Evil.' It had spread to both the optic and auditory nerves, leaving him almost blind in the left eye, while also impairing vision in the right, and deaf in the left ear." His mother, "unwilling to admit that an action of the parents could have been even indirectly responsible, preferred to think that the boy inherited the disease, and pathetically cited a small inflammation discovered on his buttock" (pp. 6–7) that had appeared and quickly healed before he was sent to the wet nurse.

3. Johnson is widely known not only as the subject of Boswell's biography but as author of the *Dictionary of the English Language,* written between 1746 and 1755. Composing a dictionary is a monumentally laborious task and not the way many of us would choose to spend our afternoons. Johnson wrote definitions of more than 40,000 words, illustrated by 114,000 quotations from all fields of learning; he was aided by only six assistants, of whom probably three or four were working at any one time.

Placing events in their context is one of the major services of narrative, and the meaning of Johnson's accomplishment is magnified by placing it in historical and comparative context. Johnson composed the first major dictionary of the English language in a span of nine years. In comparison, the national dictionaries of France and Italy were both composed by learned academies. The Italian dictionary had taken the Accademia della Crusca twenty years to prepare. More recently, the French Academy, working with forty members, had taken fifty-five years to complete its dictionary (1694). The *New English Dictionary* (10 vols., 1888–1928), which finally replaced Johnson's, was begun in 1858, drew on the help of more than 2,000 scholars, and took seventy years to complete. In this comparative context, Johnson's accomplishment takes on new meaning.

In summary, this examination of three samples of biographical narrative has both raised issues about the empirical and theoretical foundations of biographical narrative and suggested the utility of narrative methods for accomplishing important tasks in analyzing a life history. The examples illustrate how life history narrative is composed of elements such as proposed explanations with supporting evidence, descriptive generalizations followed by corroborative detail, and idiographic generalizations derived from a study of patterns within the individual case. The examples also indicate the utility, if not the necessity, of narrative methods for tasks such as conveying the meaning of important relationships and experiences, placing events in context, revealing the relationships between intentions and the effects of actions, and indicating the historical significance of a life. In short, narrative methods seem extremely useful in the study of life histories, and their theoretical and empirical foundations could profitably be subject to more systematic examination.

Selected Issues in the Structure of Narrative

The structure of life history narrative can be explored from many different perspectives, with different facets illuminated by different angles of approach. This section proposes a more extensive set of questions about theoretical and empirical aspects of biographical narrative than raised by the previous examples. These questions are derived from the reading of biographies, from discussions of the art or craft of biography (Aaron, 1978; Altick, 1966; Bowen, 1969; Clifford, 1962, 1970; Edel, 1957; Garraty, 1957; Gittings, 1978; Kendall, 1965; Pachter, 1979); and from analyses of narrative in literary theory (Chatman, 1978; Scholes and Kellogg, 1966; Toliver, 1974), the social sciences (Bower, 1978; Bromley, 1977; Cohler, 1982; Ricouer, 1977; Schank and Abelson, 1977; Sherwood, 1969), and the philosophy of history—where narrative methods have been extensively examined (Atkinson,

1978; Collingwood, 1946; Danto, 1965; Dray, 1957, 1971; Gallie, 1964; Hexter, 1971; Hook, 1963; Mandelbaum, 1977; Nash, 1969; Walsh, 1967; and White, 1965).

A sample of the relevant issues raised in these literatures includes the following:

1. *Conceptual framework.* What language or conceptual framework should be used in describing life histories? What use should be made of the everyday language of the author and intended audience, the language and concepts of the subject's world, or the technical language and conceptual framework of the social sciences?

2. *Content.* What is the content of life history narrative? What relative emphasis is given to characteristics of the person, to details of setting and historical context, to specific actions and experiences, or to other topics?

3. *Selection.* What information is selected for inclusion or omission in life history narrative, according to what criteria and processes? What kinds and degree of detail are appropriate for different purposes, and for accounts of different scale?

4. *Facts.* What degrees of certainty or consensus can or cannot be obtained about biographical facts? Are there "facts" about lives, or only "factual hypotheses"? How does the biographer establish and then indicate the different levels of certainty associated with different biographical "facts"?

5. *Generalization.* What kinds of generalizations are found in biographical narrative, and what is their place within the narrative structure? To what extent are these generalizations derived from conceptual classifications, conventional wisdom, idiographic analyses, or quantitative social science?

6. *Explanation.* May an adequate biography be purely descriptive, or must it include explanations and interpretations as well? What are the major forms of explanation and interpretation, and what is the place of each in the writing of biographies and clinical histories?

7. *The causal structure of narrative.* Does narrative consist of noncausal descriptive statements arranged in temporal order, of a sequentially ordered chain of causal statements, or of some other causal structure?

8. *Values and objectivity.* Can biography be "objective," in

the sense of being uncontaminated (or uninformed) by the author's values? What influence do values and moral judgments have (inevitably, according to one line of argument) upon biographical description and interpretation?

9. *Use of the social sciences*. Although psychology, sociology, and anthropology are all devoted to the study of human behavior in its social context, most biographies seem, paradoxically, to make little explicit use of social scientific concepts, theories, and data. Is this because the social sciences are of little help in understanding the course of experience in individual lives, because biographers are unaware of their potential contributions, or for some other reasons? What can and can't the social sciences contribute to the writing of biographies?

10. *Historical influence*. What kinds of statements are made about the historical influence of a person's life and work? What are the grounds for these statements, and how can they be critically evaluated?

This list of questions is intended to suggest, although not to exhaust, the range of questions that can be asked about the epistemological foundations of biographical narrative. The following pages contain brief discussions of the issues of selection, the causal structure of narrative, and historical influence.

Selection

It is widely agreed that a history cannot contain a "complete" description of a subject (Dray, 1962; White, 1965). As events contain innumerable aspects, it is not even possible to give a complete description of a single event (Hempel, 1965, p. 422). Inevitably, a biography cannot contain a complete account of a life. What processes and principles are used, and should be used, in selecting information to include in a biography?

Before responding to this query, let us try to imagine what a comprehensive description of a life might entail. If a life history is defined as the sequence of events and experiences in a life from birth until death and the sequence of personal states and encountered situations which influence, and are influenced by, this sequence of events, then a comprehensive description of a life would include everything that the person said, thought, felt, sensed, and perceived, including the subjective meaning of things, events, and relationships; a portrait of the social and historical context; a medical history and a record of bodily states and processes, at least as they affected acting and experiencing; a record of the situational career, or the sequence of encountered environments and situations, and the processes of entering, creating, modifying and leaving each of them; an historical record of the subject's occupational career, interpersonal career, sexual career, economic career, spiritual career, and recreational career; and finally, an account of the meaning and consequences of the person's life and work for other individuals, groups, and institutions.

According to this outline, it is clear that a complete account of a life history never has been recorded and never will be. The vision of a complete life history can, though, be used to reveal the gaps in any particular account or to suggest the range of information that may be drawn upon in writing a life history for a particular purpose or context.

A number of conditions outside the author's control contribute to the inevitable selectivity of life history accounts. Among others, there are: (1) technical-methodological limitations, in that all data collection methods yield incomplete information; (2) historical limitations, in that much information about past lives is lost or unattainable; (3) ethical limitations, in that some life history information may not be appropriate to collect or reveal; and (4) economic limitations, in that the costs of collecting as much information as possible are often prohibitive.

The series of events in a life is "indefinitely dense" (Mandelbaum, 1977, p. 15), and an account of a life can be constructed on many different scales, each with a different level of detail. On a continuum ranging from minimally to maximally detailed accounts of a life, we can identify a number of standard forms, such as: (1) bare identifying characteristics, including name, date, and nationality; (2) minimum descriptions, as contained in biographical dictionaries, with records of any cultural contributions or historical importance, and bare outlines of family and career; (3) biographical sketches or essays, as in magazines or collections such as Untermeyer's *Makers of the Modern World* (1955); (4) standard full-scale biographies, such as Quentin Bell's *Virginia Woolf* (1972) or W. J. Bate's *Samuel Johnson* (1977); and (5) massive, multivolume biographical studies, such as Leon

Edel's five-volume study of Henry James (1953–72) or Nicolay and Hay's ten-volume biography of Abraham Lincoln (1890).

A lengthy biography may feel to the reader like a block of granite, solid and complete. Yet, in relation to all the information that could be recorded, it is fragmentary and highly selective. The subjective completeness of a life history account is judged though, usually not in reference to a complete description, but rather in relation to an implicit script or template, or to particular needs and purposes.

Within the limits of accessible data, the biographer has the responsibility for selecting that information to be included in the narrative. There are at least two sets of criteria that may be used in this process. First, decisions about what events or facts to include in a life history must be made upon value judgments about what is important, interesting, or significant (Dray, 1962), or relevant for the practical purpose at hand (e.g., clinical or legal). Second, after this pool of basic events is identified, derivative statements can be made about the causes and effects of these events (White, 1965). Derivative statements may also explore the meaning and significance of basic events, such as Bate's comparative information on the writing of dictionaries in his biography of Johnson.

In describing the life of a seventeenth-century "witch," for example, one would want to include basic statements indicating that she had fits and fainting spells. In a seventeenth-century biography, these fits might be explained in terms of possession by demons, while in a twentieth-century biography, the same fits would most likely be explained in terms of psychopathology or social pressures. The two biographies could contain similar sets of basic statements about important events in the life, yet substantially different derivative statements about the causes of these events.

The construction of biographical narratives involves the formation of intelligible stories and the use of generalizations and explanatory arguments, and thus is more complex than a simple two-part structure of basic statements plus derivative statements. Nevertheless, evaluative decisions about what is important or interesting, and derivative explorations of the causes and effects, the meaning and significance of such events are an important part of the total process of selection.

The Causal Structure of Narrative

A distinction is often made between chronicle and narrative (White, 1965), between descriptive and explanatory history (Dray, 1964), or between plain and significant narrative (Walsh, 1967). Most simply, a chronicle consists of a set of temporally ordered descriptive statements, while narrative or explanatory history also contains causal analyses. Narrative accounts in general, and particularly narrative accounts of lives, are designed to give a coherent account of the development of a central subject. The objective of this section is to examine the causal structure of biographical narrative.

One of the simplest possibilities is that narrative accounts consist of a sequence of causal statements, with each event in a sequence leading to the next. For example, "The King of England died, which led the Queen to grieve, which led the Princess to worry, and so on" (Dray, 1971, p. 162). This may be referred to as the "causal chain" model of narrative accounts. Although causal chains may be embedded in narratives, it is evident that narrative accounts are generally far more complex than suggested by this model.

A second and somewhat more flexible model might be called (after Dray, 1971) the "causal input" model of narrative accounts. In following the sequence of events and experiences in a life, causes need not flow from prior states of the central figure, but may be drawn on from the outside as needed in order to explain the course of experience. For example, a causal explanation of the infant Samuel Johnson's health problems does not flow primarily from his prior state of health, but from the fact that the woman chosen as his wet nurse happened to have tuberculosis. "Causes now enter the series, as it were, from the outside" (Dray, 1971, p. 164).

A third and still more flexible model suggests that events in a narrative account need not receive causal explanations, but are presented in such a way that we can accept them "as plausible and relevant developments of the theme or subject under consideration" (Dray, 1971, p. 166). Narrative, according to this "followable contingency" model, consists of an intelligible sequence of events, with explanations needed only when the chain of events would otherwise be difficult to follow. This has been a necessarily brief discussion of the causal structure of narrative, intended primarily to suggest the relevance of this line of analysis in the philosophy of history for understanding biographical narrative (cf. Danto, 1965; Dray, 1971; Gallie, 1964; Hexter, 1971; Mandelbaum, 1977; White, 1965).

It seems that biographical narrative almost never follows a causal chain model, but often exhibits features of a followable contingency model, and sometimes of a causal input model. Many biographies, and excellent ones, contain few explicit explanations of any form. This was surprising to me, as I began with the assumption that biographies could be construed as the description and explanation of the course of a life. There are, though, at least two different perspectives on the aims of biography which need to be recognized. The historical-scientific perspective emphasizes description and explanation of the course of events, while a literary-aesthetic perspective suggests that biography is "the simulation, in words, of a man's life" (Kendall, 1965, p. 15). This latter view suggests that biography aims to convey the feel of an individual's experience, rather than our thoughts about causes of that experience. The biographical enterprise is, however, spacious enough to encompass the development and practice of both approaches to the writing of lives.

Historical Influence

Biographical literature is filled with statements about the influence of a subject's life and work upon history, culture, or our own experience. The following examples are drawn from a series of biographical portraits by Untermeyer (1955). "Richard Wagner . . . changed the whole course of modern music." Karl Marx "wrote a treatise which has had a cataclysmic effect on modern history." "The dogged seventy-five-year campaign of prodding, petitioning, and pleading that emancipated modern women owed its strength and its strategy to Susan Brownell Anthony." Tolstoy "was the largest figure and the greatest moral force in Russian literary history." "Isadora Duncan brought about a revolution not only in the dance but in the modern mind, healthier for her pioneering art." "The influence of William James is as definite as it is demonstrable. It affected not only the political thinking of men like President Woodrow Wilson and both Roosevelts, but the judicial opinions of such great jurists as Oliver Wendell Holmes and Louis D. Brandeis, the social theories of Jane

Addams, and the spiritual convictions of incalculably large groups of people." Sigmund Freud's "sweeping theories had touched almost every shore of human thought. Only two other contemporary revolutionaries—Karl Marx and Albert Einstein— had produced so profound an effect upon the character of the world they lived in."

What kinds of data and argument are needed to support such statements? How may claims about the historical influence of a life be critically evaluated? A classic discussion of this problem is contained in Hook (1943), who attempts "to work out some generalization of the types of situations and conditions in which we can justifiably attribute or deny causal influence to outstanding personalities" (p. xiv). According to Pascal, "Cleopatra's nose, had it been shorter, the whole aspect of the world would have been different." The implication is that, if less beautiful, Cleopatra would not have had the influence she did with Julius Caesar and Mark Antony, and thus, the history of the Roman Empire would have been different. Hook argues that Cleopatra's influence would not have been less with a different nose, as her attraction came primarily from her personality, will, and presence rather than appearance; that Caesar would have defeated Pompey without her; and that Antony would have lost his struggle to succeed Caesar even without her. In short, "the history of Rome would have been substantially the same if there had never been a Cleopatra" (p. 177).

Other causal analyses of the influence of historical figures are more strongly supported. In an analysis of the historical importance of Lenin, Hook argues that the Russian Revolution had an important influence upon the political, cultural, and economic life of the world; that the Revolution was not inevitable; that other Revolutionary leaders such as Zinoviev, Kamenov, or Trotsky would not have been effective substitutes for Lenin; and that the Revolution "was triumphant because of the directing leadership of Lenin and that without him it would have been lost" (p. 184).

Regardless of the accuracy of Hook's conclusions about Lenin and Cleopatra, it should be evident that assessing the influence of a life is no simple matter. One of the serious difficulties is in identifying the appropriate alternatives, or relevant counterfactual conditions (Goodman, 1973), indicating what would have happened *if* Cleopatra's nose had been shorter, or *if* Lenin had not existed. The historical influence of a person may be judged: (1) by comparing his or her actions and their estimated consequences with other courses of action available to the person; (2) by comparing the person's work and achievements with a likely alternative candidate occupying the same position (such as leadership of the Bolshevik Party); or (3) by trying to imagine the course of history without the existence of the person in question and without any likely replacement (as with Alexander the Great or Einstein).

Each of these alternatives poses substantial, and sometimes insurmountable, intellectual difficulties. Statements about the historical influence of a life may feel commonplace and perfectly natural, perhaps because of their prevalence, but upon reflection, such statements often seem problematic in their dependence upon counterfactual inferences about what would have happened otherwise that are difficult to test or verify. The purposes of commemoration, historical analysis, or moral judgment may require us to assess the effects of lives as best we can, but the complexity of the enterprise should not be ignored.

Conclusion

Biographical narrative has an intricate structure, consisting of elements such as particularistic descriptions, quotations, idiographic generalizations and supporting evidence, comparative and contextual information, and sometimes explicit interpretations and causal analyses, moral judgments, and assessments of historical influence, all organized in light of concerns such as temporal order, thematic organization, manageable length, and intelligibility in story or argument.

Tasks such as portraying the social and historical contexts of actions and events and conveying their subjective meanings are not handled easily, if at all, by methods such as measurement, correlation, and experimentation. Biographical narrative can help us to understand how people thought and felt about their experience, how they saw their worlds, what they said and did, how they were perceived by others, and the processes by which they interacted with their environments over time. Narrative, it seems, is indispensable for understanding the course of experience in individual lives, a problem which is of crucial importance in the social sciences and clinical professions. As such, the structure of life history narrative, its strengths and limitations, and the processes involved in its construction and use deserve far greater critical attention than they have yet received in the social sciences.

PART II

Conceptualizations of the Life Course

6

The Life Course
as a Theoretical Orientation

This chapter and the following one which comprise Part II are intended to present the life course as a theoretical orientation and to outline two different ways of conceptualizing the life course. These conceptual frameworks suggest ways of analyzing the causal and probabilistic structure of the course of experience and of thinking about problems in the prediction and intentional change of groups of lives. Such conceptual frameworks also provide tools or resources which can be drawn upon in the study of individual life histories. These two chapters are, however, not necessary background for Part III, and those whose sole or primary interest is in the study of individual life histories may want to skip or skim over this material and move directly to Part III, where studies of individuals are again dealt with more directly in chapters on the case study method, the idiographic approach, and psychobiographical methods.

The function of a theoretical orientation is to "indicate types of variables which are somehow to be taken into account rather than specifying determinate relationships between particular variables" (Merton, 1968, p. 142). In the history of the behavioral sciences, we can identify a number of theoretical orientations which have each had a profound influence upon the questions that psychologists ask, the puzzles they try to solve, and the empirical research which they conduct. Psychodynamic, trait, behavioral, and phenomenological orientations have each directed our attention to a specific range of phenomena, suggested a kind of order which may be discovered in the world, and had distinct implications for theory construction, research design, and practical affairs.

The intentions of this chapter are to outline the life course as a theoretical orientation and to suggest that order may be discovered in the analysis of sequences of person × situation interaction. The life course may be defined as the sequence of events and experiences in a life from birth until death and the chain of personal states and encountered situations which influence and are influenced by this sequence of events. The generative questions for a life course orientation are: What kinds of order or regularity may be found in the sequence of events and processes in individual lives, groups of lives, or lives in general? What is the causal and probabilistic structure of the course of experience? What are the meanings of events and experiences through the life span, including the prospective, concurrent, and retrospective meanings of events? What processes (cognitive, affective, physiological, social, and historical) are responsible for the flow of subjective experience and overt behavior over time? Most simply, how do lives work?

A life course orientation is concerned with the enduring problems of describing, understanding, making predictions about, and designing and evaluating efforts to change the course of lives. Specific generalizations about the life course may come and go (cf., Cronbach, 1975; Gergen, 1973), but these problems remain. It should be noted that this chapter takes a microperspective on the life course, focusing on the processes influencing the course of experience within lives, and regarding the social and historical context primarily as a background against which individuals act. This is in contrast with a sociological or macroperspective on the life course which puts greater emphasis on the influences of changing social, demographic, and historical conditions upon the collective life course (Elder, 1981b).

The objectives of a life course orientation are significantly different from those in the study of personality. Consider the following question: What are the aspirations of personality psychologists? If personality psychologists could know anything in the world, what would they most like to know? Answers will undoubtedly vary widely, but representative aspirations might be described as (1) understanding the psychological mechanisms and processes which regulate the expression of impulses, the satisfaction of needs, and the contents of consciousness, (2) identifying and measuring the major dimensions of personality, determining their correlational structure, and assessing their relationship to outcomes in the natural environment, (3) understanding the ways in which behavior is controlled by situational stimuli, (4) understanding how phenomenological awareness and self-concepts affect behavior, or (5) understanding how persons and situations reciprocally interact in determining behavior. In contrast, studies of the life course have more explicit temporal and ecological dimensions and are concerned with questions about the causal structure of sequences of experience, about the processes through which persons and situations interact over the course of time, and about the movement of persons through social and historical worlds. The analysis of persons or personalities is not the same as the analysis of lives. Persons are one component of "the life structure" (Levinson et al., 1978), or of the life history process. These distinctions have not always been made, and it should be noted that study of the life course is congruent with several streams within the history of personality psychology, such as the personology of Henry Murray (1938), Robert White's (1966) study of lives, and recent investigations in interactional psychology (Magnusson and Endler, 1977).

The term "life course" is being used here to indicate the course of experience in individual lives, groups of lives, or lives in general; while the term "life history" refers primarily to the course of experience in an individual life. The bulk of this book is devoted to issues in the study of individual life histories, but this chapter and the following one are concerned with conceptualizations of the life course. This chapter focuses specifically on the analysis of sequences of person-situation interaction as an approach to conceptualizing the life course. First is an outline of this sequential interactionist conceptualization, then an illustration of it through an analysis of careers of heroin use. Last is an examination of the implications of a life course orientation for the prediction of behavior.

A Sequential Interactionist Conceptualization
of the Life Course

The life course may be conceptualized as a sequence of person × situation interactions, or, more specifically, as a sequence of person × behavior × situation interactions. This is certainly not the only way of conceptualizing the life course, but it is a useful one, and one which relates the life course to current discussions of interactionism in personality and social psychology (e.g., Alker, 1972; Argyle and Little, 1972; Bem and Allen, 1974; Bowers, 1973; Ekehammar, 1974; Endler and Magnusson, 1976; Magnusson and Endler, 1977; Wachtel, 1973; and Yinger, 1965). Although I use the term "interaction," the argument could also be presented in terms of "transactions," putting a more explicit emphasis on the mutually determining nature of persons and situations.

A life course orientation is concerned with sequences of experience in the natural environment and thus with the processes through which persons, situations, and behaviors influence each other over the course of time. This is interactionism with an explicit temporal dimension and is consistent with what Olweus (1977) and Bandura (1977) describe as reciprocal interaction, or Magnusson and Endler (1977) describe as "dynamic" interaction. It is also interaction with an explicit ecological dimension, in its concern with persons' movements through a social structure and an historical world over the course of time. It is widely agreed (e.g., Magnusson and Endler, 1977; Overton and Reese, 1973; Pervin, 1978) that recognizing interaction is not sufficient, and that attention needs to be paid to the *how* of interaction, or to the cognitive, affective, physiological, and social processes which determine how persons function within situations.

The life course can be conceptualized as a sequence of processes, as well as a sequence of interactions (cf., Haan, 1977, who argues that personality can best be conceptualized as processes and their organization). Three of the most general processes that need to be considered are (1) *behavior-determining processes,* resulting from the interaction of persons with situations, (2) *person-determining processes,* or the processes which create, maintain, and change personal states and characteristics, and (3)

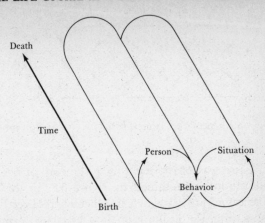

Figure 6.1   An interactional model of the life course.

situation-determining processes, or the processes through which people select, create, and influence the situations they encounter. The relationship between these three processes over time is represented in an interactional model of the life course in Figure 6.1.

Each of the arrows in Figure 6.1 represents one of the three causal processes mentioned above. There are no arrows directly linking persons and situations with each other, which represents the assumption that the effects of persons upon situations are usually mediated through their behavior, and that the effects of situations upon persons are typically mediated by the person's experience within the situation. However, for a few analytical purposes, such as studying the effects of physical attractiveness, it will be useful to consider causal arrows which directly link persons and situations with each other. It should be noted that the person component of this diagram is not restricted to psychological variables, but also includes biological, social, and economic variables, such as sex, appearance, credentials, and wealth.

Personal variables, such as intelligence or self-concept, and situational variables, such as home or college, are frequently of greater duration than behavioral or experiential variables, such as a specific act, thought, or feeling. At the risk of using a clumsy metaphor, the stream of behavior flows through banks of personal and situational variables which are of relatively greater stability.

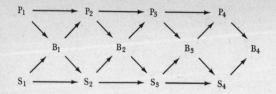

Figure 6.2   Sequences of person × behavior × situation interaction.

An alternative way of representing a sequence of person × situation interactions is contained in Figure 6.2. In this diagram there are no causal arrows which link behaviors directly to each other, representing the assumption that behaviors cannot cause each other, except as mediated through changes in the organism, or less directly, through changes in the situation. For some purposes, it would be useful to add arrows coming from outside the system to indicate maturational or nonexperiential sources of change upon person variables, and to indicate situational changes not caused by the person.

Figures 6.1 and 6.2 may be used for conceptualizing the temporal context of a specific behavior; for examining a particular sequence, process, or career; or for conceptualizing the entire life course. It should be clear that these diagrams of person × behavior × situation interaction represent only one way of conceptualizing the life course and may be expected to prove useful for many, but not all, analytic purposes.

Analysis of Heroin Use from a Life Course Perspective

A specific substantive example, such as an analysis of heroin use, can help to illustrate the implications of a life course orientation and to compare it with other orientations. Using a trait or psychodynamic view, one is led to raise questions about the relationships of heroin use to personality variables. The personality characteristics of addicts have been assessed with the Rorschach, TAT, interviews, MMPI, CPI, Rotter Internal-External Control Scale, and the Edwards Personal Preference Schedule (Kurtines, Hogan, and Weiss, 1975; Reith, Crockett, and Craig, 1975). Drug addicts have been characterized as maladjusted, hostile, immature, dependent, manipulative, and narcissistic (Feldman, 1968). One weakness of this approach is that most people with these characteristics do not become heroin addicts. A second problem is that the causal relationships between personality variables and heroin use are often unclear. Which personality characteristics led to heroin use and which are a consequence of heroin use? There is, for example, evidence that elevations on the Hypochondriasis and Hysteria scales of the MMPI are a temporary consequence of the addict's stressful life on the street, rather than indicators of enduring personality characteristics which led to heroin use (Sheppard, Ricca, Frachchia, and Merlis, 1973; Sutker and Allain, 1973).

Using a situational orientation, one is inclined to ask questions about the contexts or environments associated with narcotics use. Heroin use in New York City has been found to be heaviest in neighborhoods with the highest poverty rates, the most crowded dwelling units, the highest incidence of broken families, and so on (Chein, Gerard, Lee, and Rosenfeld, 1964). A limitation of this approach is that most people exposed to these conditions do not become heroin users. A second problem is that some features of the environment may be a function of heroin use as well as a cause of it. A similar difficulty arises in ecological studies of mental illness and criminal behavior, in which it is unclear to what extent people with deviant tendencies move into high prevalence areas, and to what extent deviant behavior is elicited by the social environment (Moos, 1976).

Using an interactionist position, one is led to formulate questions about which individual tendencies interacting with what situational conditions will lead to heroin use. This orientation permits greater precision than the first two, but it does not provide an understanding of which persons get into which situations, or of how their behavior affects them and affects their environment, which will in turn affect future behavior.

A life course orientation builds on an interactionist perspective and suggests a more complex set of questions about the temporal course of behavior. The questions about heroin use suggested by a life course orientation are (1) What kinds of persons in interaction with what kinds of situations lead to initial use of heroin? (2) How do these person × situation configurations come about? (3) What are the consequences of initial use for the person and for the situation? (4) Which new person ×

situation configurations will result in continuation vs. termina-tion of opiate use? (5) If heroin use continues and leads to addiction, what are the further consequences for the person and the situation? (6) What person × situation processes will lead to continuation or termination of addiction? (7) If the person breaks the habit, what new person × situation configurations lead to relapse or continued abstinence?

The temporal course of heroin use can be usefully divided into the four stages of experimental use, occasional use, addic-tive use, and termination of use. How can the initial or experi-mental use of heroin be explained? In Chein et al.'s (1964) study of heroin users in New York City, the first opportunity for heroin use came through offers of a friend, or in a group setting. Few addicts actively sought this first opportunity. Even so, ex-posure to these situations was not random. The Chein study compared the experiences of four groups: nondelinquent addicts, delinquent addicts, nonusing delinquents, and controls with similar social characteristics living in the same neighborhoods. Fifty percent of the control group had an opportunity to try heroin, compared to two-thirds of the delinquent nonusers, and to 100 percent of the delinquent and nondelinquent users.

Differential exposure to situations where heroin was available is a partial explanation of initial use but not a complete one. Re-sponses to this opportunity differed radically among the four groups. Of the nonusing delinquents, only four out of the thirty-six who had the opportunity tried it.

How can the differential response of these groups to the op-portunity to try heroin be explained? Only 17 percent of the users (interviewed in 1953) claimed that they knew anything before age sixteen about the harmful effects of heroin, while 79 percent of the delinquent nonusers said that they were aware of its negative consequences in areas such as health, pressure toward criminal activity, and effect on character. Although part of these differences may be due to retrospective distortion, the data still suggest that the anticipated consequences of heroin use differ-entiated those who responded to the opportunity from those who refused it.

Second, what explanation can be given of the transition from experimental to occasional use of heroin? One variable is the effect of initial use on the person. Those who experience a positive reaction are more likely to progress to occasional use than those who do not. In Chein's sample, about half of the users reported a positive reaction upon first use, while a third reported negative reactions. This first reaction influenced the timing of subsequent use. Of those with favorable reactions, two-thirds continued immediately; while of those with unfavorable reactions, only two-fifths continued immediately. Given the appropriate individual predispositions, occasional use of a drug may continue largely as a function of its easy availability (Clausen, 1966).

Third, the transition from occasional to addictive use has been conceptualized in a variety of ways. When heroin is used regularly, physical tolerance develops, and increased doses are needed in order to obtain the same subjective effects. A major aspect of the transition to addiction is the growth of physical dependence and the desire to avoid the pain of withdrawal (Lindesmith, 1947). Habitual narcotics users, however, are motivated by a continuing desire for euphoria, as well as by avoidance of withdrawal symptoms (McAuliffe and Gordon, 1974).

Another theory emphasizes that the person may become labelled as a deviant, perhaps be fired from his job, and be cut off from participation in more conventional groups (Becker, 1963). This labelling process can be accompanied by changes in self-conception and changes in attitudes toward society. In addition, the heroin user may choose to disengage himself from people who disapprove of drugs and to select new friends primarily among other users (Feldman, 1968). Thus, the heroin user can create an environment for himself in which narcotics are more readily available and heroin use is not looked upon with such disapproval.

Heroin has fewer direct physical effects than is generally realized (Goode, 1973), but depending upon social, legal, and economic conditions, addictive use of heroin may radically alter the person's whole way of life. For physicians, who have relatively free access to narcotics, addiction does not necessarily cause major life changes. There are wide variations across cultures and historical periods in the social, medical, and criminological correlates of heroin use, but for the contemporary street addict in the United States, addiction frequently leads to health problems, to crime, to alienation from family and friends, and to prison.

Fourth, heroin use may be terminated or reduced through a wide variety of person × situation processes. The breaking of physical dependency does not, however, ensure the end of addiction. Out of 1,912 addicts living in New York City who were discharged from the drug rehabilitation program in Lexington, Kentucky, more than 90 percent were re-addicted six months after discharge (Hunt and Odoroff, 1962).

In spite of high re-addiction rates, there is a tendency for heroin use to decrease over time and to decrease with increasing age. In a subsample of the Hunt and Odoroff group, 9 percent were voluntarily abstinent six months after discharge, 17 percent two years after discharge, and 25 percent five years after discharge (Duvall, Locke, and Brill, 1963). Behavior change may come through a change in the situation (no drugs available), through changes in the person (physical detoxification, a decision to change), or through some interaction of personal and situational factors (losing a supplier and deciding not to make the effort to locate a new one). However, the various sequences of changes in person × situation interaction which lead to the termination of heroin use are not well understood.

In review, let us formally conceptualize a sequence of processes involved in the four stages of a drug use career. At each stage, rough estimates of the state of selected person variables, situation variables, and behavior probabilities can be given. Although somewhat schematic, this suggests a general approach to analyzing sequences of person × behavior × situation interaction.

At stage one, the period of experimental use, heroin is available infrequently, the person's desire for it is low to moderate, and the probability of taking the drugs is moderately low. At stage two, the period of occasional use, heroin is available occasionally, but perhaps not much more frequently than at stage one. If the individual has found this first experience pleasurable, the probability of taking heroin rises.

At stage three, the period of regular or heavy use, the whole person-behavior-situation configuration may change dramatically. The addict may be in a situation where heroin is readily available and most of his friends are drug users. His desire for heroin may be so intense that he is willing to do anything in order to obtain it. In situations where drugs are available, the probability that he will take them rises to near certainty. As a product of his increased desire, and of the increased availability of drugs, the frequency of heroin use may jump from once a month or once a week to three or four times a day.

At stage four, the period of discontinued use, change may occur in a variety of ways, such as a decision to withdraw on one's own, methadone treatment, or involvement with a treatment community. The probability of taking heroin, if it is available, may shrink to near zero. Environmental changes, such as being placed in prison, may make temporary withdrawal inevitable. However, termination of use is not necessarily permanent, and depending upon an individual's characteristics and later environments, the whole process may begin again.

It is also important to recognize that there are substantial contextual variations in almost every aspect of the course of heroin use. There are significant variations across cultures and historical periods in the characteristics of users (on age, race, social class, etc.), in the reasons for initial use, in the probability of moving from one level of use to another, in the paths out of addiction, and in the correlates and consequences of use for physical health, social contacts, and criminal behavior (Brecher, 1972; Judson, 1974; Platt and Labate, 1976). Thus, investigation within a sequential interactionist framework (as in psychodynamic, trait, or behavioral orientations) should proceed with the expectation that many relationships will not be universal and that models of the course of behavior have to be developed which are sensitive to variations across cultures, groups, and historical periods.

In summary, a history of heroin use is characterized by a sequence of person × behavior × situation interactions. Psychodynamic, trait, behavioral, sociological, or interactive orientations all shed light on some phases of narcotics use, but the career of a heroin user cannot be adequately understood without considering sequences of behavior-determining, person-determining, and situation-determining processes.

Similar analyses may be made of histories of aggressive behavior, sexual behavior, altruistic behavior, abnormal behavior, creative behavior and other forms of behavior which vary with both changing personal states and encountered situations. A sequential process orientation can also be used for analyzing the temporal trajectory of personal characteristics which are subject to influence by situations and by experience, such as self-concept, level of anxiety, values, or attitudes. Finally, a life course orientation can be used to study "environmental histories" or "situational careers," and to explore the processes responsible for an individual's movement through a sequence of situations. In short, a life course orientation provides a common conceptual framework for analyzing sequences of behavior, sequences of personal states, and sequences of encountered situations.

The utility of a life course or sequential process orientation can be suggested by considering research examples from a number of other substantive areas. In a study of disturbed pre-adolescent boys, Raush (1965) examined the "contingencies through which the antecedent action of one child exerts control on the subsequent actions of another" (p. 488). Normal and hyperaggressive boys, aged 9–12, in groups of six, were systematically observed in six different situations (e.g., breakfast, or structured games). The two control groups produced 85 percent and 89 percent antecedent acts that could be classified as friendly, while the hyperaggressive group produced 58 percent friendly acts. In response to unfriendly antecedent acts, the control and disturbed boys both responded in an unfriendly way about 80 percent of the time. However, in response to antecedent acts which the staff saw as friendly, the normals responded in an unfriendly way only 8 percent of the time, while the hyperaggressive group responded in an unfriendly way 45 percent of the time early in treatment, and 19 percent of the time after 1.5 years of treatment. The hyperaggressive and control groups did not differ in their response to hostile acts, but did differ in response to friendly acts. Putting together a sequential chain of five behaviors, the hyperaggressive boys were behaving in a friendly way 40 percent of the time by the fifth behavior, while the two normal groups were behaving in a friendly way approximately 80 percent of the time.

Wachtel (1977), in an effort to integrate features of psychodynamic and behavioral theory, has spoken of "interaction cycles," in which early psychodynamic processes affect subsequent experiences and later environments, which in turn affect the continuation or change of earlier psychodynamic processes, and so on. Within this interactional-cyclical view, "the critical role of childhood is understood in terms of the way in which the particular patterns of behavior one develops skew the kinds of later experience one is likely to encounter and hence create an idiosyncratic environment of a sort likely to maintain the very pattern which produced that kind of environment in the first place" (Wachtel, 1977, p. 320). As an example, Wachtel considers the case of a man with a reaction formation against intense rage. He is frightened by feelings of anger, so acts in excessively meek or conciliatory ways, which lead others to take advantage of him. This mistreatment arouses further feelings of resentment and anger. His defensive strategy has led to experiences which generate anger, and to the continued need to defend against it.

As a third example, Elder (1974) examined the life courses of a group of 167 persons born in 1920–21 in Oakland, California, and studied periodically since 1932 at the Institute of Human Development, University of California, Berkeley. He compared the life experiences of middle class and working class children growing up in families that were deprived (35 percent or more reduction in income) or nondeprived during the Depression. One surprising finding was that within each social class (middle vs. working class), economic deprivation in childhood did not lead to substantially lower occupational attainment at age forty-seven. Within the working class, economic deprivation for male children did reduce educational attainment, but this was largely offset by a sequence of events which went roughly as follows: men from deprived working-class families were faced earlier with adult-like responsibilities in the family, which led to earlier crystallization of vocational goals, and to earlier establishment of a stable career line, which led to higher occupational attainment. In this example, and in others throughout the book, Elder's work illustrates the possibilities for studying sequences of person × situation interaction in the natural environment.

The importance of studying sequences and processes of person × situation interaction has recently been stated in a number of general theoretical formulations (e.g., Bandura, 1977; Magnusson and Endler, 1977; Pervin, 1978), and in analyses of interpersonal relationships (Peterson, 1977), marital interaction (Raush, Barry,

Hertel and Swain, 1974), and processes of stress and coping (Lazarus and Launier, 1978).

Implications for the Prediction of Behavior

The limitations of atemporal perspectives in personality theory become particularly apparent when one is concerned with the issue of prediction. A life course orientation, considering the interaction of personal, behavioral, and situational variables over time, provides a more adequate foundation for predictive efforts than do orientations focusing primarily on traits, psychodynamic processes, or situational influences on behavior.

The utility of predictions based on inferences about global traits has been seriously questioned. It has been argued that trait-based predictions have not been very successful, except in the domain of intelligence and ability variables (Mischel, 1968; Peterson, 1968; Vernon, 1964).

According to one view, the disappointing results of predictive studies indicate that the trait paradigm is faulty (Mischel, 1968, 1973), while another view is that predictive failures are often a result of seriously defective research and that adequate research does provide examples of predictive success (Block, 1977). Alternatively, as will be argued here, the trait paradigm may be appropriate under a limited and specifiable set of conditions.

If one assumes that behavior is a function of stable individual traits, then it makes sense to measure these traits, and to use these measurements in predicting future behavior. This strategy can be effective only under a restricted set of conditions. If a trait, such as intelligence or introversion-extraversion, is relatively stable over time, and is fairly consistent across situations, then trait assessments can yield valid predictions. Conversely, to the extent that behavior is situationally or interactively determined, and to the extent that person variables change as a result of experience, a trait approach to prediction cannot be expected to be widely effective.

A behavioral or social learning orientation is frequently proposed as an alternative to trait approaches. The implications of a social learning orientation for the assessment and change of behavior are fairly clear, but what are its implications for the prediction of behavior? A social learning orientation emphasizes the specificity of behavior or its dependence upon the environmental conditions which maintain and change behavior. The predictive implications of this view are that, most generally, future behavior will depend upon future situations. In conditions where the future situation is known, assessment and prediction proceed by taking "samples" of a person's behavior in similar situations. "A person's relevant past behaviors tend to be the best predictors of his future behavior in similar situations" (Mischel, 1968, p. 135). If behavior is determined largely by situations, the strategy of predicting future behavior from samples of past behavior can be successful only to the extent that future situations are similar to past situations. The prediction of future situations has never received much attention, but if social behaviorists, or interactionists, seek to accurately predict future behavior, research on situation-determining processes in the natural environment seems to be a necessity.

Even in those circumstances where future situations are known, the social learning paradigm will be useful under only a limited set of conditions. To the extent that relevant person variables change during the time interval between assessment and criterion periods, predictions from behavior samples are likely to be inaccurate. For example, suppose that we want to predict the response of a woman with a snake phobia to handling a live snake three weeks from now. As part of a systematic desensitization treatment, she has constructed an anxiety hierarchy ranking situations related to snakes from least to most anxiety provoking, with "handling a live snake" as the most frightening situation. The strategy of predicting future behavior on the basis of past behavior in similar situations would lead one to assess her response to this situation at T_1, and predict that if exposed to the same situation at T_3, her behavior would most likely be the same. The weakness in this predictive strategy is obvious. If the subject spends the intervening time period working her way through the stimulus hierarchy, then her response at T_3 is likely to be quite different. Knowledge of likely intervening experiences enables one to improve over predictions based solely on past behavior in similar situations.

In itself, this is a minor example, chosen for its transparency. But in principle, is the situation any different in the prediction of vocational performance, criminal behavior, or interpersonal behavior? The accuracy of behavioral prediction depends upon assuming that person variables remain stable. To the extent that relevant person variables change over the predictive interval, predictions based on behavior samples are likely to be inaccurate.

If an interactionist position is taken seriously what are its implications for the prediction of behavior? An interactionist orientation implies that future behavior will be determined by an interaction of future person states with future situations. This suggests that the problems of assessment and prediction cannot be solved by the consideration of personal or situational variables alone.

A life course orientation suggests a strategy for integrating person-centered and situation-centered assessment, enabling us to avoid some of the limitations inherent in either approach taken individually. This strategy focuses on the assessment of person-situation configurations and on the likelihood of alternative person-situation configurations developing out of this initial system. For example, in an effort to predict the termination of heroin addiction, assessments would be made of personal characteristics and of the person's location in an environmental network. For men living in New York City, the probability of voluntary heroin abstinence one year after treatment for addiction was about 10–15 percent (Duvall et al., 1963). For addicts in the army in Viet Nam, the probability of abstinence one year after return to the United States was greater than 90 percent (McGlothlin, 1975). Our best predicitions of the termination of heroin use would depend upon assessment of subjects' locations in environmental networks, and upon their likelihood of moving to alternative future environments, as well as upon assessment of their personal characteristics.

In summary, trait-based approaches to prediction are useful only when person attributes can be assumed to be stable over time, and only to the extent that behavior is stable across predictor and criterion situations. Situational or behavioral approaches are useful only when relevant person variables can be assumed to be stable and only to the extent that future situations are known or that behavior is invariant across the range of expectable future situations. If behavior is determined by the interaction of persons with situations, then a comprehensive approach to prediction must assess person-behavior-situation configurations and estimate the probability of alternative configurations developing out of this initial system. This more complex view of the prediction problem suggested by a life course orientation will, in some domains, enable us to increase our predictive capacities, but in other areas, it can help us to recognize exaggerated predictive claims and to better understand those conditions which inevitably limit the possibilities of accurate prediction.

Conclusion

There is little doubt that order can be found, and has been found, by those pursuing psychodynamic, trait, behavioral, and phenomenological orientations. By using a criterion of "statistical significance," some empirical support can be found for each of these orientations. No single orientation has a monopoly upon empirical support. By using the more rigorous criterion of proportion of variance accounted for, or of complete predictability, it also becomes apparent that no single orientation provides a completely adequate theory of behavior.

Each orientation seems to find its strongest support in different methodological foundations and to be particularly suited for different applications. For example, a behavioral view seems to receive its strongest support on experimental grounds and to be particularly suited for problems of behavior change. A psychodynamic view seems to receive its strongest support from clinical observation and from personal experiences in therapy and to be most useful for the interpretation of disturbed thought, affect, and behavior. A phenomenological view seems to receive some support from both clinical and scientific contexts and to be most useful in the conduct of interpersonal relationships. A trait-factor approach seems to receive its strongest support from correlational research and to be most useful for purposes of selection and decision making. (This comparative assessment is not intended to imply that all orientations are equal in scope, power, or utility, but rather is an effort to comprehend the relationships of the different orientations to each other and to understand how intelligent and well-meaning scientists can be so passionately divided in their theoretical loyalties.)

Each orientation may appear unimpressive when viewed from

different epistemological bases, or when applied to different uses. For example, a psychoanalytic view does not receive very strong support when tested experimentally, or, a trait-factor approach is not that useful for the conduct of psychotherapy. Although the strengths and weaknesses of these orientations might well be characterized in other ways, it is unlikely that this would lead to disagreement with the view that each of these orientations has discovered some form of order in the world, each has relied upon somewhat different procedures for discovering this order, and each has proven useful for some practical concerns but not for others. Similarly, a life course orientation (1) suggests a type of order that may be found in the world, (2) requires methods and strategies appropriate for discovering this kind of order, and (3) has implications for a particular range of practical concerns.

To expand briefly on these points, a life course orientation suggests that order may be found in the causal structure of the flow of experience and in the accompanying processes of person × behavior × situation interaction. It directs our attention to a fundamental and enduring set of problems in describing, understanding, making predictions about, and intentionally changing the course of lives.

The methodological problems are enormous and demand our creative attention. Understanding of the course of lives may be pursued through (1) quantitative experimental and correlational research, (2) historical and biographical research, (3) analyses of personal experience, and (4) clinical and professional practice.

We need research designs capable of studying sequences of person × behavior × situation interaction, in both natural and controlled settings. However, understanding the course of lives demands more than the development of more complex research designs; it also requires a shift in our strategies of explanation and prediction away from purely deductive-nomological ones in which individual cases are subsumed under general laws. Due to the enormous variety and change in the course of experience across cultures, across historical periods, and even across individuals, greater attention must be paid to the development of idiographic methods, $n = 1$ methodology, and explanation via context-specific case studies. Such methods for the detailed study of individuals will be examined in Chapters 8–10.

Skeptics may feel that the study of lives is impractical or hopelessly complex. It is granted that research on the life course may be methodologically complex, and that absolute certainty in the understanding of lives may continue to elude us. Nevertheless, assumptions about the causal structure of the course of experience and about the long-range effects of different courses of action upon this experience are inextricably bound into our personal lives, intellectual and professional lives, and social policies. The following chapter develops one approach to analyzing the causal and probabilistic structure of the course of lives.

7

A Stage-State Analysis
of the Life Course

The search for useful ways of conceptualizing the course of human lives has been a long and difficult one, approached from many different theoretical perspectives, each with distinct assets and limitations. To provide a partial list, the life course has been conceptualized as a sequence of episodes and proceedings (Murray, 1938, 1959); a sequence of tasks or issues (Erikson, 1963); a sequence of stages (Levinson, Darrow, Klein, Levinson, and McKee, 1978; Loevinger, 1976); a sequence of transitions (Lowenthal, Thurnher, and Chiriboga, 1975); a sequence of personality organizations (Block, 1971); a sequence of changing environments and organismic responses (Skinner, 1953); a sequence of dialectical operations (Riegel, 1975); a sequence of person-situation interactions (Baltes and Schaie, 1973); and, in the previous chapter, as a sequence of behavior-determining, person-determining, and situation-determining processes. The life course has also been conceptualized from sociological and social structural perspectives that focus more on roles, life-long socialization, age norms, and the flow of populations through socially and historically structured pathways (e.g., Clausen, 1972; Elder, 1975, 1977; Neugarten and Datan, 1973; Riley, Johnson, and Foner, 1972).

This chapter presents a stage-state analysis of the life course, which can be used for identifying types of life courses and their relative frequency, estimating the likelihood of moving from a given state through a sequence of future states, and analyzing the routes and processes connecting initial states with a variety of potential outcomes. This conceptual framework is intended to address an important set of questions not adequately dealt with in other orientations, but like each of the other perspectives, it also has a certain "range of convenience" and is useful for only a particular range of theoretical and practical purposes. A stage-state approach does not allow us to analyze the process of living in all its complexity, but it does provide a method for examining the movement of persons through a social structure over time; for investigating the alternative routes, or sequences of processes, through which initial person-situation configurations may be linked with an array of potential outcomes; and for analyzing aspects of the probabilistic and causal structure of the course of lives.

A stage-state analysis makes the simplifying assumptions that the life course can be divided into a sequence of stages and that a person can exist in one of a limited number of states within each stage. For example, if the course of early experience is divided into Freud's psychosexual stages, then individuals can be characterized according to whether they have been excessively frustrated, excessively gratified, or normally satisfied at the oral or anal stage. Conditions of inadequate or excessive gratification may be conceptualized as possible states (or outcomes) within each psychosexual stage. If the life course is divided according to Erikson's eight psychosocial stages, then persons can presumably be characterized by their ratios of basic trust versus mistrust experienced or acquired at the oral-sensory stage, of identity versus role confusion in adolescence, intimacy versus isolation in young adulthood, and so on. In both examples, potential differences in experience can be conceptualized as possible states within relatively common stages.

The stage-state approach combines aspects of the search for common sequential order pursued in stage theories along with a concern for individual differences in the way that stages are negotiated and experienced. As expressed by Levinson et al. (1978), "Everyone lives through the same developmental periods in adulthood, just as in childhood, though people go through them in radically different ways" (p. 41). As will be discussed in a later section of this chapter, a stage-state analysis can also be used for examining the possibilities of experience open to individuals and for analyzing some of the ways in which the course of experience is not solely the unfolding of invariant developmental progressions but is also (as stressed by Tyler, 1978) a function of individual goals, plans, and choices.

Both stages and states can be defined by personal, situational, or behavioral-experiential variables, or by combinations of the three. The concept of *stage* is being defined here in a broad way to indicate periods in a process and not necessarily in the more technical sense used in developmental psychology of a hierarchy of qualitatively different structures (Kitchener, 1978; Kohlberg, 1969). The most sophisticated conceptualizations of states within a stage will identify specific kinds of persons behaving in particular ways in particular social and historical circumstances. Although the present focus is on a stage-state analysis of the life course, stage-state analyses may also be made of the course of experience within more specific domains, such as within educational careers, occupational careers, or interpersonal relationships.

A particular set of stage and state definitions permits an exhaustive classification of possible life courses, with a life course defined by a person's movement through a particular sequence of states. The empirical distribution of people among alternative life courses can be computed. This provides a way of thinking about types of life courses and about their relative frequency within a population. In some cases, it would be possible to compare the frequency of different types of life courses across age cohorts, or across cultures and ethnic groups.

By studying the movement of numbers of people through a sequence of stages, multistage flow tables or transition matrices can be constructed that indicate the probabilities of a person's moving from any given state through an array of possible future states. These multistage flow tables can also be used to identify the variety and likelihood of routes between a given early state, or origin, and a specific later state, or destination. This specification of routes provides a way of analyzing one class of life history processes.

This chapter presents a quantitative illustration of a stage-state analysis of the life course and suggests that empirical data from a stage-state model can be examined in relationship to the three reference points of statistical independence, complete predictability, and implicit theories about the course of lives. Finally, there is a brief discussion of the ways in which data from stage-state analyses can and cannot be used by conscious agents in thinking about the future course of life experience.

Types of Life Courses and Their Distribution

For this initial exposition of the stage-state approach, I will use a relatively simple set of four stages, with four possible states within each stage. The analysis will focus on transitions between type of family background, level of educational attainment, type of first job, and type of last job. It cannot be emphasized too strongly that the stages and states proposed here are illustrative and in no sense final. They are used to give a quantitative illustration of a form of analysis that can be applied to a range of substantive phenomena and that may employ a variety of alternative conceptualizations of stages and states.

The data come from the Occupational Changes in a Generation data file (Blau and Duncan, 1967), which is a representative national sample of more than 20,000 American men between the ages of twenty and sixty-nine, taken in 1962. The present analysis uses a random subsample of 614 men between the ages of thirty-five and forty-five.

The four stages are family background (indicated by father's occupation), level of educational attainment, type of first job, and type of last job (most recent job at the time of the survey). Occupations are divided into four levels or states: professional and executive, skilled, semiskilled, and unskilled and farm (hereafter abbreviated as unskilled). Educational attainment is also divided into four states: elementary school, some high school, high school graduation, and college or higher.

What are the possible courses among these stages? The number of possible courses can be calculated by multiplying the number of states within each stage; in this case, there are $4 \times 4 \times 4 \times 4 = 256$ possible life courses. Life courses are defined by a pattern of movement through a sequence of states, rather than by characteristics at any single stage, and a life course can be identified or classified according to any one of these 256 possible state sequences.

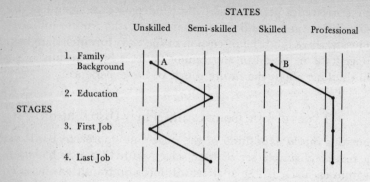

Figure 7.1 Alternative paths through a sequence of stages and states. (The four states for Stage 2—education—are, respectively, elementary school education, some high school, high school graduation, and college or higher.)

This set of stages and states, and the variety of courses through them, is illustrated in Figure 7.1. Of the 256 possible paths, Person A followed the particular course of movement from an unskilled family background to some high school to an unskilled first job to a semiskilled last job, and Person B followed the path from a skilled family background to a college or higher education to a professional or executive first and last job. (The model could be made more complex by considering changes in personal characteristics and behaviors as different kinds of people moved along the various paths.)

What is the empirical distribution of people in this sample among each of the possible life courses? If people were distributed randomly among each of the 256 possible courses, there would be 1/256, or approximately .4 percent, of the population within each life course. The single most frequent course, containing 5.8 percent of the population, was defined by movement from family background with an unskilled father to elementary education to unskilled first job to unskilled last job. The second most frequent course, containing 5.1 percent of the sample, consisted of movement from a family with an unskilled father to elementary education to unskilled first job to semiskilled last job, and the third most frequent course, followed by 3.0 percent of the sample, was defined by movement from a family with a professional or executive father to college education to professional first job to professional last job.

To account for the majority of men, it is necessary to consider only a small portion of the theoretically possible life courses. Of 256 possible courses, 27, or 11 percent of the total, were pursued by 1 percent or more of the population. These 27 courses accounted for 54 percent of the population. The other 46 percent of the men were distributed among the remaining possible courses.

Not all of the theoretically possible courses actually occurred. Of the 256 possible courses, 99 were not followed by any member of the sample. For example, there was no one who had a professional father, got a college education, a professional first job, and an unskilled last job. Neither was there anyone in the sample who had an unskilled father, received an elementary education, and ended up in a professional or executive last job. There are 62 other possible courses that were followed by only one person, or by .2 percent of the sample.

Why are some life courses so much more common than others? Why, for example, were there so many sons of unskilled workers who received an elementary education and got unskilled first and last jobs? Was upward mobility prevented by deficits in skills or intelligence, by low levels of aspiration and expectation, by class biases of schools or employers, by an interaction of social-structural constaints with deficits in personal and economic resources, or by other factors and processes? A detailed answer will probably require different explanations for different individuals and groups, and will need to consider the sequential interaction of persons with their social environments. In any case, the discovery of nonrandom transition probabilities suggests questions about the causal structure of the course of lives that can then be investigated through experimental, quasi-experimental, and naturalistic research methods (Blalock, 1964; Campbell and Stanley, 1966; Cook and Campbell, 1979).

Multistage Flow Tables

Using a stage-state analysis of the life course, a set of multistage flow tables or transition matrices can be constructed that make it possible to estimate the probabilities of a person moving from

Table 7.1   Population Percentages for Each State

Education	%	Type of work	Percentage Father's job	First job	Last job
College	27	Professional	15	10	30
High school	29	Skilled	26	28	30
Some high school	19	Semiskilled	17	28	23
Elementary	25	Unskilled	42	34	17

Note. Each cell contains a percentage of the column total.

any given state through an array of future states. One can then study how these transition probabilities are affected by prior background and can estimate the probabilities of taking different routes from a given origin to a particular destination. Thus, multistage flow tables allow us to address a set of questions that cannot be handled through the use of base rates or standard two-stage flow tables.

The base rates or population percentages for each state within each stage are contained in Table 7.1. Of the entire sample, 15 percent of the men had fathers with professional jobs, and 26 percent had fathers with skilled jobs. As for education, 27 percent of the sample received a college education, and 25 percent obtained an elementary school education.

In the absence of any other information, these base rates can be used for making predictions. With base rates alone, it would be estimated that a person would be most likely to receive a high school education, to get an unskilled first job, and to get a professional or skilled last job. Base rates have the limitation of not indicating the differential probabilities of outcome dependent on the values of earlier states. For example, men from professional versus unskilled families could be expected to have significantly different educational and occupational careers. To examine differential probabilities, a set of flow tables is needed. For a model with four stages, there are six possible two-stage flow tables (e.g., stage one to two, two to three, or one to four), one of which is produced in Table 7.2.

These percentages are significantly different than those that would be expected on the grounds of base rates alone. Knowing father's occupation is of substantial help in predicting a man's

Table 7.2   Father's Job to Education:
Outflow Percentages

Father's job	Level of education			
	Elemen- tary	Some high school	High school	College
Professional	3	11	23	63
Skilled	8	16	34	42
Semiskilled	21	24	34	20
Unskilled	43	21	26	10

likely level of education. For example, men with professional fathers had a 63 percent chance of attending college, whereas men with unskilled fathers had only a 10 percent chance. Similarly, knowing a person's level of education helps in predicting his type of first job and type of last job.

Two-stage flow tables are common analytic tools in the social sciences, yet there are several important kinds of questions that they cannot answer and for which the multistage tables in a stage-state analysis are required. First, can life courses be regarded as Markov processes, in which transition probabilities are contingent only on current states (Tibbitt, 1973), or does knowledge of previous states aid in predicting? For example, of all those holding a skilled first job, do men with different family backgrounds have equal chances of attaining a professional last job? Second, by what processes or routes have people moved from their initial family background to their last job? For example, what variety of routes or state sequences were followed by men moving from families with unskilled fathers to professional last jobs?

Questions about differential transitions from one stage-state to later ones depending on previous background and questions about intervening processes can be answered by flow tables containing three or more stages. In this case, we can construct a multistage flow table that indicates movement through a sequence of four stages and that represents all of the 256 possible sequences of state transitions. This complete table can be broken down into sixteen 4 × 4 subtables, each of which has a fixed level of family background and educational attainment. One of these subtables, describing the experience of men from unskilled fam-

Table 7.3   Example of a Multistage Flow Table (Subtable for Men with Unskilled Fathers and Elementary School Educations)

Type of first job	Type of last job				
	Professional	Skilled	Semi-skilled	Unskilled	Total
Professional					
N	—	—	—	—	0
% column total	—	—	—	—	
% row total	—	—	—	—	
% subtable total	—	—	—	—	0
% grand total	—	—	—	—	
Skilled					
N	—	3	2	1	6
% column total	—	24.7	3.8	2.3	
% row total	—	56.6	27.3	16.1	
% subtable total	—	3.3	1.6	.9	5.8
% grand total	—	.6	.3	.2	
Semiskilled					
N	—	4	10	7	21
% column total	—	33.7	25.6	17.6	
% row total	—	20.1	47.3	32.5	
% subtable total	—	4.5	10.5	7.2	22.3
% grand total	—	.8	1.8	1.3	
Unskilled					
N	4	5	28	31	68
% column total	100.0	41.7	70.6	80.2	
% row total	5.8	7.7	40.5	46.0	
% subtable total	4.2	5.6	29.1	33.1	71.9
% grand total	.7	1.0	5.1	5.8	
Total N	4	12	40	39	95
%	4.2	13.3	41.2	41.3	100.0

Note. This is a weighted sample, so there is sometimes a discrepancy between the number of persons in a cell and their percentage of the sample total.

ily backgrounds with elementary educations, is presented in Table 7.3.

The meaning of these figures can be illustrated by considering the lower right-hand cell. The top figure is the number of men in the cell. It indicates that thirty-one men followed the particular life course from unskilled family background to elementary education to unskilled first job to unskilled last job. The second figure is the percent of the column total. It indicates that of men with unskilled last jobs, 80.2 percent came from unskilled first jobs. The third figure is the percent of the row total, indicating that 46.0 percent of men with unskilled first jobs ended up in unskilled last jobs. The fourth figure is the number of men in this cell over the subtable total, showing that 33.1 percent of men from unskilled family backgrounds and elementary educations ended up in unskilled first and last jobs. The fifth figure is the number of men in this cell over the total for the inclusive table; it indicates that 5.8 percent of the sample followed this particular course from unskilled family background to unskilled last job.

What are the effects of background states on transition probabilities? As indicated by data from the comprehensive multi-stage flow table from which Table 7.3 was drawn, men with skilled first jobs have widely different chances of attaining professional last jobs, depending on their preceding history. For men having skilled first jobs, even with family background held constant at the level of unskilled fathers, those with elementary educations have little or no chance of getting a professional last job, those with some high school have a 16 percent chance, those graduating from high school have a 30 percent chance, and those with at least some college have a 43 percent chance of attaining a professional last job. In short, previous background has a substantial effect on later state transitions, and these data cannot be accurately fitted by a Markov model.

Second, what variety of routes were used by people moving from a given family background to a particular type of last job? With this particular model, there are sixteen different ways such transitions may be made. Let us consider, for example, the forty-one men in the sample who moved from an unskilled family background to a professional last job. All together, 14/41 (34 percent) of these men got college educations, and 13/41 (32 percent) got a professional first job. The chances are 9/41 (22 percent) that a man making this transition followed the specific route of going to college *and* getting a professional first job. The chances are 0/41 that he followed the specific route of getting an elementary education and a professional first job. The probability of following any of the fourteen other routes between an unskilled family background and a professional last job can also be calculated.

In general, given a transition between any two nonadjacent states, a stage-state model can indicate the number of possible transition routes and the probability that each of these routes was followed.

So far, the discussion has considered probabilistic transitions between a sequence of states, but a stage-state model can also be used to study causal chains. Working with this same set of stages and states, causal inferences could be made about chains of effects by introducing treatments such as special educational programs or family financial assistance to a sample of children and then examining the sequence of effects on educational attainment, first job, and last job. A quasi-experimental study tracing the effects of an early life experience, in this case economic deprivation, on a sequence of later life stages is reported by Elder (1974).

Comparison with a Path Analytic Approach

Multiple regression and path analytic techniques are frequently used in the analysis of quantitative life course data, so it may be useful to briefly compare the issues addressed by these techniques with those addressed by the multistage transition matrices presented here.

A path analysis of the relationships between family background, level of education, first job, and last job in this sample is presented in Figure 7.2. The straight lines connecting one

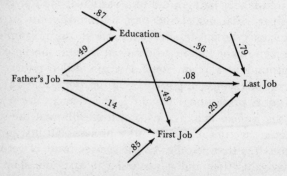

Figure 7.2   A path analysis of occupational attainment.

variable with another show the magnitude of the direct relationship between the two variables. For example, the magnitude of the direct influence of education on last job is .36. These path coefficients are partial regression coefficients, with the other variables in the system controlled for. The lines with no sources indicate the residual paths standing for all other influences on the variables, such as unmeasured causal variables, errors of measurement, and departures of the relationships from additivity and linearity.

What kinds of questions can be addressed with a path analytic model versus a multistage conditional probability model? Path analysis allows us to give quantitative interpretations to the causal relationships among variables in a system. "The technique of path analysis is not a method of discovering causal laws but a procedure for giving a quantitative interpretation to the manifestations of a known or assumed causal system as it operates in a particular population" (Blau and Duncan, 1967, p. 177). Path analysis permits the calculation of the magnitude of direct and indirect effects of earlier variables on later ones, such as the influence of educational attainment on level of last job. The data in Figure 7.2 indicate that an increase of one standard deviation in education should lead to an increase of .36 (direct effects) plus .43 × .29 (indirect effects) = .48 standard deviations in level of last job.

The advantages and uses of path analysis are considerable, yet it seems that a stage-state analysis provides access to a somewhat different set of questions. In general, a path analytic model elucidates the quantitative relationships among variables and reveals variable-to-variable relationships that can be abstracted across contexts or across person-situation configurations. On the other hand, a stage-state model allows us to think more easily about persons in situations and about different processes or different sequences of conditions that may emerge from these person-situation configurations.

In particular, a stage-state model allows us (1) to calculate the probabilities for an array of qualitatively different outcomes, (2) to estimate the probabilities of particular sequences of states or sequences of person-situation configurations, and (3) to analyze the variety of routes or processes connecting initial states with later outcomes. These are three kinds of questions that seem to be handled more effectively by a stage-state approach than by a path analytic approach.

On the other hand, one of the limitations of a stage-state analysis is the large number of cases required to fill in the cells for complex sets of stages and states. When a large number of personal and situational variables are considered in the definition of stages and states, it may be necessary to find ways, perhaps through factor analysis or cluster analysis, of reducing the number of discrete stages and states.

A second limitation of the stage-state approach, which is shared by path analysis, is that it can be applied only under conditions in which the course of experience can be divided into a relatively common sequence of stages. The stage-state model is only one approach to finding order in the probabilistic and causal structure of the course of experience; and for studying less structured sequences, other models, such as a state-sequential approach discussed further on, will need to be developed.

Comparison with Statistical Norms and Implicit Theories
In this stage-state model, statistical significance of the results can be assessed by comparing expected with observed transition frequencies from one stage-state to later stage-states. Expected transition probabilities are calculated on the assumption of random movement between stage S and stage $S + 1$, or in other words, on the assumption that all of the states in stage S have equal access to the array of states at stages $S + 1$. The χ^2 test provides a simple method for comparing the information in flow tables to the null hypothesis of statistical independence between stages.

A second reference point to use in assessing the information in these conditional probability tables is that of total predictability or total regularity. Complete regularity is approached as each of the transition probabilities approaches .00 or 1.00. An index, or "hit rate," varying from 0 to 100 percent can be used to assess the degree of predictability permitted by the data. Prediction is used here in the sense of estimation from known to unknown variables within a population. Due to the pace of social and historical change (e.g., Cronbach, 1975; Gergen, 1973), generalization to other cohorts and predictions to future time periods can be made only with considerable caution.

To illustrate the index of predictive efficiency, consider the problem of predicting an individual's last job. On the basis of population percentages alone, the best strategy for each individual is to predict a professional last job, which will be accurate 30 percent of the time and inaccurate 70 percent of the time.

What happens to predictive accuracy if information about an earlier stage, such as father's occupation, is made available? This can be calculated according to the following formula, where A_i represents each category of father's occupation:

$$\text{Probability of hit} = \Sigma P(\text{hit}/A_i) \times P(A_i).$$

Drawing on the two-stage table relating father's occupation to last job and on Table 7.1, which gives the likelihood of each category of father's occupation, we get:

$$\text{Probability of hit} = (.57 \, (.15) + (.46) \, (.26 + (.36) \, (.17) \\ + (.30) \, (.42) = .40.$$

Knowing father's occupation has raised the accuracy in predicting last job from 30 percent to 40 percent.

If information about several previous stages, such as father's occupation and level of education, is made available, then predictive accuracy can be computed according to a similar formula, in which A_i represents each level of father's occupation, and B_j represents each level of education:

$$\text{Probability of hit} = \Sigma P(\text{hit}/A_i B_j) \times P(A_i B_j) = .503.$$

Given knowledge of father's occupation and of level of educational attainment, type of last job can be accurately predicted 50 percent of the time, rather than the 30 percent accuracy obtainable through base rates alone. By defining more stages and differentiating more states within each stage, predictive accuracy can often be increased so that it rises progressively farther above base rates. This same index of predictive accuracy can also be used to assess predictions about sequences of future states.

As a third reference point, observed probabilities can be compared to "common knowledge," or to individuals' implicit theories about the course of lives. For example, people could be asked to estimate the proportion of men with high school educations who ended up in each job level, or to estimate the frequency with which given routes connected a particular origin, such as unskilled family background, with a particular outcome, such as professional last job. Using alternative conceptions of stages and states, respondents could be asked to estimate the likelihood of orally deprived children ending up with different type of adult characters, or to estimate the likelihood of generative older adults having successfully mastered identity and intimacy at earlier life stages, and so on.

In addition to having implicit theories of personality (Schneider, 1973) and implicit theories of events (Ajzen, 1977), people also have implicit theories of the life course, or implicit theories about the structure of the course of experience, and about the probabilities and processes of moving from one state to a set of later ones. Implicit theories about the life course undoubtedly influence the ways in which individuals plan, make decisions within, and conduct their lives. It would be valuable to investigate the implicit theories of life courses that people hold and the processes through which these theories are constructed and revised in changing social and historical circumstances.

Generalization and Applications

Stage-state analyses are not restricted to any particular substantive domain, but may be applied to the analysis of sequences of state transitions within parent-child relationships, educational careers, occupational histories, interpersonal relationships, and the "natural histories" of psychological disorders, criminal behavior, or drug abuse. Most generally, stage-state analyses can be used to examine the temporal course of behaviors, personality characteristics, encountered situations, or sequences of person-situation interaction. The minimal requirements are that there be individual differences in the course of the phenomena under investigation, and that there be enough comparability across cases to permit quantitative analysis.

If, for example, one were interested in the temporal course of aggressive behavior, a stage-state framework could be used to divide the relevant time period into a number of stages (such as childhood, adolescence, early adulthood, and middle adulthood), to identify three or four levels or states within each stage, and to trace the relative frequency of different diachronic patterns (such as continual antisocial aggression, high-level aggression only in adolescence, or high-level aggression in childhood that gradually tapered off).

For some analytic purposes, it may be advantageous to relax the assumption of a set of common stages and to examine instead sequences of selected states and events and the relative likelihood of alternative sequences. This could be termed "state-sequential" analysis. For example, one might want to examine the probability of alternative sequences of events such as finishing formal education, starting a full-time occupation, getting married, and having a first child. In studying the sequential arrangement of the first three of these events, Hogan (1978) found that 45.7 percent of his sample of men followed the particular sequence of completing formal education, starting first full-time job, and then getting married; 4.6 percent followed the sequence of completing education, marriage, and first full-time job; 6.0 percent followed the sequence of full-time job, completing education, and marriage; and so on. The probability of different event sequences varied depending on conditions such as birth cohort and ethnic background.

Evaluation Research

A stage-state framework may also be employed in evaluation research for assessing the sequential effects of intervention programs. The net value of an intervention is determined not by its effects at a single point in time, but by its effects on a sequence of future experiences. Insofar as possible, this sequence of effects needs to be considered in assessing the desirability of alternative forms of treatment (Ricks, 1974; Runyan, 1977). In the short term, thalidomide may have been effective as a sleeping aid, but in the long term, if taken in the first trimester of pregnancy, it could also lead to deformed babies. In the realm of psychosocial intervention, the Cambridge-Somerville delinquency prevention program appeared to have few short-term effects, but a thirty-year follow-up (McCord, 1978) indicated that men who had been in the treatment group were more likely than controls to commit a second crime, show signs of alcoholism and serious mental illness, have occupations with lower prestige, and to report high blood pressure or heart trouble, without any compensating advantages.

In these two examples, negative long-term effects clearly outweigh short-term benefits, but in other cases, such as the use of psychotropic drugs with potentially damaging side effects (Klein and Davis, 1969), more differentiated knowledge about short- and long-term risks and benefits for different kinds of patients is needed in order to make informed treatment decisions.

The Relationship of Conscious Agents to Studies of State Sequences

Stage-state and state-sequential analyses provide a framework for analyzing sequences of states and events through the life course. The study of extended sequences of states and events raises questions about the relationships between empirical inquiry and our status as conscious agents with particular force, in a way that is not as immediately apparent in most correlational, experimental, or case study research.

Can the study of state sequences lead to knowledge about predictable sequences of events and processes that will inevitably unfold in the course of lives? Are we helplessly embedded in an unfolding sequence of events that is beyond our conscious control? To some extent, we undoubtedly are. The course of biological aging, of aspects of psychological development, and of age-related changes in social constraints and expectations are all pretty much beyond individual control.

In other ways, however, the course of life experience is at least partially under conscious control. As conscious agents, we have at least some control over choice of an occupation, what to do with our vacations, or who we decide to marry. To the extent that people function as rational agents (as at least some of us do some of the time), the analysis of state sequences can be used not only for providing a glimpse of what is to come, but also for visualizing an array of possible paths and outcomes, designing plans and strategies for the pursuit of desired goals, and for making decisions in light of the expected short- and long-term consequences of alternative courses of action.

Consider, for example, a college student attempting to get into medical school, a graduate student thinking about the prospects of getting an academic job, or a cancer patient faced with an array of alternative forms of treatment. In each case, a rational actor needs to estimate the likelihood of alternative outcomes, to identify methods believed to increase the probability of desired outcomes, and to make decisions and pursue courses of action in light of these considerations. Stage-state or state-sequential analyses of the experiences of other applicants to medical school, other aspiring professors, or other cancer patients can provide information about what those in similar situations, who may have been more or less knowledgeable about the structure of their worlds, attempted to do and were or were not able to do. Such information about what has proved possible and probable in the lives of others can often be useful to those engaged in planning and decision making in similar circumstances.

There are two related questions that need to be distinguished. Descriptively, how *do* conscious agents make use of the experience of others in thinking prospectively about the course of their own lives? (Studies of social cognition suggest that there may be substantial errors and biases in such processes, e.g., Nisbett and Borgida, 1975; Ross, 1977; Tversky and Kahneman, 1974.) Second, normatively or rationally, what inferences *should* be made from the experience of others in thinking about the future course of one's own life? Both of these questions deserve investigation in their own right, but the more specific point being made here is that stage-state analyses of the life course are at least potentially useful to conscious agents in thinking prospectively about the course of life experience.

Conclusion

In summary, a stage-state analysis makes the simplifying assumptions that the course of experience can be divided into a sequence of common stages, with a limited number of possible states within each stage. This approach provides a method for examining the relative frequencies of different courses of experience, estimating the probability of movement from given states through a sequence of future states, and analyzing the routes or processes connecting initial states with a variety of potential outcomes.

There are opportunities for applying such an analytic framework to research on the temporal course of behaviors, personal attributes, encountered situations, and interaction processes within a wide range of substantive areas, such as parent-child relationships, stability and change in personality characteristics, histories of deviant behavior, or assessment of the sequential effects of intervention efforts.

Due to factors such as the pace of historical change, the operation of random processes, and even the transforming effects of inquiry itself, there are real limitations in the extent to which the sequential structure of the course of lives can be known. Within these limits, however, stage-state and state-sequential analyses can be of use in analyzing aspects of the probabilistic and causal structure of groups of lives, and these analyses can in turn be of use in thinking about the course of individual life histories.

To illustrate this latter use, in clinical contexts stage-state analyses can be used in attempting to predict the short-term, intermediate-term, and long-term effects of various treatment alternatives, such as psychotherapy, drug treatment, or electroconvulsive therapy for a severely depressed individual. (This problem of predicting and evaluating the likely consequences of alternative forms of therapy is discussed in more detail in Arthur, 1966, and Runyan, 1977).

One other application is for individuals in looking at the future course of their own lives, visualizing an array of possible futures—with regard to educational career, occupational career, relationships, parenting, choice of medical treatments, or whatever—and attempting to anticipate the sequential effects of different decisions or courses of action. This may be done either intuitively and imaginatively, trying to visualize what would lead to what, or more systematically and empirically, by attempting to draw inferences from the life histories of those in similar circumstances with similar experiences.

Many important problems in analyzing the life course are not touched on by the conceptual frameworks outlined here in the chapters that make up Part II, nor by other existing frameworks. There is, obviously, a great deal that remains to be done. In Part III, we return more directly to problems and issues in the study of individual life histories, with discussions of the case study method, idiographic methods, and the psychobiographical enterprise.

PART III

Theory and Method
in the Study
of Individual Lives

8

The Case Study Method

The case study method involves the presentation and interpretation of detailed information about a single subject, whether an event, a culture, or of primary interest in this chapter, the case study of an individual life. Although widely used, the case study approach has been the subject of considerable controversy among social scientists. Adherents of the method argue that it has unusually great theoretical and practical importance. For example, "The case study method is the traditional approach of all clinical research. . . . Much of the knowledge common to all clinicians today was discovered by the case study method" (Bolgar, 1965, p. 28). The study of individual lives, as presented in detailed case histories, provides "the only possible way of obtaining the granite blocks of data on which to build a science of human nature" (Murray, 1955, p. 15). The case studies of Freud are "rare works of art and a record of the human mind in one of its most unparalleled works of scientific discovery" (Kanzer and Glenn, 1980, p. 43). Or finally, "Life history data are usually necessary in any serious attempt to explain, predict, or influence the person's behavior" (Bromley, 1977, p. 129).

On the other hand, there is a widespread view that the case study method is severely defective, or is useful only as a source of hypotheses which must then be tested with more rigorous research methods. One early formulation of this view is presented by Lundberg (1926): "(1) The case method is not in itself a scientific method at all, but merely the first step in the scientific method; (2) individual cases become of scientific significance only when classified and summarized in such form as to reveal uniformities, types, and patterns of behavior; (3) the statistical method is the best, if not the only, scientific method of classifying and summarizing large numbers of cases" (p. 61). Thus, in Lundberg's view, "the only possible question" as to the relative value of the case method and statistical method is whether generalization shall be carried out by the random, qualitative, and subjective methods commonly used in case studies or by the systematic and objective procedures of statistical methods.

Such sweeping criticisms are not limited to the earlier parts of the century. One of the most widely used methodology texts, by Campbell and Stanley (1966), states that "one-shot" case studies "have such a total absence of control as to be of almost no scientific value. . . . Such studies often involve tedious collection of specific detail, careful observation, testing, and the like, and in such instances involve the error of *misplaced precision*. . . . It seems well-nigh unethical at the present time to allow, as a thesis or dissertation in education, case studies of this nature (i.e., involving a single group observed at one time only)" (pp. 6–7). (It should be noted, however, that Campbell has since retracted his "earlier dogmatic disparagement of case studies" (Campbell, 1975, p. 191).)

Another representative criticism is that, "Case study methodology was typically characterized by numerous sources of uncontrolled variation, inadequate description of independent and dependent variables, and was generally difficult to replicate" (Kratochwill, 1978, p. 5). This "made case study methodology of little scientific value," and led to the rejection of single-case methods by "more sophisticated" experimental methodologists (Kratochwill, 1978, p. 5). Kazdin, while also acknowledging some advantages of case studies, states that limitations of the traditional case study "pertain to the fact that the information obtained is scientifically weak and often completely unacceptable. The type of information usually solicited and the manner in which it is obtained make the case ambiguous. The information usually consists of anecdotal reports filtered through extensive interpretations or inferences on the part of the therapist. Even if objective measures are relied upon, the case study does not

control for factors that might account for the same pattern c.
results" (Kazdin, 1980, p. 25).

Conceptualization of the Case Study Method

This controversy about the value of case studies stems in part
from the conflation of a variety of underlying issues. Identification and disentanglement of these issues may help us to obtain a
deeper and more balanced appreciation of the virtues and limitations of case studies.

One underlying issue is that of possible errors introduced
through use of the retrospective method. Substantial data on
biases and inaccuracies in retrospective reports (e.g., Brekstad,
1966; Yarrow, Campbell, and Burton, 1970) raise questions about
the value of such retrospective reports for scientific purposes.
These deficiencies of retrospective reports are sometimes used
as grounds for criticizing the case study method.

Although case studies of individual lives *may* rely on retrospective reports, and, in clinical settings, often do, they *need not*
rely on such reports. Instead, case studies can, and often do (as
in biographies), rely on the collection and interpretation of
letters, diaries, observations by contemporaries, archival data,
and so on. Alternatively, case studies may be based upon systematic longitudinal studies, such as those conducted at the
Institute of Human Development, University of California,
Berkeley (Jones, Bayley, Macfarlane, and Honzik, 1971, Eichorn,
Clausen, Haan, Honzik, and Mussen, 1981). Case studies can be
conducted with prospective "follow-up" methods, which start
with a sample of individuals in childhood and follow them
into adulthood, or with "follow-back" methods (Ricks, 1970),
which start with adults and explore their pasts through the
search of existing school, medical, court, and hospital records.
Limitations of the retrospective method are not adequate
grounds for dismissal of the case study method, as retrospective
methods are only one of the techniques which may, but need
not, be used in the construction of case histories.

A second issue is that of qualitative versus quantitative
methods. It is sometimes suggested that quantitative methods
are an essential characteristic of scientific endeavor (e.g., Lundberg, 1926). This is a highly questionable position, but even

if it were true, it would not provide adequate grounds for dismissal of case studies, as there are substantial possibilities for quantitative and statistical studies of single cases (e.g., Baldwin, 1942; Chassan, 1967, 1979; Davidson and Costello, 1969; Hersen and Barlow, 1976; Kratochwill, 1978; Neufeld, 1977).

A third issue is that of "subjective" versus "objective" data. Life history studies have been praised for their value in providing information on the subjective side of social experience. "Herein lies the tremendous value of the life history—it permits sociologists to balance the 'objectivism' of the experiment, the survey, and participant observation with the internal, covert, and reflective elements of social behavior and experience" (Denzin, 1978, p. 252). In a climate in which operational and positivistic doctrines predominated, the life history method was valued as a way in which to introduce individuals' subjective perceptions and interpretations of social life. As the study of cognitive processes became more acceptable in the behavioral sciences, a variety of other methodological channels for the study of subjective experience opened up, and the life history was no longer the only or primary avenue for studying subjective perceptions and interpretations.

The use of subjective reports has also been a grounds for criticism of case studies, as evidence accumulated about possible errors and biases in introspective reporting methods (e.g., Nisbett and Wilson, 1977; Nisbett and Ross, 1980). Although introspective reports are often used in case studies, they are not an essential part of the method, as case studies can be written without them. Whatever the merits and deficiencies of introspective reports, the value of case studies is somewhat independent of this particular issue. Introspective reports are only one of many sources of data which may be used in the construction of case histories. Thus, the value of case studies is a distinguishably different issue than that of the value of introspective reports.

A fourth issue is that of the place of case studies in the generation and testing of causal generalizations. Case studies are seen as having low "internal validity," in that it is difficult to rule out competing causal explanations, and low "external validity," in that it is difficult to generalize findings from a single case to the population at large.

Case studies are often criticized for their "lack of controls." According to this view, "the fundamental weakness" of a case study "is that it provides no basis for comparison, and comparison is essential to science" (Carlsmith, Ellsworth, and Aronson, 1976, p. 39). In collecting an immense amount of detail on a single case, "all this care and precision is misplaced, because no comparison has been made. Conducting such a study is analogous to building a castle on quicksand" (Carlsmith et al., p. 40). From the perspective of the experimentalist, case studies may be useful in suggesting interesting hypotheses, but these hypotheses must then be tested through more rigorous experimental research.

What is the force or weight of such criticisms? First, it is certainly true that for the specific purpose of testing general causal relationships, the case study is, compared to the experiment, a relatively ineffective method. For the particular purpose of testing causal generalizations, case studies unquestionably do have limitations; they are, as commonly stated, useful in an adjunctive way for suggesting causal hypotheses but do not provide a powerful means for testing such generalizations.

For other purposes, however, the case study may be the single most effective method. If one's purpose is to describe the experience of a single person, to develop interpretations or explanations of that experience, or to develop courses of action and to make decisions appropriate for this particular individual, then the case study method is an extremely useful one. It is necessary to consider the merits and deficiencies of case studies from a broader context, a broader range of purposes than solely for testing causal theories.

Studies of individual cases can sometimes be useful for testing causal generalizations, as when intersubject variability is low, when opportunities for observing a given class of events are limited, or when a negative instance can be found for a supposedly universal relationship (Dukes, 1965), but this is not their primary function. Case studies are primarily useful for tasks such as describing an individual's experience, for developing idiographic interpretations of that experience, and for developing context-specific predictions, plans, and decisions.

In summary, questions about the value of the case study method need to be distinguished from questions about the limitations of retrospective reports, about qualitative versus quantitative methods, and about the strengths and limitations of introspective reports. Strong opinions, both positive and negative, about qualitative methods and about retrospection and introspection have sometimes been directly transferred to the case study method, and have contributed to the diversity of opinion about case studies. The empirical fact that case studies often employ retrospective, qualitative, and introspective methods should not be allowed to obscure the important conceptual point that such methods are not essential features of case studies and that case studies are not restricted to such methods.

Once it is established that case studies are analytically separable from any particular method of data collection, attention needs to be turned to identifying those methods, and combinations of methods, which have the most to contribute to producing insightful studies. A full consideration of the strengths and limitations of each available method is beyond the scope of this discussion. It should be noted, however, that even to the extent that the writer of a case study chooses to employ retrospective, introspective, or qualitative methods, some of the limitations of these methods are correctable, and are not as great as often implied by critics.

For example, recollections can often be checked by comparing them against various forms of documentary evidence, as was done by Herbert Spencer in the writing of his autobiography, or B. F. Skinner in his. Both retrospective and introspective data can be used without assuming that they are unfailingly accurate, by indicating that this is how events were perceived or interpreted by the person at a given point in time, which is often important information in its own right. At the same time, the accuracy of such reports can be checked against as many independent sources of evidence as possible. Also, qualitative methods are not necessarily inferior to quantitative ones. For purposes such as presenting meanings, lines of reasoning, perceptions of the situation, or the interpretation of actions, qualitative and narrative methods have (as argued in Chapter 5) substantial advantages over purely quantitative methods.

In short, case studies can be constructed using a full range of retrospective and nonretrospective data, qualitative and quantitative data, introspective and nonintrospective data. No matter what methods are employed, conscientious efforts need to be made to be aware of the potential limitations of each method, to correct for these limitations insofar as possible, and to construct the final case study within the boundaries established by the available methods and sources of data.

Definition and Types of the Case Study Method

Thus far, we have been proceeding with an implicit definition of the case study. If a case study is not a person's telling of his or her own story, then what is it? If a case study need not involve retrospective reports, or qualitative data, or introspective reports on subjective experience, then how is it to be defined?

A case study may be defined as the systematic presentation of information about the life of a single unit, and for this discussion, we will be focusing on the lives of individuals as the unit of analysis. A case study may be defined as "a *reconstruction* and *interpretation,* based on the best evidence available, of part of the story of a person's life" (Bromley, 1977, p. 163). The case study may be based upon a synthesis of evidence attained from all available sources, including interviews, projective or objective tests, observations in the natural environment, longitudinal studies, personal documents, public archives, the testimony of others, experiments, or any other method capable of producing relevant information. According to this definition, the case study is not a particular method of collecting information, such as a lengthy life history interview, but is rather a form for organizing and presenting information about a specific person and his or her circumstances, which may draw upon a variety of specific techniques of data collection.

A case study is typically undertaken in response to a problem in understanding, and/or a problem requiring practical action. The case study is necessarily selective, in that the whole story of a person's life is overwhelmingly detailed and complex, with much that is irrelevant to the purpose at hand. A case study inquiry is focused on a limited number of issues pertaining to the person and his or her circumstances, and is organized about the critical examination of evidence and arguments related to these issues (Bromley, 1977).

Looking specifically at clinical case studies, it is possible to identify at least three different types of case studies, distinguished by their place in the course of treatment. One form of clinical case study examines a person's problems and circumstances leading up to treatment, including material on presenting problems, assessment, diagnosis, relevant past history, and so on. A second type of case study gives major attention to the treatment process, to the interaction of client and therapist during the course of treatment, such as Dewald's (1972) 655-page presentation of the course of psychoanalytic treatment with a single patient. A third type of case study places greatest emphasis upon assessing the effects of treatment (e.g., Hersen and Barlow, 1976; Jayaratne and Levy, 1979; Kratochwill, 1978). In these single-case experimental designs, emphasis is placed on assessing the effects of a particular intervention which is usually, although not necessarily, a behavioral one. Actual clinical case studies may, of course, consist of combinations of two or three of these different types. It might be more useful, then, to consider these as three possible foci of case studies, with particular case studies having different combinations of these three emphases. In general, psychodynamic case studies place greatest emphasis upon preceding history and the course of treatment, while behavioral case studies place greater emphasis upon assessing the effects of particular interventions.

A more elaborate classification of types of case studies is suggested by Light (1980, p. 195), who outlines six types of case conferences. Each type of case conference suggests a possible focus of a case study. An *analytic* case conference, and correspondingly, an *analytic* case study, would focus on a person's psychological history and psychodynamics. A *diagnostic* case study would center upon issues of differential diagnosis. A *neurological* case study would focus on the extent to which a patient's problems could be attributed to neurological disorders. A *therapeutic* case study would concentrate on the process and problems of conducting therapy with a particular patient. An *administrative* case study would center on administrative problems, such as how to deal with a disruptive or violent patient on the wards. Sixth, a *discharge* study would focus on alternatives and plans for a person's life or treatment after discharge from the hospital. It is not included in Light's classification, but it is certainly also possible to have *evaluative* case studies, focusing on assessment of the effects of treatment.

A case study may also be differentiated from a psychological report and from a life history, recognizing that the distinctions must be rough, as usage of the concepts has not been uniform. A psychological report, which can be defined as a document containing psychological information relevant to clinical plans and decisions (Tallent, 1976), might be in the form of a case study, but it might also be more limited or specific, such as reporting the results of a single test or battery of tests. On the other hand, a life history, as represented by a biography or psychobiography, may contain a sketch of the entire course of a person's life and experience, and thus be broader and more inclusive than a clinical case study. "A case-study usually deals with a problem of adjustment during a relatively short and self-contained segment of an individual's life, although the case-report may contain some life-history information as context" (Bromley, 1977, p. 162).

One overall objective of this chapter is to begin moving toward clarification and improvement of case study methodology. The following section discusses three well-known cases—King George III and two of Freud's famous cases, Dr. Schreber and Little Hans—in order to illustrate several of the methodological issues involved in the construction, evaluation, and reformulation of case studies. The third section discusses a relatively recent development in the field of case studies, that of single-case experimental designs, and briefly discusses their relationship to more traditional case studies. The fourth section discusses the criteria which are used, and those which could or should be used, in evaluating case studies. The fifth section explores several promising ideas and recent lines of work which may lead to improvements in case study methodology.

Three Case Studies

George III

The case of George III, King of England from 1760 to 1820, provides an illustration of some of the processes through which case studies may be formulated and reformulated, as reflected in assessments by his own physicians and through a succession of interpretations of his disorders by later generations. During his lifetime, King George III had five distinct periods of disturbance, with none except for the last enduring more than a few months.

The most fully documented attack, which also had the greatest political implications, occurred in 1788–1789 and is the one that will be discussed here.

First reports of the disorder came in June 1788, when the King complained of a fever and violent pains in his stomach and bowels. He recovered shortly, but in October of that year, signs of delirium appeared, accompanied by symptoms such as weakness of the limbs, hoarseness, sleeplessness, excitement, and confusion. On November 5, Fanny Burney, a resident of the court, reported that, "The King, at dinner, had broken forth into positive delirium, which has long been menacing all who saw him most closely; and the Queen was so overpowered as to fall into violent hysterics. All the Princesses were in misery, and the Prince of Wales had burst into tears. No one knew what was to follow—no one could conjecture the event" (Macalpine and Hunter, 1969, p. 25). Another member of the court, Lady Harcourt, recorded in her diary that, "Every alarming symptom seemed increased; the bodily agitation was extreme, and the talking incessant, indeed it was too evident that his Majesty had no longer the least command over himself . . . the veins in his face were swelled, the sound of his voice was dreadful; he often spoke till he was exhausted . . . while the foam ran out of his mouth" (p. 25). In December of 1788, "He was as deranged as possible. . . . Among his extravagancies of the Moment He had at this time hid part of the Bed Clothes under his bed, had taken off his Night Cap, and got a Pillow Case round his head, and the Pillow in the bed with Him, which he called Prince Octavius [his youngest son, who died at the age of four in 1783], who He said was to be new born this day" (p. 68).

A summary of his symptoms can be provided in more modern terms as a background for the succession of alternative diagnoses and explanations of his illness.

His medical history shows that he suffered periodically from attacks which followed the same pattern and in which he manifested the same symptoms. These are indicative of a recurrent, widespread and severe disorder of the nervous system. It affected the peripheral nerves, which supply movement and sensation to all parts of the body, causing painful weakness of the arms and legs, so that he could not hold a cup or pen, or walk or stand unaided (even when still able to sit on horseback), hoarseness and difficulty in articulation and swallowing; his muscles wasted and it took months before he regained normal strength and vigour. He suffered from pain in the head and face, became over-sensitive, so that he could not bear the touch of clothes or bedding, wig or necktie, and at times lost the power of feeling, as when he was not aware of blisters being placed upon his legs. Affection of the autonomic nervous system, which controls the heart, blood vessels, gastro-intestinal system and sweat-glands, led to nausea, colic and constipation due to paralysis of the gut; at times the pain was so severe that Baker [one of his physicians], for instance, found him doubled up in bed; at times breathing was embarrassed and he had pain and stitches in the chest; racing pulse, flushing and sweating made his doctors think he had "fever." When attacks became more severe, the brain was involved, leading to giddiness, visual and auditory disturbances, mounting agitation, excitement, over-activity, non-stop rambling, irritability and persistent sleeplessness, confusion typically first by night and then also by day, producing delirium, tremor, rapid movements of his eyes (nystagmus), rigors, stupor and convulsions (Macalpine and Hunter, 1969, p. 172).

The King's disorder was of great concern, not only for the sake of his personal well-being, but also for political reasons, in that if he was judged insane, then the Prince of Wales would be appointed regent, with powers of the king. Thus, the understanding of his disorder became a subject of public as well as medical importance. A number of physicians became involved in the King's treatment, with an expectable diversity of opinions. When other explanations failed, physicians of the time fell back on the ancient theory of an imbalance between the four humours: black bile, yellow bile, phlegm, and choler. According to Lord Grenville, "The cause to which they all agree to ascribe it, is the force of a humour which was beginning to show itself in the legs, when the King's imprudence [he failed to change out of wet stockings] drove it from thence into the bowels; and the medicines which they were then obliged to use for preservation of his life have repelled it upon the brain" (Macalpine and Hunter, 1969, p. xiii). The attending physicians and psychiatrists differed as to whether the disturbance should be attributed to physical problems, to excessive psychological pressures, or to unknown causes.

One issue in the formulation of the case which carried great weight was whether the King's disturbances should be seen as the result of a physical problem with accompanying fever and delirium, in which case one could expect recovery or death; or whether his symptoms indicated insanity, in which case recovery was relatively unlikely, and he might have to be declared incompetent to rule. Different political factions lined up behind different medical opinions, with the King's supporters favoring an explanation in terms of physical disturbance, while his opponents were more inclined to consider the disturbance a mental one. By March 1789, the King had apparently recovered, lending support to the theory of physical origins of the problem.

In the decade following the attack of 1788–1789, a number of physicians besides those attending the King developed their own analysis of his problems. They varied substantially in assessment and recommended treatment but generally agreed that the King suffered from a physically based delirium and not from insanity.

In 1855, Dr. Isaac Ray disagreed with the royal physicians' earlier assessment of delirium, and argued, rather, that the disturbances had all the characteristics of "ordinary acute mania," resulting from an abnormal mental state. After the Kraepelinian classification scheme became accepted in the early twentieth century, Dr. Smith Ely Jelliffe suggested in 1931 that King George's disturbance could be more accurately diagnosed as "manic-depressive psychosis," rather than a simple "mania."

After Isaac Ray's study of 1855, the next extended study did not appear until 1941 when Manfred Guttmacher published a psychoanalytic study titled *America's Last King: An Interpretation of the Madness of George III*. He argued that the King's disturbances could be understood in psychodynamic terms, and that his attacks could be understood as breakdowns under the pressure of political and domestic events which overwhelmed his vulnerable defenses and led him to decompensate. "The mental disorder which seized George III on five separate occasions was manic-depressive insanity. . . . Believing that, as a king, he should be all-powerful, he became unbalanced when he found himself impotent and unable to act . . . minor attacks followed frustration imposed on him by the outside world . . . major attacks came, as a rule when he felt that he thwarted himself by a lack of decisiveness intolerable in a king. . . . Self-blame, indecision and frustration . . . destroyed the sanity of George III.

. . . Had it been his lot to be a country squire, he would, in all probability, not have been psychotic" (Guttmacher, 1941, quoted in Macalphine and Hunter, 1969, pp. 357–358.)

A persuasive argument has recently been made (Macalpine and Hunter, 1969) that the King's puzzling array of symptoms resulted from porphyria, a rare metabolic disorder not identified until the 1930's. Porphyrins are purple-red pigments which exist in every cell in the body and which give blood its red color. In the disease of porphyria, there is a disturbance of porphyrin metabolism, which leads to an accumulation of toxic chemicals throughout the body, resulting in symptoms such as acute abdominal pain, discolored urine, and mental disturbance.

The range of symptoms of George III, which are extremely puzzling from a psychological perspective, fit almost exactly with those of porphyria. Porphyria is hereditary, and those who carry it may remain symptomless, or experience attacks of varying frequency and severity. At the height of attacks, patients are described as ill, delirious, and in agonizing pain, which closely fits the attacks of George III. "Indeed, his symptoms and their sequence read like a textbook case" (Macalpine and Hunter, 1969, p. 173).

Although urinalysis was not a systematic practice at the time, there are six different instances in which the King's physicians noted that his urine was dark or bloody at the height of his attacks. If porphyria is hereditary, then one would expect to find symptoms of it in the King's ancestors and descendents. Laboratory methods verified the existence of porphyria in four living descendents, and analysis of historical and medical records also provide evidence of porphyria in relatives such as Mary, Queen of Scots; James VI of Scotland; George III's four sons; and his granddaughter, Princess Charlotte. In short, a variety of lines of evidence converge in pointing to the conclusion that the King suffered from porphyria.

The life of George III provides a vivid illustration of how a case history can be formulated and reformulated in light of changes in scientific beliefs. To summarize the history of alternative formulations, "His own physicians puzzled what bodily disorder had caused his mind to become deranged; in the asylum era of the middle of the nineteenth century it was simply called mania, and in the descriptive era of classification, manic-depressive psychosis. In the recent past, when psychodynamics entered the field, it was ascribed to stress and conflict and with it the King's personality and character were denigrated. Reviewed in the light of modern medical knowledge and applying to it the clinical corrective of investigative science, it emerges as porphyria, an inborn error of metabolism" (Macalpine and Hunter, 1969, p. 363).

Dr. Daniel Paul Schreber

In 1903, Dr. Daniel Paul Schreber, a distinguished German jurist, published a detailed account of his mental illness, which today would be called paranoid schizophrenia. In 1911, Freud published an analysis of these memoirs, entitled "Psychoanalytic Notes upon an Autobiographical Account of a Case of Paranoia (Dementia Paranoides)." Freud's analysis of these memoirs has been called his "most important contribution to the psychoanalytic exploration of psychotic illness" (Niederland, 1974, p. xiii). This section will outline some of Schreber's symptoms, summarize aspects of Freud's interpretation, and then provide additional data about the case, examining the way these data have influenced later interpretation of the case.

Schreber was born in 1842, and in 1884, after losing in an attempt to be elected to the Reichstag, had a nervous illness which led to hospitalization through June 1885, when he was discharged, apparently recovered. His second and more severe disturbance, which was the subject of his *Memoirs* and Freud's analysis, occurred in the fall of 1893, when he was fifty-one years old. In June 1893 he was promoted to the Office of Senatspresident in Dresden, that is, presiding judge in the Superior Court of Appeals. Shortly thereafter he had dreams that it must be nice to be a woman, submitting to the act of copulation. He then developed a delusional system of which the central features were that he must personally be transformed into a woman, that he would become God's mate, and that he was thus responsible for restoring the world to a lost state of bliss. Schreber consulted with a Dr. Flechsig in November 1893 and was hospitalized from later that month until 1902.

A more detailed account of Schreber's symptoms is presented by the director of the sanitarium. The patient was troubled by hypochondriacal ideas, complained that he had softening of the brain, that he would soon be dead, etc. . . . Later, the visual and auditory illusions became much more frequent, and, in conjunction with coenaesthetic disturbances, dominated the whole of his feeling and thought. He believed that he was dead and decomposing, that he was suffering from the plague; he asserted that his body was being handled in all kinds of revolting ways; and, as he himself declares to this day, he went through worse horrors than anyone could have imagined, and all on behalf of a sacred cause. The patient was so much occupied with these pathological phenomena that he was inaccessible to any other impression and would sit perfectly rigid and motionless for hours" [Freud, 1911, pp. 108–109].

Over the next few years, Schreber's degree of disorganization decreased, and he became capable of meeting the demands of everyday life, except that a delusional system crystallized.

The culminating point of the patient's delusional system is his belief that he has a mission to redeem the world, and to restore mankind to their lost state of bliss. . . . The most essential feature of his mission of redemption is that it must be preceded by his *transformation into a woman* . . . neither he nor the rest of mankind can win back their immortality except by his being transformed into a woman (a process which may occupy many years or even decades) by means of divine miracles. He himself, of this he is convinced, is the only object upon which divine miracles are worked, and he is thus the most remarkable man who has ever lived upon earth. Every hour and every minute for years he has experienced these miracles in his body, and he has had them confirmed by the voices that have conversed with him [Freud, 1911, p. 112].

How is such a delusional structure to be understood? Freud's analysis cannot be presented in all its detail, but several central features may be summarized. Freud argued that paranoia resulted from a defense against homosexual impulses, and that the exciting cause of Schreber's illness was an outburst of homosexual libido toward Flechsig, his physician. The initial feeling of "I, (a man) love him" is unacceptable, so it is negated by the thought, "I hate the man." This feeling is projected onto the other, so that "He hates (persecutes) me which will justify me in hating him." In short, "I do not love him—I hate him, because HE PERSECUTES ME" (Freud, 1911, pp. 165–166).

Freud speculated about what led to the relatively satisfactory adjustment of Schreber in the years immediately following his release from the sanitarium, and, with the lack of direct evidence, suggested: "It may be suspected, however, that what enabled Schreber to reconcile himself to his homosexual phantasy, and so made it possible for his illness to terminate in something approximating a recovery, may have been the fact that his father-complex was in the main positively toned and that in real life the later years of his relationship with an excellent father had probably been unclouded" (Freud, 1911, p. 181). This synopsis does not do justice to the rich detail of Freud's interpretation, but it does present one of the central components of his interpretation. Freud is able to argue that this case is consistent with the psychoanalytic view "that the roots of every nervous and mental disorder are chiefly to be found in the patient's sexual life" (Freud, 1911, p. 127).

Since Freud's interpretation of the case, additional evidence, not contained in the *Memoirs* which Freud worked from, has come to light. This additional information is about the character, beliefs, and child-rearing practices of Schreber's father. The father of Dr. Daniel Paul Schreber was Dr. Daniel Gottlieb Moritz Schreber (1808–1861), a leading German physician and educator, and promoter of therapeutic gymnastics. He had published close to twenty books on education and child rearing and claimed that he used these methods in rearing his own children, of whom Daniel Paul Schreber was the second son.

The elder Schreber's philosophy was that children should be sternly and rigidly brought up, both physically and emotionally, in order to prevent problems in later years. He believed that the straightest possible posture was important for young children, whether standing, sitting, or sleeping, and he constructed a number of mechanical devices to be used for such purposes. He had a horizontal metal bar attached to desks to assure a rigidly straight sitting posture, a harness to assure good posture in the sleeping child, and a head holder to assure the symmetrical growth of the jaw and skull (Niederland, 1974, p. 51). His books offer detailed rules and instructions for almost every aspect of the child's daily behavior. In a discussion of children under one year old, he states, "Our entire effect on the direction of the child's will at this time will consist in accustoming it to absolute obedience. . . . The thought should never even occur to the child that his will could be in control, rather should the habit of subordinating his will to the will of his parents or teachers be immutably implanted in him" (Schreber, 1858, p. 66, in Schatzman, 1973, pp. 21–22). And, "the most important thing is that the disobedience should be *crushed* to the point of regaining complete submission, using corporal punishment if necessary" (Schatzman, p. 24).

Apparently the senior Dr. Schreber had been a sickly and frail child, who, although never reaching five feet one inch, had built himself into an excellent gymnast, swimmer, and horseman through systematic exercise and calisthenics. Even though extreme rigor in child rearing may have been more prevalent then than now, Dr. Schreber carried it to excess. He drove his sons "into a state of complete submission and passive surrender. He made of them the earliest targets and examples of his aggressive efforts toward the development of a better and healthier race of men. Although the authoritarian regimentation of children with its emphasis on coercive disciplinary measures was probably typical of the country and era in which Dr. Schreber lived, it is a matter of record that the straps, belts, and other forms of mechanical restraint were his personal inventions. They obviously sprang from his own pathology and were recommended and applied by him, though rationalized as educational reform" (Niederland, 1974, p. 57).

It is possible to see a number of correspondences between the delusions of the son and specific child-rearing practices of the father (following quotations from Schatzman, 1973, pp. 35, and 41–51).

1. Son (in *Memoirs*): "Books or other notes are kept in which for years have been written down all my thoughts, all my phrases, all my necessaries, all the articles in my possession or around me, all persons with whom I come into contact, etc. . . . The writing-down system . . . became a mental torture, from which I suffered severely for years and to which I am only slowly getting

a little accustomed; because of it, I had to endure trials of patience as they had probably never before had to be borne by a
human being."

Father (in child-rearing text of 1858): "In families . . . a quite
effective means of education is a punishment board, which is to
be stuck upon the wall of the children's room. Such a board
would list the children's names and against them every committed misdeed: all ever so little signs of omission, all instances
of insubordination, would be chalked up by a tick or by a re-
mark. At the end of each month everybody would assemble for
the hour of reckoning. According to what transpired, reproach
or praise would be assigned. If one or other of the children had
shown some recurring faults or weaknesses, particular mention
should be made of these" (p. 35).

2. Son (in describing the so-called "coccyx miracle.") "This was
an extremely painful, caries-like state of the lowest vertebrae. Its
purpose was *to make sitting and even lying down impossible.*
Altogether I was not allowed to remain for long in *one and the
same position* or at the same occupation: when I was walking,
one attempted to force me to lie down, and when I was *lying
down one wanted to chase me off* my bed. Rays did not seem to
appreciate at all that a human being who actually exists must
be somewhere."

Father: "One must see to it that children always sit straight
and even-sided on both buttocks at once . . . leaning neither to
the right nor left side. . . . As soon as they start to lean back
. . . or bend their backs, the time has come to exchange at least
for a few minutes the seated position for the absolutely still,
supine one. If this is not done . . . the backbones will be deformed. . . . *Half resting in lying or wallowing positions should
not be allowed*" (p. 44).

3. Son: "This was perhaps the most abominable of all miracles—next to the compression-of-the-chest-miracle; the expression
used for it if I remember correctly was 'the head-compressing
machine'. . . . The 'little devils' . . . *compressed my head as
though in a vice* by turning a kind of screw, causing my head
temporarily to assume an elongated almost pear-shaped form. It
had an extremely threatening effect, particularly as it was accompanied by severe pain."

Father: The father had invented a head-holder to prevent the child's head from falling forward or sideways. This device pulled the child's hair if the head was not held straight.

Further similarities between the son's delusions and the father's child-rearing practices are noted by Schatzman (1973) and Niederland (1974). How is this additional data on the father's actions to be interpreted? Niederland suggests that "these fantasies turned out to be *distorted memories of realistic experiences in his early life*" (1974, p. 27). The discovery of this additional evidence "has made it possible to correlate the bizarre mental formation in Schreber's delusional system (including florid fantasies, distorted images, hallucinatory experiences) to specific events in the early father-son relationship and thus to demonstrate the nucleus of truth in the son's paranoid productions" (Niederland, 1974, p. xvi).

Niederland believes that this additional evidence has "sharpened" and "clarified" Freud's original interpretations. In contrast, Schatzman believes that "radically new hypotheses" are called for; he attempts to reinterpret the case in light of existential-phenomenological ideas, double-bind theory, and theories of interpersonal and family systems. In terms of phenomenological theory, the current delusions are seen as images or transforms of earlier experiences, and in terms of double-bind theory, the young Schreber is punished, but not allowed to acknowledge who it is that is harming him. There are, in short, conflicting opinions about the impact of this additional evidence on Freud's original interpretation, but regardless of the specific interpretation chosen, the Schreber case clearly illustrates how the emergence of additional historical evidence can serve to revise prior understandings of a particular case.

Little Hans

Little Hans was the child of a musicologist and his wife; the latter a onetime patient of Freud's. Little Hans' parents were among Freud's "closest adherents," and regularly reported observations of their child to Freud. In January 1908, when Hans was four and three-quarter years old, his father reported that a problem had developed. "My dear Professor, I am sending you a little more about Hans—but this time, I am sorry to say, material for a case history. . . . He is afraid *that a horse will bite him in the street*. Apart from his being afraid of going into the street and from his being depressed in the evening, he is in other respects the same Hans, as bright and cheerful as ever" (Freud, 1909, p. 63).

In one of the first days of January, Little Hans woke up crying in the morning and reported that he had had a bad dream in which he thought his Mummy was gone and that he had no one to cuddle with. Several days later while the nurse was taking him to the park, he began to cry in the street, saying that he wanted to go home to Mummy and to cuddle with her. The next day he went out with his mother, yet still appeared frightened, and told her that he was afraid a horse would bite him. That evening, he grew frightened again, and wanted to caress his mother. "He said, crying, 'I know I shall have to go for a walk again tomorrow.' And later, 'The horse'll come into the room' " (Freud, 1909, p. 65).

Freud's interpretation of Little Hans' horse phobia is that it stems from Oedipal conflicts, which erupted during a period of intensified sexual attraction toward his mother. "Hans was really a little Oedipus who wanted to have his father 'out of the way,' to get rid of him, so that he might be alone with his handsome mother and sleep with her" (Freud, 1909, p. 148). Little Hans experienced "hostile and jealous feelings against his father, and sadistic impulses (premonitions, as it were, of copulation) towards his mother. These early suppressions perhaps have gone to form the predispositions for his subsequent illness. These aggressive propensities of Hans's found no outlet, and as soon as there came a time of privation and of intensified sexual excitement, they tried to break their way out with reinforced strength. It was then that the battle which we call his 'phobia' burst out" (Freud, 1909, pp. 173–174). Freud argued that Little Hans transposed his fear of his father onto horses, and that he was most afraid of horses with muzzles and blinkers, which may have resembled his father's moustache and eyeglasses. The phobia served to keep Little Hans at home with his beloved mother, and thus was successful in attaining his libidinal aims. This is necessarily an abbreviated account of Freud's analysis, and a reading of the original case is highly recommended. (The reader may be interested to note that Little Hans has since been identified as Herbert Graf, for many years the story director of the Metropolitan Opera in New York, and author of three books on operatic production (Silverman, 1980, p. 101).)

A valuable example of a critique of the logic, methods, and evidential foundations of a case study is provided in a behavioral reinterpretation of this study by Wolpe and Rachman (1960). The point of citing this example is not to imply that behavioral theory is superior in any general way to psychoanalytic theory, a position I would not necessarily want to argue, but rather to illustrate the process by which the conclusions, inferences, and evidential foundations of a clinical case study may be critically examined and challenged by an alternative formulation.

Wolpe and Rachman argue that "there is no scientifically acceptable evidence showing any connection" (1960, p. 135) between Little Hans' sexual life and his phobia for horses.

"It is our contention that Freud's view of this case is not supported by the data, either in its particular or as a whole. The major points that he regards as demonstrated are these:

1. Hans had a sexual desire for his mother,
2. He hated and feared his father and wished to kill him,
3. His sexual excitement and desire for his mother were transformed into anxiety,
4. His fear of horses was symbolic of his fear of his father,
5. The purpose of the illness was to keep near his mother, and finally,
6. His phobia disappeared because he resolved his Oedipus complex" (p. 143).

Taking these claims one at a time, Wolpe and Rachman (pp. 143–145) argue:

1. Hans clearly did derive satisfaction from his mother, and once while bathing wanted her to touch his penis. "But nowhere is there any evidence of his wish to copulate with her. . . . Even if it is assumed that stimulation provided by his mother was especially desired, the two other features of an Oedipus complex (a wish to possess the mother and replace the father) are not demonstrated by the facts of the case."
2. Hans never spontaneously expressed either fear or hatred of

his father, but was told by Freud that he possessed these emotions. "On subsequent occasions Hans denied the existence of these feelings when questioned by his father. Eventually, he said 'Yes' to a statement of this kind by his father. This simple affirmative obtained after considerable pressure on the part of the father and Freud is accepted as the true state of affairs and all Hans's denials are ignored."

At one point Little Hans knocked over a toy horse, which Freud interpreted as a "symptomatic act." This interpretation rests on the questionable assumptions that the horse represents his father, that knocking over the horse was not accidental, and that the act indicates a wish for removing whatever the horse symbolizes.

3. Freud's argument that Hans' sexual desire for his mother was transformed into anxiety is based on the theoretical assumption that what is today the object of a phobia must once have been the source of pleasure. This assumption is contradicted by experimental research indicating how previously neutral stimuli can be made the subjects of phobias through simple conditioning.

4. "The assumed relationship between the father and this horse is unsupported and appears to have arisen as a result of the father's strange failure to believe that by the 'black around their mouths' Hans meant the horses' muzzles."

5. The claim that the purpose of Hans' phobia was to keep him near his mother is contradicted by the fact that Hans experienced anxiety even when he was out walking with his mother.

6. The claim that the phobia disappeared because Hans resolved his Oedipus complex is brought into question both by the fact that there is no adequate evidence that he ever had an Oedipus complex; and that during the course of treatment, there seems to have been no systematic relationship between the psychoanalytic interpretations made and the course of his phobia.

Wolpe and Rachman argue that the origin and course of Little Hans' phobia can more plausibly be interpreted in terms of learning theory. Phobias are seen as conditioned fear reactions which can arise through the pairing of any neutral stimulus with a fear-producing situation. They argue that such a conditioning process may well have been the source of Little Hans' fear of horses, and that what Freud saw as "merely the exciting cause of Hans's phobia was in fact the cause of the entire disorder. Hans actually says, 'No, I only got it [the phobia] then. When the horse in the bus fell down, it gave me such a fright, really.' That was when I got the nonsense" (Wolpe and Rachman, 1960, p. 146). The fact that the anxiety broke out immediately afterwards was confirmed by Hans' mother. Two other incidents may also have sensitized or "partially conditioned" Hans to fear horses. One was a warning from a father of one of his friends to avoid a horse so that he wouldn't get bitten, and in a second incident, one of Hans' friends fell and cut himself while playing horse.

Wolpe and Rachman say that the actual mechanism responsible for Hans' recovery cannot be identified because of a lack of relevant information, but that remission may have been due to repeated exposure to the phobic stimulus in a nonthreatening context, so that the aroused anxiety responses were weak enough to be inhibited by other concurrently aroused emotional responses. They suggest that the gradualness of Little Hans' recovery is consistent with an explanation of this type.

It seems to me that in this particular case, a learning theory interpretation appears more compelling than a psychodynamic one, and that a critique of the inferential procedures used by Freud seems warranted. This single case does, of course, not provide any substantial grounds for assessing the relative merits of psychodynamic and learning theoretical systems as a whole. It is hoped that the case does, however, provide a useful illustration of the process by which the evidential, inferential, and theoretical foundations of a case history may be critically examined, and the data reformulated in light of an alternative theoretical orientation.[1]

It should be noted that the Wolpe and Rachman analysis has not been without its critics.[2] In one psychoanalytic response, Neu (1977) states that their critique "contains so many misunderstandings that one hardly knows where to begin enumerating them" (p. 125). For example, in relation to Freud's claim that Little Hans had a sexual desire for his mother, Wolpe and Rachman say, "That Hans derived satisfaction from his mother and enjoyed her presence we will not even attempt to dispute. But nowhere is there any evidence of his wish to copulate with her"

(Wolpe and Rachman, 1960, p. 143). Neu responds, "It is virtually incredible that they should use such a narrow notion of the 'sexual' " (p. 124), as Freud shows, even in this case, that the sexual desires of children are based on their own sexual theories, correspond to their own level of development, and must be understood far more broadly.

To take a second example, Wolpe and Rachman argue that there is no independent evidence that Hans hated or feared his father, and reject as evidence his knocking over of a toy horse, which supposedly symbolizes his father. Neu suggests that there is other evidence consistent with Freud's interpretation that horses represented his father for Hans. For instance, Hans tells his father not to "trot away from me," parents are expected to have penises as big as horses, and his father had played at being a horse for him. Finally, Neu argues that reinterpretations of Hans' phobia in terms of learning theory concepts such as "stimulus" and "generalization" "will yield only vacuous descriptions and explanations" (p. 127), and cannot possibly explain the complexities of Hans' entire disorder.

In sum, the three cases of Little Hans, Dr. Schreber, and King George III bring to life a number of the methodological issues involved in the interpretation, critical evaluation, and subsequent reformulation of studies of single cases. Although not always arriving at a single consensual conclusion, the case studies illustrate how the critical examination of evidence, inferences, and conclusions can lead to increasingly plausible and more tightly argued interpretations of single cases.

The Relationship of Single-Case Experimental Designs to Naturalistic Case Studies

After naturalistic case studies, a second tradition in the study of individual cases is that of single-subject experimentation, or single-case experimental designs (e.g., Chassan, 1979; Davidson and Costello, 1969; Hersen and Barlow, 1976; Jayaratne and Levy, 1979; Kratochwill, 1978; Leitenberg, 1973; Shapiro, 1966). This approach has its historical roots in experimental laboratory research with animals, in disaffection with the clinical utility of group-comparison or extensive designs, and in the development of behavior therapy for humans (Hersen and Barlow, 1976).

Single-case experimental designs focus on the experimental manipulation of independent or treatment variables and the objective assessment of dependent variables in order to determine if observed changes in behavior are causally related to therapeutic interventions. For example, a baseline for the frequency of a particular behavior, such as percentage of time paying attention in class for a child, is established. Then an invervention, such as verbal praise or a financial reward for attending in class is introduced, and changes in the target behavior measured. Finally, the reinforcement may be removed to see if this leads to a subsequent decrease in the target behavior. A variety of forms of single-case experimental designs, such as withdrawal designs, reversal designs, and multiple baseline designs (Hersen and Barlow, 1976; Kratochwill, 1978) are used in order to make systematic inferences about the effects of specified treatment procedures, and to control for different threats to internal validity (Campbell and Stanley, 1966; Cook and Campbell, 1979).

From the perspective of experimental analysts of the single case, the traditional naturalistic case study is seen as seriously deficient. Traditional case studies "do not try to experimentally isolate the effects of 'the' therapy from the effects of other therapeutic factors which might be acting on the patient simultaneously" (Leitenberg, 1973, p. 89). Another expression of this view is that "case study methodology was typically characterized by numerous sources of uncontrolled variation, inadequate description of independent and dependent variables, and was generally difficult to replicate" (Kratochwill, 1978, p. 45).

From the viewpoint of the single-case experimentalist, the naturalistic case study does have functions such as suggesting new hypotheses for subsequent experimental examination, providing data on extremely rare clinical phenomena, or communicating novel psychotherapeutic techniques (Hersen and Barlow, 1976; Kazdin, 1980). However, some (but not all) experimentalists still believe that design defects made the traditional case study method of little scientific value (Kratochwill, 1978).

Is it fair to conclude that traditional naturalistic case studies are no more than poorly controlled single-case experiments? Do developments in single-case experimental design make the naturalistic case study obsolete, or assign it to a purely auxiliary role, such as generating hypotheses for more rigorous experimental tests? No, I think not, even though writers in this tradition sometimes create a history, or a context, within which this seems a perfectly natural conclusion.

First, there is no doubt that single-subject experimental designs are an important and extremely useful methodological advance. They have contributed both to clinical practice and to our theoretical understanding of individual cases, and it is hoped that further developments along these lines will be made. On the other hand, in the process of developing and promoting these relatively new single-case experimental designs, it seems that some of the advantages of and needs for naturalistic case studies are being overlooked. I want to argue that too limited a set of criteria is being used in comparing naturalistic with experimental case studies, and that a broader context or broader perspective is needed in order to develop a balanced appreciation of the strengths and weaknesses of the two methods.

This defense of naturalistic case studies is not to deny that they have flaws and limitations, or that they have often been used in irresponsible or indefensible ways, such as in biased "testimonials" or as grounds for insupportable generalizations. The misuses of case studies are no more grounds for abandoning the method than it would be to go from the observation that one can lie with statistics to the conclusion that we should stop using statistics. A more appropriate solution is to be aware of the limitations and potential misuses of the method and to learn how to use it with proper constraints.

As a background for discussing the respective strengths and weaknesses of naturalistic and experimental case studies, recall the distinction noted earlier in this chapter about the three foci that a case study may have: (1) assessment-formulation of the problem, either in terms of a current baseline and/or a reconstruction of its origin and course through the life history, (2) description of the treatment process, of techniques used, and of interactions between therapist and client, or (3) assessment of the effects of treatment.

I want to suggest that single-case experimental designs and naturalistic case studies have relatively different emphases within the array of possible goals of case studies, and thus may prove to be complementary. The single-case experimental design is devoted primarily to assessing the effects of treatment, or to controlling for threats to internal validity in drawing causal inferences about the effects of specific treatment procedures upon selected outcome variables. In contrast, the traditional case study places a relatively greater emphasis upon identifying the origins and historical course of a client's disorder, or upon searching for the causes and meanings of a person's problems within the context of his or her entire life history. Traditional case studies may also give detailed information about the course of treatment, as in Dewald (1972).

This is not to deny that each form of case study may also devote some attention to other goals. For example, single-case experimental designs typically present descriptive information on the problem, often in the form of a baseline indicating the current frequency and intensity of target behaviors, but usually without much information on the initial causes and historical course of the disorder. Information on intervention techniques and methods is also presented, but usually not in the form of detailed reports on verbal exchanges between client and therapist or on their changing personal relationship. Naturalistic case studies may, but do not inevitably, contain statements about the presumed effects of treatment, as with Freud's follow-up notes on Little Hans, but the assessment of effects is frequently not as rigorous or as systematic as in single-case experimental studies.

In summary, single-case experimental designs seem relatively more effective for assessing the effects of therapeutic interventions, for recording behavior baselines in the current time period, and for measuring changes in quantifiable aspects of behavior and functioning. On the other hand, traditional or naturalistic case studies seem relatively effective for interpreting the origins and historical course of disorders; for providing a context for understanding the meaning of specific acts, statements, or feelings; for providing a sketch of the entire life history as a background for understanding current problems and potentials; and for representing aspects of the relationship with the therapist. The reader may want to characterize the functions of experimental and naturalistic case studies in somewhat different ways, but the central point is that experimental and naturalistic case studies need to be compared not solely for the purpose of assessing the effects of interventions but also for their relative value in light of the broader range of functions suggested above.

Criteria for Evaluation

What criteria are used, and should be used, in evaluating case studies? How are we to distinguish a good case study from a bad one, and if a case study is revised or reformulated, how do we tell if it is better or worse than the original? Such questions are not just idle speculation, as it seems that some minimal or provisional answers to them must be formulated in order to develop methodological procedures for improving case studies.

One early study attempted to assess "The Reliability of Life-History Studies" (Cartwright and French, 1939). Two researchers both worked from similar amounts of information about the same subject, including four hours of interviews by each researcher, one interview with a friend of the subject, and the subject's responses to intelligence and personality tests. Reliability was assessed by seeing how accurately each of the researchers could predict the subject's responses to several self-report instruments, including Allport and Vernon's *A Study of Values,* and Watson's *A Survey of Public Opinion on Some Religious and Economic Issues.* Each of the researchers had a higher percentage of agreement with the subject than they did with each other. Thus, they concluded that "the total validity of the judgments of each experimenter was greater than the total agreement (reliability) between them" (Cartwright and French, 1939, p. 113). Regardless of the merits of this particular study, consideration of it raises the question of whether reliability is an appropriate criterion to use in assessing life history studies.

Chapter 2 has shown the extreme diversity of biographical accounts which can be produced about the same individual, suggesting how difficult, or perhaps even impossible, it is to attain "reliable" accounts of a single life. One line of reasoning, explicitly or implicitly, goes as follows:

1. Research methods should be "reliable," in the sense of yielding similar results if employed by different persons.
2. Many alternative accounts of individual lives can be constructed using the case study method.
3. Therefore, the case study method is "not reliable," and perhaps should be avoided in favor of more reliable methods,

such as standardized measurement scales, questionnaires, or experiments.

This is, I believe, an unfortunate line of reasoning. Reliance on too narrow a methodological criterion of "reliability" may lead us to avoid some of the most interesting and important problems in understanding human lives, to unduly restrict our substantive concerns, and to exclude a method—the case study method—which has no adequate replacement. If "reliability" is not an appropriate criterion for evaluating the case study method, what are the appropriate criteria?

An early work attempting to identify appropriate criteria for the evaluation of life histories is John Dollard's *Criteria for the Life History* (1935), which proposed seven specific criteria. The life history is defined as "a deliberate attempt to define the growth of a person in a cultural milieu and to make theoretical sense of it" (Dollard, 1935, p. 3), a definition which corresponds closely enough to our sense of the case study or case history. The seven criteria proposed by Dollard are

> I. The subject must be viewed as a specimen in a cultural series. II. The organic motors of action ascribed must be socially relevant. III. The peculiar role of the family group in transmitting the culture must be recognized. IV. The specific method of elaboration of organic materials into social behavior must be shown. V. The continuous related character of experience from childhood through adulthood must be stressed. VI. The "social situation" must be carefully and continuously specified as a factor. VII. The life-history material itself must be organized and conceptualized [Dollard, 1935, p. 8].

These criteria were then applied to six notable life history documents, including Freud's "Analysis of a Phobia in a Five-Year-Old Boy," *The Jack Roller* by Clifford Shaw, and H. G. Wells' *Experiment in Autobiography*.

Another study examined six different forms of case studies and evaluated them in light of the criterion of their efficiency "in promoting an understanding of the lives by the reader" (Polansky, 1941, p. 188). The six approaches were the *structural* approach (emphasizing temporary traits, attitudes, and ambitions), the *cultural* approach (emphasizing community, family standards, and the like), the *genetic* mode (stressing longitudinal patterns and early events), the *episodic* approach (presenting anecdotes of typical behavior), an approach focusing on *major maladjustment* (reflecting the psychiatric point of view), and lastly, an approach in terms of *individual differences* in test scores (a psychometric account) (Allport, 1942, p. 34.)

As evaluated by their success in enabling judges to successfully predict aspects of the behavior of three subjects described with each of the modes, the modes arranged from most to least successful were the structural, cultural, genetic, episodic, individual difference, and major maladjustment. In terms of subjective interest to the judges, the structural mode was the most interesting and the individual difference mode least interesting.

One problem in evaluating case studies is that they are often judged by people who have no outside knowledge of the subject, and thus, the case study is evaluated solely on internal criteria, such as its style, vividness, coherence, and apparent plausibility. Case studies need to be judged not solely on internal criteria, but also, as a check on their validity, by the criterion of their correspondence with external sources of information about the subject. To be complete, the process of evaluation cannot be carried out solely by reading the case itself, but also must involve judgments by people who either know the subject or are familiar with other sources of evidence about the individual.

In a more practically oriented context, Dailey (1953) suggested that clinical reports (including clinical case studies) be evaluated in light of their utility for clinical decision making. Clinical reports were evaluated in light of their impact upon thirty-two frequently made clinical decisions, such as "Should the patient have been admitted to the psychiatric ward?" "Should he receive sedative drugs?" "Should she receive intensive interpretive individual psychotherapy?" and "Should the patient be watched for suicidal tendencies?"

Another set of criteria is suggested by Tallent (1976) in his survey of complaints about psychological reports (of which many, although not all, take the form of case reports). More than 1,400 clinicians responded to questionnaires asking them to complete the root sentence: "The trouble with psychological reports is. . . ." A sample of the criticisms, with evaluative criteria either explicit or implicit, are given below.

One frequent criticism was that reports have an improper emphasis, such as too much on personality dynamics, as for example, "They seem to emphasize the personality state of an individual whereas I think more emphasis should be placed on the functioning of an individual in terms of what he is doing to and with other people. If the patient is to be seen in psychotherapy, the psychological report should include some predictions about how he will probably act toward the therapist, how he will see the therapist, some goals for the therapist, and how the therapist might try to accomplish these goals and why he might do it in the way suggested" (pp. 33–34).

Another common complaint was that case reports often contained irresponsible interpretation, or overspeculation. For example, "Too much speculation, reading between the lines, personal interpretation rather than reporting facts as observed." Or, "Data is frequently overinterpreted. One can speculate but should label it as such." Or, "The distinctions between reasonable deduction from the data, speculative extrapolations from the data, and the psychologist's clinical impression are not clear." Or, "They sometimes seem to reflect the psychologist's feelings about the patient rather than the data revealed by the patient's responses to the tests" (pp. 36–37).

A third common criticism is that the reports are not practical or useful enough. "They are not pertinent to the purpose desired," or, "They're too sophisticated, too impractical for the people who rely upon the information they dispense." Or, "They often are too theoretical or academic in language to be comprehensible or meaningful in terms of future treatment goals for the client. They occasionally give us the feeling that no client was present at the time" (pp. 38–40).

A fourth criticism is in terms of word usage, as either too technical, or ambiguous, or just too many of them. For example, "Gobbledygook." "Too much jargon." "They are too often written in a horrible psychologese—so that clients 'manifest overt aggressive hostility in an impulsive manner'—when, in fact—they punch you on the nose." "Most of them are too long. Few people, if any, will take the time to read them." "Too often the completed report is too long. Often I might go to the summary to get the gist of the examination" (pp. 42–43).

A fifth criticism is that there is not enough well-developed

psychological science or theory behind them. "The greatest defect is inadequate and unsympathetic personality theory on
which to hang our observations." "Interpretation is too often
based on theories which are yet poorly validated."

This is just a sample of the variety of criticisms of case reports.
Others are that they omit essential information; they contain
too much raw data, or not enough; they are too authoritative,
or too exhibitionistic; they hedge too much; they are poorly organized; and so on. Each of these criticisms suggests criteria
which are implicitly applied to case studies, such as that they
should consider social context as well as personality dynamics,
avoid unsupported interpretations, address practical treatment
issues, and be written concisely and without unnecessary jargon.

Taking a more positive approach, case studies can be praised
in terms of a substantial list of criteria, among which I would
want to include:

1. Providing "insight" into the person, clarifying the previously meaningless or incomprehensible, suggesting previously
   unseen connections;
2. Providing a feel for the person, conveying the experience of
   having known or met him or her;
3. Helping us to understand the inner or subjective world of
   the person, how they think about their own experience, situation, problems, life;
4. Deepening our sympathy or empathy for the subject;
5. Effectively portraying the social and historical world that the
   person is living in;
6. Illuminating the causes (and meanings) of relevant events,
   experiences, and conditions; and
7. Being vivid, evocative, emotionally compelling to read.

In addition, if the case study is carried out in a clinical context, it might be evaluated in terms of criteria such as:

8. Delineating the "problem" requiring decision or action;
9. Identifying the need for collecting additional types of information;
10. Suggesting possible goals and courses of action; and
11. Sensitizing us to the likely consequences of alternative courses
    of action.

It is difficult to come up with a comprehensive set of criteria for evaluating all case studies. In fact, it may be inappropriate to come up with one single set of criteria, as case studies are carried out in different contexts for different purposes, and various criteria may be differentially important within different contexts. For example, there may be somewhat different criteria appropriate for case studies used in a theoretical argument, in an historical study, or for clinical purposes. There are, however, a core set of primary criteria which should be met by case studies in any context, such as being based on accurate data and avoiding one-sided selection and interpretation of the data. Beyond such basic criteria, there could be partially overlapping sets of secondary criteria appropriate for each of a number of different contexts and purposes.

Methods for Improvement

In this section, I will consider methods which have been used, and which might be used, in attempting to improve case studies. The aim is not to find a method leading to perfect or flawless case studies (which can be a paralyzingly ambitious goal), but rather to produce case studies which alleviate some of the common problems and which are at least incrementally better than current ones.

OSS Assessment Program

One of the early methods for systematically conducting case studies was that of Henry A. Murray, used in the Office of Strategic Services (OSS) Assessment Program for selecting men for overseas intelligence work in World War II. Each personality sketch was originally the product of two assessors "who, though covering different phases of the personality, were obliged to arrive at conceptions acceptable to both" (OSS Assessment Staff, 1948, p. 55). This initial personality sketch was read before a staff conference, and the purpose of the staff discussion was "to change or eliminate statements unjustified by the evidence, and, if necessary, to add other statements to cover manifestations of the personality which escaped the notice of the writer" (p. 55). "Each generalization had to be supported by sufficient evidence to make it plausible, and no generalization that seemed unwarranted or disregarded contradictory data was permitted to go unchallenged. Thus each personality sketch corresponded to the conclusions of several different minds" (p. 55).

Their working hypothesis was that individual judgments would be improved by the group discussion, assuming that "group discussion brings into each man's sphere of reflection more facts and more interpretations than were there before. Thus the errors that come from ignorance of all the available evidence and the errors that come from an inability to conceive of all plausible interpretations will be reduced" (pp. 55–56).

The dangers of this group discussion and persuasion process were, as recognized by Murray, that a person's influence upon the group analytic process might be due to personality characteristics such as verbal facility, desire to persuade, reputation, or authority, rather than solely the quality of his analysis.

The work of the OSS staff conferences proceeded, however, on the assumptions that these forces balance out over time, eventually "leaving diagnostic ability as the chief factor in deciding the course of group opinion" (p. 56); and on the assumption that "the judgments of the majority are, in the long run, more valid than the judgments of any one member of a group, assuming that the disparity in ability among the members is not great" (p. 56). Both of these assumptions could be, and to different degrees have been, subjected to empirical test since this pioneering work.

Later, in rating returnees, a conference of one senior and two junior staff members rated individual returnees on six dimensions. If there was agreement among the three raters, the ratings were recorded. "When there was disagreement, the conferees tried to see if they could come to agreement by discussion; if they could not, the case was continued in order to get more data" (p. 406). Here is an example in which high social consensus led to the termination of inquiry, and disagreement or conflict led to the continuation of inquiry, a theme noted earlier in Chapter 4 on the course of explanatory endeavors. The OSS assessment program pioneered the idea of improving case analyses through a combination of scaled rating and group discussion, identified several of the advantages and liabilities of such group processes, and in their detailed self-criticisms and recommendations for future research, made a significant contribution to the holistic approach to the assessment of individuals.

Rules for Writing Life Histories

Developing methods or procedures for writing case studies of individual lives has not been an easy task. In his autobiography, Gordon Allport states that a central question throughout his intellectual career was: "How shall a psychological life history be written?" (Allport, 1967, p. 3). In the late 1930's or early 1940's, he composed a set of thirty-eight rules to be used in the preparation and evaluation of life histories and case studies. The rules make such suggestions as (1) the purpose for which the life history is written should be clear to author and reader; (2) all sources of data should be specified; (3) completeness of information should be sought, so that omissions in the written product are due to judgment rather than neglect; (4) all statements regarding the objective situation by the subject should be checked against independent sources of evidence whenever possible; (5) extensive use should be made of the subject's own language in describing subjective experiences and his or her view of major life events; (6) statements about general personality characteristics should be followed by specific illustrations which particularize them for the individual; and (7) avoid irrelevance and unnecessary repetition, striving for maximum brevity (Garraty, 1981). But Allport felt that the rules were a failure, and never published them during his lifetime. Thus, they have been publicly available only through a summary in Garraty (1957) and a post-mortem release (Garraty, 1981). Near the end of his life, Allport concluded, "It is true that we designed a set of rules and composed cases to fit the rules, but at the end we were distressed by the hollowness of the product. . . . I still do not know how a psychological life history should be written" (Allport, 1967, pp. 3–4).

A variety of other suggestions and guidelines for the writing of life histories have been proposed (e.g., Lemert, 1951; Young, 1952; Garraty, 1957). To give one more recent example, Denzin (1978) suggested a set of nine steps to follow in preparing life history studies. These move from the first step of selecting a series of research hypotheses and problems to be explored in the life history, through the subsequent steps of selecting subjects, recording events and experiences in their lives relevant to the central problems, and obtaining their subjective interpretations of these events. At this point, the collected reports and statements are to be analyzed in terms of internal coherence and external validity, with the intention of resolving conflicts and assessing the credibility of alternative sources of information. One can then begin to test initial hypotheses, search for negative evidence, and generate and test additional hypotheses. After a draft of the entire life history is prepared, it should be submitted to the subjects for their reactions, and modified in light of these reactions. The completed life history study should include a presentation of the hypotheses and propositions that have been supported and should indicate the relevance of the report for theory and subsequent research. Denzin's rules seem reasonable, and a valuable next step would be to test and report on their value in use, to see if they prove more satisfying than Allport's guidelines.

Configurational Analysis

The recent work of Mardi Horowitz (1979) provides an illustration of the kinds of improvements which can be made in case study methodology. He presents "configurational analysis" as a strategy for the recognition of individual patterns in human personality and psychotherapeutic change. Configurational analysis consists of both a particular theoretical framework and a more general strategy for identifying patterns or configurations in the study of individual persons. The substantive theoretical framework has three principal components, which are conceptualizations of (1) states of behavior and emotional experience; (2) role relationships, including images of self, of others, and the process of interaction; and (3) information processing, or the relationships between ideas, emotions, and controls of thoughts and feelings. Although these substantive ideas are of considerable intrinsic interest, the current discussion will focus on those strategic aspects of configurational analysis which have more general implications for case study methodology.

One of the traditional problems with case history formulations is the lack of replicability in observation and interpretation. In clinical settings, a case study is often based on the observations and interpretations of a single therapist or diagnostician, who may have been the only staff member to have any direct experience with the client, which makes it difficult for others to have an independent evidential base for critically assessing the initial formulation. Horowitz addresses this problem with the use of videotaped clinical interviews, so that it is possible to make repeated observations of the same clinical material, either by the original clinician, or by those with alternative points of view. The existence on videotape of enduring records of primary data makes possible "a sequential process of observation, theory revision, reobservation, and further theory revision" (p. 128). It becomes possible both to test theoretical formulations and interpretations against the original data, and to have the process of theory formation and testing pursued by a variety of different observers having different interests and alternative theoretical perspectives.

The writer of clinical cases is often on the horns of the nomothetic-idiographic dilemma. On the one hand, "if we approach the complexity of human personality and change with a rigid preformed theory of categories, we will make observations only according to these restrictive classifications" (p. vii), and often miss distinctive and important features of the individual case. On the other hand, an effort to avoid preformed categories has its own difficulties. If the scientist attempts to start "from ground zero . . . he always starts at the beginning, is not alert to certain signals and so misses them, and leaves no scientific foundation upon which others can build" (p. vii).

Between the extremes of naïve empiricism and rigid theoretical stances lies an opportunity for a flexible method of description and explanation based on repeated observation of videotaped clinical material. Clinical interactions are often so complex that they cannot be fully grasped upon initial observation. Initial descriptions and interpretations can be checked against the descriptions and interpretations of others, and points of disagreement can be checked against repeated observations of the clinical material, leading to gradual clarification of initially cloudy issues.

Configurational analysis can be used in moving between different levels of analysis in interpreting a specific case. Consider, for example, the problem of describing different states, or different recurring patterns of behavior and experience, in the case of Janice, a twenty-four-year-old therapy patient. Janice complained of depressions, which were characterized by apathy, withdrawal with feelings of fogginess and unreality, and overeating. This might be described in a general way as "depressed mood," but it is also possible to use individualized state descriptions which "go beyond generalities to individual nuances of experience and behavior. Labels such as 'phobic' fear are elaborated to include the way a particular person senses and displays such fear" (p. 30). A more individualized description of Janice's depressed state that she used in describing herself was "hurt and not working." Other common states for Janice were "dramatic animation, when she felt as if she were pretending for the benefit of another person. In another frequent state she continued her efforts to work but felt and appeared as if her feelings were hurt. This was labeled the *hurt but working* state. Using her own words for the animated episodes, this was called the *tra-la-la* state" (p. 36).

For the purposes of clinical work and writing individualized case studies, the person's states can be described in individualized categories, but for purposes of research and theory construction, the same material may be formulated in terms of more general nomothetic categories. Janice's problems, for example, were formulated both in terms of states characterized by idiographic patterns of behavior and experience, and also in terms of her response to standardized measures such as the ninety-item Hopkins Symptom Checklist.

Configurational analysis suggests ways of doing systematic and progressive research on the description and interpretation of individual cases. "In each step of configurational analysis assertions are made about patterns that characterize the person in a specific context. Once these statements are clear, it is possible to check their reliability using the raw data retained by recording or other notation and thus available to review. Reliability of the configurational analysis method rests with the degree to which a second or third person, blind to the pattern judgments of the first reviewer, can follow the same system and produce comparable results" (p. 196). For example, initial observation suggested that the frequency of a number of Janice's states changed over the course of twelve sessions of short-term therapy. In particular, she seemed to experience a decrease in the tra-la-la state, and an increase in the hurt-but-working state. This assertion was tested by having two independent observers view ten-minute segments from each of the twelve therapy sessions, randomized so they did not know the place of each segment in the sequence of sessions. They agreed 73 percent of the time on when each state was entered or left. Their controlled observations clearly supported the initial claim about the decrease in the frequency of the tra-la-la state and increase in the hurt-but-working state. In the initial sessions, Janice spent approximately half of her time in each of these two states, but by the final five sessions, she was in the hurt-but-working state more than five-sixths of the time and in the tra-la-la state less than one-sixth of the time.

When independent clinicians reach similar conclusions after reviewing the basic data, those issues can be set aside as agreed upon, or as reliably established. Issues about which they disagree can be used in order to identify areas "in need of closer observation, sharper classification, and clearer theoretical formulation" (p. 197). Thus, a clearer understanding of individual cases can be reached through a sequential procedure of observation, interpretation, discussion of conflicting interpretations, reobservation, and so on. This sequential process will not always lead to unanimous agreement, but can lead to expanded areas of agreement and to the sharpening and clarification of topics of disagreement.

A Quasi-judicial Methodology for Case Studies

Another valuable perspective on the case study enterprise, which will be discussed in some detail, is that of Bromley in his book *Personality Description in Ordinary Language* (1977). Bromley's analysis is useful for thinking about both the logical and empirical foundations of case studies and the social organization of the process through which case studies are formulated, critically evaluated, and revised. This dual approach provides a useful perspective for thinking about case studies as they are, and as they could be.

According to Bromley, "A psychological 'case-study' is a scientific account, in ordinary language, of an individual person in normal or problematic circumstances" (p. 163), and "is essentially a *reconstruction* and *interpretation,* based on the best evidence available, of part of the story of a person's life" (p. 164). A case study is undertaken in response to a problem in understanding, and/or a problem requiring practical action. For example, a case study might be undertaken in order to help a therapist understand a rare clinical problem, to help a teacher in dealing with a troubled student, or to help a judge in making a decision about a delinquent. A case study usually focuses on a small number of issues, which determine the relevance of the evidence and arguments to be considered.

It is impossible for a case study to tell the whole story of a person's life and circumstances, because the whole story is overwhelmingly complex and detailed. Rather, a more appropriate goal is to tell the story in such a way that the omitted information makes little or no difference in understanding the main structure of the events and arguments in question.

A central feature of Bromley's argument is that the preparation of case studies follows a "quasi-judicial" procedure. A case study presents a theory about how and why a person behaved as he or she did in particular circumstances, and this theory needs to be tested by collecting evidence and formulating arguments relevant to the claims put forward in the theory. This quasi-judicial method "is based on methods evolved in law for ascertaining the truth and conducting fair trials. . . . The quasi-judicial method requires, among other things, that the main issues be stated clearly at the outset, that sufficient empirical data be available to support or refute claims, that evidence be admissable and relevant to those claims, that arguments be relevant and rational, and that conclusions which have important practical implications be supported by a greater weight of evidence than conclusions of lesser importance" (p. 165).

The judicial analogy seems apt in that it suggests that alternative parties may have competing interests (whether legal, theoretical, or practical interests) which often seem relevant to understanding debates surrounding particular cases, whether in courts of law, historical-political controversies, or scientific debates. For example, Freud's case of the Wolf Man was written partly in order to further his side of the argument with Adler and Jung about the primary importance of childhood sexual disturbance in adult neurosis. Or, Wolpe and Rachman's critique of the Little Hans case was written in order to criticize the evidential foundations of psychoanalytic interpretation, as well as to argue for the superiority of learning theory formulations.

Such competing theoretical interests often seem to lie behind and to motivate the collection of evidence, the drawing of inferences and conclusions, and the critical analysis of alternative formulations of cases in clinical and scientific work.

This quasi-judicial construal of case studies, which considers both the logical-empirical and social-political aspects of the process of formulating and critically evaluating case studies, also seems appropriate from a contemporary philosophy of science perspective, which would argue that science cannot be understood solely through rational reconstruction of its logical procedures (e.g., Hempel, 1965; Nagel, 1961), or primarily as a social phenomenon (Kuhn, 1970), but rather as a joint interplay of both logical-empirical and social-political considerations (Laudan, 1977; Suppe, 1977). This notion of a quasi-judicial procedure is also related in its emphasis on both rational and social factors to discussions in earlier chapters about the processes through which alternative accounts of lives are formulated in different social and historical contexts, and of the interaction of rational and social processes in shaping the course of particular explanatory inquiries.

A criticism of traditional case studies is that they are commonly produced by a single individual and often presented to an audience which shares similar perspectives and orientations. "One of the limitations of the case-study method as traditionally practiced in psychology and social work is that it tends to present a one-sided account of the person in a situation, i.e., it fails to consider and compare alternative accounts . . . , and so fails to show that one account is more acceptable than another when judged in terms of a common standard of evidence and argument" (Bromley, 1977, p. 174). One practical implication of a quasi-judicial perspective is that the evidence, inferences, and arguments in a case study ought to be subject to critical examination by others, and that furthermore, there seems to be some advantage to having this examination conducted by someone with an alternative theoretical perspective or with a competing interest in the outcome of the case.

Bromley also suggests six rules to be followed in the writing of case studies. To present them in summarized form: "The first and most important rule is that the investigator must report truthfully on the person, his life and circumstances, and must be accurate in matters of detail. . . . The second rule is that the aims and objectives of the case-study should be stated explicitly and unambiguously. . . . The third rule is that the case-study should contain an assessment of the extent to which the stated aims and objectives have been achieved. . . . The fourth rule is that if, as is often the case, the inquiry deals with episodes of deep emotional significance to the person, then it can be carried out properly only by someone trained and equipped to establish and manage a close, fairly long, and possibly difficult, personal relationship. . . . The fifth rule is that the person must be seen in an 'ecological context'; that is to say, a full account must be given of the objects, persons and events in his physical, social and symbolic environment. The proper focus of a case-study is not so much a 'person' as a 'person in a situation.' . . . The sixth basic rule is that the report of a case-study should be written in good plain English in a direct, objective way without, however, losing its human interest as a story" (Bromley, 1977, pp. 170–172).

Bromley also outlines ten kinds of information which may be included in case studies and presents ten procedural steps to follow in preparing them. For reasons of space, as well as the reader's patience, these rules will not be presented here, but the interested reader is advised to consult Bromley (1977, Chap. 8). It would be valuable to examine case studies composed according to Bromley's rules and procedures and to compare them in persuasiveness, cost, and utility with case studies prepared according to other formats (such as those of Allport or Denzin) or without any explicit guidelines (Runyan, 1978b). In a summarizing checklist, Bromley suggests that investigators check: "that the report fulfills its aims and purposes; that it satisfies its terms of reference, contains no serious omissions, and makes good psychological sense; that subjective factors have been reduced to a minimum, preferably by the incorporation of several independent opinions; that matters of detail are correct and each part is given its due weight; that the sources of evidence and methods of investigation are clearly stated and properly evaluated; that evidence and inference are not confused; that arguments are made explicit and as cogent as possible; that reasons are given for whatever conclusions are reached and for whatever action is recommended; that the evidence and its sources are properly catalogued, so that, in the event of another investigator taking over the case, the original data can be re-examined" (Bromley, 1977, pp. 202–203). I have presented Bromley's comments in some detail, because of the various guidelines for preparing case studies, his seem to me the most cleanly worded, analytically useful, and promising for future investigation.

Conclusion

The twentieth century has witnessed an impressive development of experimental and quasi-experimental methods and of quantitative and statistical methods in the social sciences (e.g., Campbell and Stanley, 1966; Cattell, 1966; Cook and Campbell, 1979; Duncan, 1975; Nesselroade and Baltes, 1979; Winer, 1971). There have, unfortunately, not been equivalent improvements in case study methods, which, at least in terms of systematic methodological attention, have been relatively neglected. An argument can be made that there is a need to rehabilitate this "sadly neglected scientific method" (Bromley, 1977, p. 164).

The aim of this chapter has been to take some preliminary steps in that direction. To briefly summarize, we began by reviewing a range of strongly positive to strongly negative opinions about case studies, and attempted to clarify the nature of the case study method by distinguishing it from debates about retrospective methods, quantitative versus qualitative methods, and subjective versus objective methods. The cases of King George III, Dr. Schreber, and Little Hans were then used to illustrate some of the possible flaws in case studies and the processes through which they might be revised and corrected.

Next, single-case experimental designs were compared with traditional case studies across a range of contexts and purposes. A discussion of the criteria appropriate for evaluating case studies indicated that we need a broader and more flexible approach than focusing on the "reliability" of case study methods or than evaluating the utility of the method solely for the purpose of testing causal generalizations, and a range of such criteria were suggested. Finally, we examined several of the methods and procedural rules which have been suggested by Murray, Allport, Denzin, Horowitz, and Bromley for improving the case study method.

There are dangers in asking for too much precision or certainty from the case study method. As Aristotle said in the *Ethics,* "Our discussion will be adequate if it has as much clearness as the subject matter admits of, for precision is not to be sought for alike in all discussion. . . . For it is the mark of an educated man to look for precision in each class of things just so far as the nature of the subject admits" (Wheelright, 1951, p. 159). Discouragement about attaining high levels of precision or certainty through the case study method can lead us to neglect systematic improvement of the method, with the result that it continues to be used in unnecessarily crude ways and that possible improvements in the method are left undeveloped.

There are vast and relatively unexplored possibilities for empirical research on the case study method and how it might be improved. Two lines of research which appear promising are (1) descriptive studies of how case studies are currently formulated, evaluated, and revised, and of the range of psychological and social factors which influence these processes; and (2) experimental studies of the utility, cost, persuasiveness, and so forth of case studies constructed according to the different rules and procedures proposed by Allport, Denzin, Horowitz, Bromley, and others. Research on the case study method could profitably draw upon methods and findings from a host of related areas, all of which study the cognitive processes involved in thinking about individual lives, such as the elegant process-tracing research in medical diagnosis and problem solving (Elstein, Shulman, and Sprafka, 1978), and research in areas such as person perception (Schneider, Hastorf, and Ellsworth, 1979), social cognition and human inference (Nisbett and Ross, 1980), clinical judgment (Goldberg, 1968), and jury decision making (Saks, 1977).

In sum, the case study deserves our systematic methodological attention as it is the method which defines the limits of our ability to understand the course of events and experiences in individual human lives.

NOTES

1. A delightful discussion of common errors in reasoning about clinical cases is contained in Paul Meehl's classic "Why I Do Not Attend Case Conferences" (1973).

2. For those interested in following up the controversy over psycho-analytic versus learning theory interpretations of Little Hans, the debate is continued in Conway (1978) and Cheshire (1979), and in an entertaining and informative exchange of letters from Stanley Rachman, Neil Cheshire, Geoffrey Thorpe, and Hans Eysenck in subsequent issues of the *Bulletin of the British Psychological Society* (1978–80).

9

Idiographic Methods

[The goal of psychology is] the development of generalizations of ever increasing scope, so that greater and greater varieties of phenomena may be explained by them, larger and larger numbers of questions answered by them, and broader and broader reaching predictions and decisions based upon them.

Leon Levy (1970, p. 5)

To generalize is to be an idiot.

William Blake

Understanding individual life histories requires not only the employment of general conceptual frameworks and theories but also methods for understanding what is particular, distinctive, or unique about the individual. Beginning in 1937, Gordon Allport argued that psychology had defined itself too exclusively as a generalizing discipline, and that in order to redress this imbalance, there should be a greater emphasis upon individuality, the organization of variables and processes within the person, and the lawful regularities within individual lives (Allport, 1937, 1961, 1962). Borrowing from the German philosopher Windelband (1904), Allport used the word "nomothetic" to characterize the search for general laws, and "idiographic" to indicate a concern for what is particular to the individual case.

   This chapter will attempt a conceptual clarification of the idiographic approach and its relationship to the nomothetic approach, review and respond to a number of criticisms of the idiographic approach, and finally, review a number of recent developments in idiographic methods. This review of the idiographic-nomothetic issue is intended to strengthen the rationale for the individual level of analysis, and to survey a range of idiographic methods, many of which can be drawn upon in the study of individual life histories.

Issues of Conception and Definition

Allport believed that "the outstanding characteristic of man is his individuality" (Allport, 1937, p. 3). He argued that psychology had been defining itself too exclusively as a nomothetic or generalizing discipline, without sufficient concern for patterned individuality. "We recognize the single case as a useful source of hunches—and that is about all. We pursue our acquaintance with Bill long enough to derive some hypothesis, and then spring like a gazelle into the realm of abstraction, drawing from Bill a 'testable proposition' but carrying with us no coordinated knowledge of him as a structural unit" (Allport, 1962, p. 406). "Instead of growing impatient with the single case and hastening on to generalizations, why should we not grow impatient with our generalizations and hasten to the internal pattern?" (Allport, 1962, p. 407). The study of individuality requires idiographic methods capable of revealing individual traits or variables and their patterned relationship within the individual. Allport believed that the comprehensive study of individuals would require both nomothetic and idiographic approaches.

The idiographic-nomothetic debate flourished from the 1950's through the early 1960's (e.g., Allport, 1942, 1946, 1961; Beck, 1953; Eysenck, 1954; Falk, 1956; Krech, 1955; Meehl, 1954; Rosenzweig, 1958; Seeman and Galanter, 1952; Skaggs, 1945), but seemed to subside as a topic of focal concern after Allport (1962) suggested that the word idiographic be replaced by the term "morphogenic," meaning accounting for pattern or structure within the individual, and Holt (1962) argued that the original dichotomy was "badly formulated and based on misconceptions" (Holt, 1962, p. 400) and had best be dropped from our scientific vocabularies. According to Holt (1962), the terms idiographic and nomothetic "continue to appear in psychological writing but largely as pretentious jargon, mouth-filling polysyllables to awe the uninitiated, but never as essential concepts to make any scientifically vital point. Let us simply drop them from our vocabularies and let them die quietly" (p. 402). The terms, however, linger on. There seems to be a persistent interest in the underlying issue of the relationship between the search for general laws and the understanding of particular individuals.

Since Allport's introduction of the term idiographic, it has been used and misused in a variety of ways, to mean not only what is unique to the individual and the particular patterning or organization of elements within the individual but also to include such things as a teleological view of man, designed to highlight "uniqueness, identity, will, and other humanistic concepts" (Marceil, 1977, p. 1047). In spite of the alternative construals, it is possible to identify a relatively stable core meaning of the term, which is a concern with the in-depth understanding of particular individuals. The idiographic approach does not apply to just a single issue, but rather to a set of related issues, all associated with its central meaning. The idiographic approach may be concerned with:

1. Individualized traits or personal dispositions (Allport, 1961)
2. The identification of central themes within an individual life (Allport, 1965; Baldwin, 1942)
3. The ipsative ordering of responses within the individual, meaning scores determined in relation to individual rather than group norms (Alfert, 1967; Broverman, 1962)
4. The patterning or organization of variables within the single case (Allport, 1937, 1961), perhaps through factor analysis (Cattell, 1966; Luborsky and Mintz, 1972)
5. The correlation of variables within the single case (Chassan, 1979; Shapiro, 1966)
6. The selection of particular traits on which to assess individuals, in the belief that all individuals are not equally consistent across common trait dimensions (Bem and Allen, 1974; Kenrick and Stringfield, 1980)
7. The causal relationship of variables within the single case (Chassan, 1979; Hersen and Barlow, 1976)
8. Descriptive generalizations about the single case (Bromley, 1977)
9. The particular subjective meanings of events and circumstances to the individual or

10. Predictions based on trends or patterns in the data about a single case.

This list is not necessarily complete, but it should be sufficient to indicate a variety of possible uses of the term idiographic, all unified by a concern with what is particular to the individual.

Three Levels of Generality in the Study of Lives

As argued in Chapter 1, the discipline of psychology is concerned with learning (1) what is true of all human beings; (2) what is true of groups of human beings, distinguished by race, sex, social class, historical cohort, and so on; and (3) what is true of individual human beings. There is order or regularity within each of these three levels of analysis, and the three levels cannot be collapsed into each other. The three levels of inquiry are semi-independent, and the solution of problems at one level does not necessarily solve problems at the other levels. In particular, research at the group or universal level can contribute to the task but is, in itself, often insufficient to enable us to understand and predict the behavior of individuals.

Consider, for example, the relationship between Milgram's research on obedience to authority and our understanding of the behavior of Adolf Eichmann in World War II. As head of the Jewish Department in the Reich's Main Security Office, Eichmann was involved in the execution of an estimated 6 million European Jews. At his trial for war crimes in 1961, Eichmann argued that he had never wished to harm a single Jew, but felt impelled to obey the orders of his superiors. "I was in the iron grip of orders," he argued, and personally, he considered "the whole solution by violence to be a dreadful thing" (Hausner, 1966, p. 366). Before being executed by hanging in 1962, Eichmann's last words were, "I had to obey the rules of war and my flag" (p. 446).

In a well-known program of experimental research on obedience to authority, Milgram (1974) found that more than 60 percent of normal subjects could be induced to administer what they believed to be extremely painful or even life-threatening shocks to innocent subjects in a learning experiment. What relationship do these experiments have to our understanding of

Eichmann's behavior? Is it fair to suggest that he was not an evil man, but that like the subjects in the experiments, he was coerced into performing destructive actions against his inner objections? Maybe this is an adequate explanation of his behavior, and maybe it is not, but how can we know?

The collection of detailed particularistic information about Eichmann through interviews, cross-examination, and the analysis of personal and historical documents suggests a somewhat different picture than that of a man driven by authority to violate the dictates of his conscience. As for the view that he was just following orders, Eichmann said in 1957 in a tape-recorded talk to a Dutch Nazi journalist, "I could make it easy for myself. I could claim it was an order I had to carry out because of my oath of allegiance. But that would be just a cheap excuse, which I am not prepared to give" (Hausner, 1966, p. 11). And "I was not just a recipient of orders. Had I been that, I would have been an imbecile. I was an idealist" (p. 11). Furthermore, Eichmann was selective in his following of orders, and attempted to sabotage or reverse requests for leniency in the treatment of Jews. In 1944, for example, Hitler authorized that 8,700 selected Jewish families and 1,000 children be allowed to emigrate from Hungary so that the Hungarian government would accede to the deportation and execution of the 300,000 Jews remaining in the Budapest ghetto. Eichmann was outraged at this leniency and appealed the matter to Himmler. In accord with Eichmann's objections, Hitler cancelled the emigration permits (Hausner, 1966, pp. 142–145).

Milgram reports that subjects frequently experienced extreme strain and tension as they administered higher-level shocks. In contrast, according to Dr. Heinrich Grueber, a German clergyman who tried to help the Jews during World War II, Eichmann "was like a piece of ice or marble. Nothing ever touched his heart. Whenever I came to plead with him on behalf of a Jew or a Jewish cause, the answer was always negative" (Hausner, 1966, p. 13). As for his sympathy for the victims, Eichmann told Sassen, "To be frank with you, had we killed all of them, the 10.3 million, I would be happy and say, All right; we managed to destroy an enemy" (p. 11).

These selected bits of evidence are, of course, not conclusive. Other interpretations drawing on other pieces of evidence can and have been offered (Arendt, 1964). The important issue here though is: What is the relationship between the general and individual levels of analysis? Eichmann's behavior might be explained by deducing it from a set of initial conditions (such as that he was embedded in an organizational hierarchy and that his superiors had ordered the destruction of Jews), plus the general experimental results showing that most people will harm others if ordered to do so by authorities. Or, an understanding of Eichmann's behavior could be pursued through collecting detailed information about what he said and did in many different situations, and trying to develop an idiographic interpretation out of the complete range of available facts about him. General theories can suggest hypotheses about the individual, but these explanatory hypotheses must then be tested through extensive research about the person in question. Research at the group or universal level can contribute to the task, but is, in itself, often insufficient for understanding and predicting the behavior of individuals.

Since progress at the universal, group, and individual levels of analysis is partially independent of progress at the other levels, research needs to be pursued independently on all three of these levels, with idiographic methods directed toward advancing our understanding of particular individuals. There is, in short, an important place within psychology for both *idiographic goals*— of describing, explaining, predicting, generalizing about, and intentionally changing the behavior of particular individuals— and *idiographic methods* capable of contributing to the attainment of these goals.

Criticisms of the Idiographic Approach

If the need for idiographic methods is as clear as suggested here, why haven't they been more widely accepted? Why are personality journals filled with between-group experiments, tests of general hypotheses, and correlation matrices, and with so few studies of individual human beings (Carlson, 1971)? Part of the reason may be found in the criticisms of and objections to the idiographic approach, a number of which will be reviewed below. Some of the criticisms are based on misunderstandings or misinterpretations of the idiographic approach, while others identify exaggerated or indefensible claims made for the approach. An attempt will be made to discover which of these criticisms are or are not justified, and to see if consideration of these criticisms can lead to an improved formulation of the idiographic approach.

Perhaps the most widespread criticism of idiographic studies of particular lives is that it is difficult to generalize from them. Holt (1962), for example, argues that "if every personality structure were as much a law unto itself as Allport implies, it would be impossible to gain useful information in this field; there would be no transfer from one case study to another" (p. 398). A common reaction to the intensive study of an individual life was expressed by a colleague of mine as follows: "So what? How can you generalize from that?" Allport's summary of these criticisms is that if a relationship is found within a single case, "We'd have to generalize to other people or else we'd have nothing of any scientific value" (Allport, 1962, p. 406).

This criticism seems based on the unwarranted assumption that the goal of personality psychology is solely to produce generalizations at the highest possible level of abstraction, preferably universal generalizations. As argued earlier, personality psychology needs to attend to goals on at least three different levels of abstraction, that of universals, groups, and individuals. Although there is some transfer between these three levels of abstraction, they are at least partially independent of each other. To the cry of "How can you generalize from that idiographic study?" the equally appropriate response is "How can you particularize from that group or population study to the individual?" Work on all three levels of analysis is necessary, and the fact that inquiry at one level does not automatically answer questions at the other two levels is not a telling criticism.

A second criticism is that there is no such thing as a unique trait or element. Emmerich (1968) says, "Any unique attribute is also common, for the only way that the two might be distinguished is in terms of the nature of the distribution of individuals on the attribute" (p. 679), and he suggests that the distinction between common and unique elements is not worth perpetuating.

This criticism is certainly technically correct, in that any trait or category, once formed, can then be applied to all other individuals. The idiographer's question, though, is whether the individual will be studied in enough detail to permit the *formulation* of idiographic traits and classes of behavior, or whether the individual will be described solely in terms of a prior set of nomothetic categories.

Consider the case of Elizabeth Bathori, a Polish countess who was discovered in 1610 to have murdered 650 young girls, so that she might renew her own youth by bathing in their blood. The category of acts of "Killing young girls in order to bathe in their blood" is one that can be meaningfully created and used for this individual. Once this category is formulated, it can then be used more widely, although it is likely to be relatively uninformative when applied to the general population.

Creating concepts and categories which apply to specific individuals is certainly what Allport means by idiographic. Emmerich is correct in that any idiographic concept or category can, once formulated, be applied to other individuals. Over time, any new concept or category can become a nomothetic one, depending upon the range of individuals it is applied to. In sum, if a concept or category is created for the purpose of describing a specific individual, it seems appropriate to call this idiographic, with the recognition that if it becomes more widely used, it could then become a nomothetic concept.

A third criticism is that the study of individual cases is useful for generating hypotheses, but not for testing them. For example, "We can surmise (or, if you will, intuit) general laws from a single case in the hypothesis-forming phase of scientific endeavour, but we can verify them only by resorting to experimental or statistical inquiry or both. . . . As excellent a way as it is to make discoveries, the study of an individual cannot be used to establish laws" (Holt, 1962, pp. 396–397).

This criticism seems to be based on several misunderstandings. First, it assumes that there are only general laws, and not laws applying to particular cases (e.g., Herbst, 1970). Second, it seems to imply that experimental and statistical inquiry cannot be carried out at the level of the individual case. It is true that universal laws can usually not be established through the study of a particular individual, but laws of the individual can be formulated and tested through rigorous experimental and statistical methods at the level of the individual case (e.g., Chassan, 1967,

1979; Hersen and Barlow, 1976; Kratochwill, 1978). This criticism is clearly outdated in light of the extensive developments in single-case designs over the last two decades.

A fourth criticism is that there is no way of determining if a particular pattern of behavior is "unique." Allport claims that "the personal patterns of individuality are unique" (1961, p. 10). Levy (1970) queries, "How can it be determined that each individual possesses a unique pattern of behavior? Clearly, this cannot be done empirically, since it would require the observation and measurement of the behavior of every person living as well as those long departed. There is no other way to satisfy the strict meaning of unique, which is 'different from all others' " (p. 74). Empirically, we can tell if a pattern of behavior is rare or relatively infrequent, but not if it is unique.

This seems a compelling criticism. In the strict sense of unique as "different from all others," the claim for uniqueness of individual patterns of behavior appears indefensible. This criticism leads me to suggest that idiographic be redefined as that which is particular or specific to the individual (which may or may not be shared with others), rather than that which is unique to the individual.

There are, however, several points that might be made in favor of retaining the concept of uniqueness. First, unique may be defined in reference to a specific context or horizon, such as all those individuals encountered in one's previous experience, or all of those described in the scientific literature. A pattern of behavior may be "distinctive," in that it serves to distinguish one individual from a particular set of others, or it may be unique and unduplicated within a specific context.

Second, the word "unique" also has a dictionary definition as "very rare or uncommon." If $unique_1$ is defined as unlike any others, and $unique_2$ as very rare or uncommon, then Allport's use of the term could legitimately correspond to $unique_2$, although not to $unique_1$. Finally, the word unique has a certain psychological appeal (Snyder and Fromkin, 1980), as it implies that the individual's particular experience is valued or appreciated, and is not merely "common" or "typical." Some clinicians and personologists might still choose to use the word for its psychological functions, even if it is logically incorrect. For academic discussions, however, I would recommend that idiographic be defined as that which is particular or specific to the individual (which may be relatively rare or relatively common, and, on occasion, perhaps even unique).

A fifth criticism is that the topic of "structured pattern" or the relationship among many variables does not effectively distinguish idiographic from nomothetic methods. This criticism was made as long ago as 1954 by Eysenck, who stated that the study of traits in combination and the ways they interacted with each other to bring about behavior is a standard part of nomothetic research (Eysenck, 1954, p. 340). This criticism has, to the best of my knowledge, not been explicitly answered by proponents of idiographic methods.

This criticism, like the previous one by Levy, seems to have an element of validity in it, which requires a more precise formulation of the idiographic approach. A concern with the patterned relationship between variables is certainly shared with nomothetic investigators in multivariate statistical and experimental inquiry. To be at all distinctive, the idiographic approach must define itself as concerned with the relationship of variables or processes *within the individual case,* a distinction that Allport made only inconsistently throughout his writings (e.g., Allport, 1937, 1961, 1962).

Another criticism suggests that it is not only impractical but literally impossible to conduct an idiographic study of every individual. If individuals are as dissimilar as Allport suggests, then "Every sparrow would have to be separately identified, named and intuitively understood" (Murray, 1938, p. 715). If all individuals are unique, then it would be necessary to formulate "as many theories as there are persons in the universe" (Levy, 1970, p. 76).

This criticism raises an important question about the costs and benefits of detailed studies of individuals. Granted that there are not sufficient resources for studying every individual in the universe, it is still entirely feasible to conduct detailed idiographic studies of individuals of particular interest to us, including historical figures such as Adolf Hitler, Sigmund Freud, Virginia Woolf, or Vincent Van Gogh; particular clinical patients; or other individuals of special theoretical, personal, or practical interest. We don't have the time and money to study all individuals, but neither do we have the resources to test all possible theories. It is necessary to be selective, both in theoretical inquiries and in studies of specific individuals.

A seventh criticism contends that there is nothing wrong with the idiographic study of individuals, but it is not science. Levy (1970), for example, argues that the meaning of data about individual cases "can only be found within the context of laws that hold for all individuals. . . . It is not possible to go beyond this and remain within the confines of science" (p. 76). Nunnally (1978) states that "the idiographists may be entirely correct, but if they are, it is a sad day for psychology. Idiography is an antiscience point of view: it discourages the search for general laws and instead encourages the description of particular phenomena (people)" (p. 548).

Is there some conflict or contradiction between the study of individual persons and the scientific endeavour? Is the study of individual persons more properly the concern of the novelist, the biographer, the historian, or perhaps the clinician? It is undeniably true that historians and biographers are concerned with the description and interpretation of individual lives. There are, however, many tasks of generalizing about, systematically describing and measuring, explaining, predicting, and attempting to change the course of individual lives which seem properly to fall within the domain of the social and behavioral sciences.

If the thrust or intent of this criticism is that it is impossible to apply systematic, reliable, quantitative or experimental methods to the study of individual cases, this criticism has been refuted by the proliferation of quantitative and experimental studies of the single case (e.g., Davidson and Costello, 1969; Hersen and Barlow, 1976; Kratochwill, 1978).

Finally, the suggestion that science as a whole is not concerned with the study of particulars is clearly untenable, as this criterion would rule out significant portions of sciences such as geology, astronomy, and evolutionary biology. These sciences are concerned not solely with general principles and processes but also with topics, respectively, such as the structure and evolution of this particular earth, the structure and origins of our solar system, and the particular sequence of species leading to the evolution of man.

An eighth criticism is that the abstract argument for an idiographic approach sounds appealing, but there just aren't adequate methods for carrying it out. "The problem with concluding that an idiographic approach represents the path to truth, however, has always been that one is never sure what to do next" (Bem and Allen, 1974, p. 511). "It is all very well to talk about personal space, for example, but no idiographically personalistic research methods were developed" (Holt, 1962, p. 386). Allport himself has been criticized on the grounds that, with several exceptions such as *Letters from Jenny* (Allport, 1965), much of his own research has employed nomothetic rather than idiographic methods (Hall and Lindzey, 1978, p. 472).

If there are not adequate methods for carrying out idiographic research, this is a serious criticism. The following section attempts to demonstrate that this criticism is unjustified by outlining a substantial array of methods and techniques that may be used in the pursuit of idiographic objectives.

An Updated Survey of Idiographic Methods

The thoughtful reader might get suspicious after reading the discussion of idiographic methods often found in textbooks in personality and clinical psychology. After briefly characterizing the idiographic approach, there is a discussion of the same limited and somewhat out-of-date set of examples, such as Allport and Vernon's matching studies of expressive behavior (1933), Baldwin's (1942) "personal structure analysis," Q-methodology (Stephenson, 1953), and Kelly's (1955) role construct repertory test. If the idiographic method is such a good idea, why aren't there more examples and more up-to-date examples of it?

The aim of this section is to draw together a number of more recent lines of research which can be characterized as idiographic. I will start by briefly reviewing the list of idiographic (or "morphogenic") methods proposed by Allport, and then make additions to the list in light of recent methodological developments. (By 1962, Allport was referring to these methods as "morphogenic," meaning accounting for structured pattern. Allport derived the term from biology, arguing that molecular or dimensional approaches study elements common to all species, and morphogenic approaches examine the development of patterned structures out of these common elements. In spite of Allport's suggestion, the term morphogenic never caught on in

psychology and is rarely used today. Idiographic refers to idiosyncratic traits or elements as well as to structured pattern, and
thus has a broader meaning than morphogenic. For these reasons, this discussion will refer to idiographic rather than morphogenic methods.)

Allport's List of Idiographic Methods

1. The first method is that of matching, in which the investigator matches different records of personal expression with each
other. For example, the task might consist of matching particular case records with test files for the same individual or of
determining which sample of handwriting goes along with
which voice. "The method requires a judge to place together
different records of *one* personality from an assortment of records
taken from many personalities. The records may be of any type:
life-histories, photographs, specimens of handwriting, scores on
various tests, artistic productions, or anything else" (Allport,
1961, p. 387). Such methods are employed in Allport and Vernon's (1933) studies of expressive behavior and reviewed in Vernon (1936).

2. A second technique is that of "personal structure analysis,"
or content analysis, which examines the frequency with which
ideas are associated in verbal material. Baldwin (1942), for
example, applied this method to a collection of more than 100
letters written by an older lady, Jenny, in the last years of her
life. If Jenny mentioned one subject, such as her son or money,
what other topics did she tend to mention at the same time?
Baldwin found that Jenny "was highly jealous of her son; she
was paranoid concerning her relations with women; she has a
strong esthetic interest; and she was scrupulous in matters of
money" (Allport, 1961, p. 369). More elaborate computerized
analyses have been conducted with these same letters (Allport,
1965; Paige, 1966). A more recent example of content analysis
was used to assess Theodore Dreiser's implicit theory of personality, as reflected in the frequency with which sets of attributes were attributed to the characters in his novels (Rosenberg and Jones, 1972).

3. On the basis of extensive interviewing with a single clinical
patient, an individualized questionnaire or set of items can be
constructed for this individual which may not directly apply to

any other individuals, but which can be used for assessing this person's improvement or deterioration over time (Shapiro, 1961).

4. A fourth idiographic method is to search for the number and range of "essential characteristics" or "major structural foci" in a life. For example, Perry suggested that William James had eight dominant trends (1936, chapters 90–91), and Allport (1962) found that students could describe their friends with an average of 7.2 essential characteristics.

5. A fifth method is a "self-anchoring scale," devised by Kilpatrick and Cantril (1960). Individuals are asked to imagine the very best or ideal state of affairs and then the very worst state of affairs in some domain. These conditions are placed on a ladder with the best scaled at 10, and the worst at the bottom. Subjects are then asked where they perceive themselves in terms of this self-constructed scale at present, five years ago, five years from now, and so on.

Allport (1962) also described what he characterizes as a set of "semi-morphogenic methods," which combine morphogenic and dimensional features, or, in current language, idiographic and nomothetic features. A number of these follow.

6. A sixth approach is to use a standard rating scale to assess only those characteristics perceived as of central importance in an individual's personality. In an early application of this approach, Conrad (1932) had teachers rate students on 231 common traits, in which the median reliability coefficient of the ratings was .48. When teachers rated only those traits they saw as centrally important in the child's personality, the reliability of their ratings increased to .95. This approach of focusing only on those characteristics perceived as salient for the individual has since been pursued in greater depth (e.g., Bem and Allen, 1974; Kenrick and Stringfield, 1980).

7. Another partially idiographic method is Kelly's (1955) Role Construct Repertory Test. Respondents are asked to identify how two individuals, such as mother and sister, are alike, and how they differ from a third individual, such as wife. This method is intended to reveal the constructs an individual commonly uses in perceptions of self and others.

8. The ipsative method is another semi-idiographic approach, in which subjects' scores on a certain measure are considered in

relation to their scores in other areas, rather than in relation to group scores or averages on this single test (Broverman, 1960, 1962).

9. The Allport-Vernon-Lindzey *Study of Values* (1960) is another example of an ipsative approach, which indicates the relative importance of six common values (e.g., economic, theoretic, religious) for an individual.

10. The Q-sort method (Stephenson, 1953) is a technique in which a standard set of propositions are arranged according to their relative salience for the individual subject. This method has been developed and extensively applied by Block (1961, 1971).

11. A final method listed by Allport is that of inverse factor analysis, illustrated in a study by Nunnally (1955) in which sixty statements selected for their particular relevance to a single woman were factor analyzed, yielding three fairly independent factors within her self-concept.

Allport intended his list to be "illustrative rather than exhaustive" (1962, p. 415), and hoped that it would stimulate the invention of idiographic methods. He would not have been disappointed, as there has been an enormous outpouring of work since the early 1960's which can contribute to idiographic analysis, although the methods are not always presented under that label. The following survey is intended to illustrate a variety of methods which may be used in pursuit of the idiographic goal of understanding those elements, structures, and relationships which are particular to the individual.[1]

Recent Developments in Idiographic Methods

1. A first type of idiographic method consists of intra-individual correlational methods, in which variables are correlated within the single individual. An example is provided by Chassan (1967, pp. 185–189) of a paranoid schizophrenic in her fifties, who had been hospitalized for many years. She was examined during seventeen interviews over a twenty-week period, and rated on a clinical rating form on items such as "general appearance, coherence and relevance of speech, orientation for person, place, and time, motor activity, various component affective states, delusions, and hallucinations" (p. 186). Several of the symptoms correlated perfectly with each other

over the seventeen observation periods. For example, in the first eight interviews, her speech was coherent and relevant *and* she was well oriented to time, while in the last nine interviews, her speech was not coherent and relevant *nor* was she well oriented to time. More surprisingly, there was a negative correlation between other symptom pairs, as between general appearance and orientation for persons. On each of the thirteen occasions when she was well oriented as to who she was, her appearance was slovenly, while on three out of the seventeen times when she was disoriented, her appearance was rated as neat and clean. Analyzing this data in a 2 × 2 contingency table, the negative correlation between appearance and orientation for persons was significant at p < .02. This is a correlational pattern which may be relatively rare, and not shared by patients in general.

A second example was originally reported by Metcalf (1956), who analyzed the relationships between a young woman's meeting with her mother and her asthma attacks. This patient was interviewed sixty-six times over an eighty-five-day period, and each day was rated as to the presence or absence of asthmatic symptoms. To test the hypothesis that meetings with her mother were connected with her asthma attacks, "the 85 days were divided into those with asthma . . . and those without asthma; the same days were separated into those during which the patient was within 24 hours of having seen her mother, and the remainder in which she had not been in contact with her mother for the preceding 24 hours. It was then found that of a total of 23 days in which the patient had been with her mother within 24 hours, nine (39 percent) were days with asthma in contrast to six asthma days out of a total of 62 days (9.7 percent) when she had not been in contact with mother over the previous 24 hours. An application of the 2 × 2 chi-square test to these data yields a chi-square value of ten, which is significant beyond the .01 level" (Chassan, 1979, p. 393). More complex examples of intra-individual correlational analysis involve the O- and P-techniques of factor analysis outlined by Cattell (1946), and illustrated by Cattell (1966), Bath, Daly, and Nesselroade (1976), and Luborsky and Mintz (1972).

2. Perhaps the most extensively developed mode of idiographic research since Allport's review is that of single-case experimental designs, in which variables are manipulated and causal relation-

ships investigated *within* single cases. This search for causal relationships within the single case, which may or may not apply to any other individuals, corresponds to Allport's interest in the structural relationship of variables within individuals.

The essential idea of single-case experimental designs is to establish a baseline for one or more classes of behavior, and then to systematically manipulate independent variables in ways that will enable one to draw relatively unambiguous inferences about the causal relationship between the independent variables and target behaviors. The literature on single-case experimental designs is so extensive that it would be impossible to review it here, but useful reviews are provided by Chassan (1967, 1979), Gambrill (1977), Hersen and Barlow (1976), Kratochwill (1978), Jayaratne and Levy (1979), and Kazdin (1980).

3. At the opposite end of the continuum of controllability from single-case experimental designs are narrative methods, which provide a qualitative description and interpretation of the course of events in a life. Tasks such as portraying the social and historical contexts of actions and events and conveying their subjective meanings are handled more effectively through narrative than through the more traditional social scientific methods of measurement, correlation, and experimentation. Narrative is (as argued in Chapter 5) useful, if not indispensable, for indicating how people thought and felt, what they said and did, how their words and actions were interpreted by others, and the processes by which they interacted with their worlds over time.

In attending to the particularities of thought, conversation, actions, subjective meanings, and social contexts, narrative qualifies as an idiographic method *par excellence*. The utility of the narrative method for representing individuals in their environments is reflected in its extensive use in biography, psychobiography, and clinical case studies.

For social scientific purposes, narrative methods have been criticized for their lack of reliability (Chapter 2). In fact, we would be suspicious if two individuals produced the same narrative account of a single life. This lack of total reliability is, however, not the same as no reliability, in that through a process of critical examination, it is possible to rigorously assess the evidence, inferences, generalizations, interpretations, and conclusions of narrative accounts. Although more flexible than standard scientific methods, narrative methods can be used with sufficient controls so that they are of considerable scientific value.

4. The case study method is one of the most important and widely used idiographic methods. The case study method does not necessarily rely on retrospective or introspective methods, or any other specific method of data collection, but is, rather, a form for organizing information about particular individuals and their circumstances. The case study, as discussed in Chapter 8, may be based upon evidence obtained from interviews, projective or objective tests, observations in the natural environment, longitudinal studies, personal documents, public archives, the testimony of others, experiments, or any other method capable of producing relevant information. Although typically narrative in form, case studies can also contain quantitative information derived from naturalistic observation, psychological testing, or experimental studies. Case studies can effectively incorporate and organize a large amount of idiographic information about individuals and their circumstances. (It should be evident that several of the items in this list of idiographic methods partially overlap with each other, in that narrative methods may be employed in case studies, and that the following methods of assisted autobiography and of psychobiography can be seen as specific types of case studies.)

5. Another idiographic method, as developed by De Waele (1971) and De Waele and Harré (1979), is that of the assisted autobiography. In this method, an individual "is assisted by a well-trained team in the production of a document which is a representation of how he views his own life-course, his own knowledge, beliefs, interpretative schemata, and principles of action and judgment" (De Waele and Harré, 1979, p. 177).

The first step in the method is for the person to produce an autobiography written in his or her own terms. A team of skilled investigators then raises a series of questions about the document, drawing upon an extensive nine-part Biographical Inventory. Questions may be raised about topics not covered in the initial autobiography, about apparent contradictions or inconsistencies in the autobiography, about the experience of producing it, about the meaning and interpretation of particular events, and so on. Accounts offered by the participant can be compared with data collected from other sources, such as naturalistic observations, performance in test situations, and questionnaires. Questions can then be raised about the relationships between this new information and the initial autobiography. Finally, through a dialogical process, a revised and negotiated autobiographical document is produced.

This final autobiography "is not a record of happenings and responses to them, but a record of interpretation of happenings, the plannings of responses to them, the understandings of successes or failures in these matters. In short, it provides a cognitive map both of how the individual now represents his life to himself and how he represents his resources by which he sees himself to have coped or failed to cope with the problems and crises of that life as it unfolded" (De Waele and Harré, 1979, p. 206).

As developed in Brussels by De Waele, the method of assisted autobiography was used with a very particular group, that of convicted murderers, for the purposes of understanding their acts of murder and of assessing their potential for parole. The method could, of course, be applied more widely. The complete method is quite complex, and for a more detailed account, the reader is referred to De Waele and Harré (1979).

6. Psychobiographical methods are those methods used in constructing and reconstructing psychological and social scientific interpretations of the lives of particular individuals. Psychobiographical methods may be seen as a special case of the case study method. They deal *explicitly* with explanatory and interpretive questions about the single case, which may be latent or unexplored in more purely descriptive case studies. Psychobiographical methods deserve, however, treatment in their own right, as such an extensive methodological literature has developed on the topic (e.g., Anderson, 1981a; 1981b; Barzun 1974; Crosby, 1979; Elms, 1976; George, 1971; Glad, 1973; Mack, 1971; Meyer, 1972; Runyan, 1981; and Stannard, 1980). The methodological discussion covers issues such as the use of psychoanalysis versus general psychology, the possibility of applying psychoanalysis to historical figures, and the dangers of psychological reductionism, and will be reviewed in Chapter 10.

7. Another recent contribution to idiographic methodology is a procedure for idiographic measurement proposed by Lamiell

(1981). Lamiell argues that differential psychology, concerned with assessing differences between groups of individuals, is distinctly different from personality psychology, which is concerned with describing, explaining, and making predictions about individuals. He argues that "the individual differences research paradigm . . . is fundamentally inadequate for the purposes of a science of personality" (1981, p. 276), since individual difference research provides aggregate level data, and with such data *"it is simply not possible to tell* how consistent or inconsistent any one individual was in the levels at which he or she manifested the underlying attribute in question. Consequently, it is not possible to determine, for any one individual, whether or not (or to what degree) the attribute in question is relevant to a description of his or her personality" (1981, p. 279).

Lamiell proposes a strategy for idiographic personality measurement in which the meaning of a person's score on an attribute is not influenced by the scores of other individuals, but is directly dependent upon the range of alternative values that could be assigned to the person within the constraints of the situation and the measurement operation. Mary, for example, can be assessed on the attribute "compliant versus rebellious" in relation to eleven possible activities over a one-week period. The perceived behavioral alternatives are (1) drinking beer or liquor, (2) engaging in premarital sex, (3) studying or reading, (4) participating in extracurricular activities, and so on. Her actual behavior for the week could include all rebellious acts or all compliant acts, and thus her behavior can be scored according to its place within this range of possibilities. Her idiographic score is .802 on the attribute "compliant versus rebellious," which is a product of her actions, the perceived relevance of each act to compliance or rebelliousness, and her score in relation to her range of possible scores, given this set of measurement procedures.

This idiographic measurement strategy is not dependent upon observations of any other individuals. "It is a rationale by which the measured status of an individual on a single attribute at a given point in time hinges entirely on information available for *that* individual at *that* point in time with respect to a set of empirical referents for *that* attribute" (Lamiell, 1981, p. 282). The essence of the strategy is to outline a range of possible actions and score values for an individual over a set of situations or occasions, and then to represent the individual's score in relation to the range of values seen as possible for that individual within that range of situations. Lamiell (1981) provides a mathematical formalization of this idiographic measurement strategy and a discussion of its implications for personality psychology.

8. Another set of idiographic methods or procedures are those concerned with idiographic prediction. Idiographic prediction may be defined as prediction made about a case based on data from that particular case and no other cases. It is possible to identify four different predictive strategies, distinguished by the number of cases used as a data base. According to this classification, there are (1) idiographic predictions, based on data from the case in question and no other cases; (2) comparative predictions, which draw upon data from several other comparable cases, cases judged to be similar on relevant dimensions; (3) statistical predictions, based on frequencies for a large number of similar cases; and (4) nomothetic predictions, based on general laws, which presumably are derived from and apply to a whole population of cases.

Idiographic prediction is related to, but also distinguishably different from, clinical prediction, as defined in the extensive clinical versus statistical prediction controversy (e.g., Gough, 1962; Holt, 1978; Meehl, 1954, 1965; Sawyer, 1966; Wiggins, 1973). In this literature, clinical refers to the source of data (clinical judgment rather than psychometric data) and method of data combination (clinical analysis rather than statistical combination). In idiographic prediction, I am referring to a strategy of prediction which relies on data exclusively from the individual case, rather than to any particular clinical or statistical methods for collecting or extrapolating from such data.

The relationships between idiographic, comparative case, statistical, and nomothetic predictions are suggested in Figure 9.1. The common objective of all four predictive strategies when applied to the single case is to predict the contents of cell 2, which is the future of the case under study. To illustrate these four logics of prediction, they will be used to make predictions about a cold, unfeminine, severely disturbed woman (given the forbidding label of Mrs. X), who was being seen in therapy as

	Predictors	Outcomes
Individual Case	1	2
Comparable Examples	3	4
Statistical Correlations	5	6
Laws, Theories	7	8

Figure 9.1 Four strategies of prediction.

part of a research project on prediction in psychotherapy. "The patient, a 41-year-old married woman and artist, was referred for psychiatric hospitalization because of panics, agitated depressive outbursts, and disturbed histrionic behavior bordering on the totally disorganized, which had risen to an intolerable crescendo during the several months of her return to live with her husband after a five-year separation" (Sargent et al., 1968, p. 71).

The logic of idiographic prediction is to make inferences about the content of cell 2 on the basis of information in cell 1. These inferences may be based upon the assumption of stability, the assumption of continuity in current trends, or upon the application of idiographic patterns derived from intensive study of cell 1. In purely idiographic prediction, no explicit use is made of previously established laws or generalizations, or of knowledge of comparable cases (the information in cells 3 to 8). For example, predictions about Mrs. X based on the assumption of stability would be that her interests in art, and her difficulties with a traditionally feminine role, will continue. A prediction based upon the stability of idiographic patterns and sequences would be that sexual relations will continue to lead to psychosomatic symptoms.

The logic of comparative case prediction is based upon the assumption that if cell 1 is enough like the example(s) in cell 3, then cell 2 will resemble cell 4. According to this predictive strategy, predictions would be made about Mrs. X based on knowledge of the experience of several women with similar characteristics in similar circumstances.

The logic of statistical prediction is to assume that the relationship between variables measured and correlated in cells 5 and 6 can be used to make inferences from cell 1 to variables of interest in cell 2. As an example of a statistical prediction about Mrs. X, since she is a white forty-one-year-old female, it could be predicted on the basis of life expectancy charts that her likely life expectancy is approximately forty more years.

Finally, the logic of nomothetic or theoretical prediction is to assume that the content of cell 2 can be deduced from a knowledge of the conditions in cell 1 in conjunction with a theoretical statement linking cells 7 and 8. An example of a theory-based prediction about Mrs. X made from a psychoanalytic perspective is that "if treated by supportive-expressive psychotherapy and if limited goals are fulfilled, then the patient will break off the present marital situation (because) the improvement of adaptive functioning resulting from supportive psychotherapy leads to a decrease in the patient's self-destructive behavior" (Sargent et al., 1968, pp. 88–89). Regardless of the limitations of this particular example, there does seem to be a meaningful conceptual distinction between these four different strategies of prediction, with idiographic prediction being one of the four major strategies, and one that is particularly useful for making predictions about individuals.

9. One final idiographic approach is that of "configurational analysis" (Horowitz, 1979), aspects of which were discussed in Chapter 8. This is a strategy for recognizing patterns of stability and change in personality functioning. One aspect of configurational analysis is concerned with identifying a set of recurrent states within an individual, and the conditions leading to transitions between states. Each state is defined by a particular pattern of conscious experience and behavior, such as in an anxious state, an enraged state, or a depressed state.

States may be identified with general nomothetic terms, or they can also be identified by idiographic terms specific to the individual. For example, Janice, a twenty-four-year-old college graduate, entered therapy shortly after her younger brother died, and complained of depressions, which were characterized by apathy, withdrawal with feelings of fogginess and unreality, and over-eating. This might be described in a general way as "depressed mood," but it is also poosible to use individualized state descriptions which go beyond generalities to individual nuances of experience and behavior. A more individualized description of Janice's state that she used in describing herself was "hurt and not working." "She could recognize herself as entering and leaving this state. When it occurred, she felt dull and lonely, had bodily concerns, and tended to withdraw from social contacts and life tasks. When she entered this state during the treatment situation, she could be observed to mumble and trail off" (Horowitz, 1979, p. 36). Another of her states was dramatic animation, in which she pretended to be cheerful and lighthearted. This was identified, again in her own words, as her "tra-la-la" state. Other significant and identifiable states for Janice were "hurt but working," crying to elicit attention, competitiveness, acute self-disgust, and an ideal state of feeling competent and authentic.

After a set of recurrent states is identified, it is then possible to search for patterns of transition between states, or for those conditions leading to entry or exit from each state. In the case of Janice, if she was confronted in therapy with difficult material, she would often shift from her tra-la-la state to a hurt-but-working state. If the material was too difficult to handle or overwhelming, she could enter a state of acute self-disgust. On the other hand, if she coped well with it or defended successfully against it, she would return to the tra-la-la state. In outside life, if abandoned by someone she was attached to, she would shift from her tra-la-la state to a hurt-and-not-working state. If someone else was present, she might shift from hurt and not working to a state of crying to elicit attention.

Horowitz outlines a system of states and state transitions for Janice, consisting of six distinguishable states and the conditions leading to transition from each state to the others. This is an excellent example of idiographic analysis in that it is composed of idiographic states and an idiographic pattern of relationships between the states, resulting in cycles or systems of state transitions for a particular individual. Through the use of videotapes of therapy sessions, these idiographic analyses can be critically assessed by having other observers see if they can reliably identify the emergence and disappearance of certain states and the conditions responsible for transitions between states.

The complete strategy of configurational analysis also includes attention to images of self and role relationships, and processes of information control, as well as to recurrent states and patterns of state transition. Horowitz's book *States of Mind: Analysis of Change in Psychotherapy* (1979) is recommended as an illustration of the possibilities of complex and systematically evaluated idiographic analysis.

This is obviously not a complete inventory of idiographic methods. Additional methods that are idiographic, or that have idiographic aspects, would include psychoanalytic methods such as free association and dream interpretation for investigating the unconscious meanings of events and experiences for the particular individual; techniques of behavioral assessment; the analysis of personal documents, such as diaries, journals, and letters (Allport, 1942; Wrightsman, 1981); and the analysis of "possibility-processing structures" used by individuals in generating perceived possibilities and choosing among them (Tyler, 1978). The reader may well be able to identify additional idiographic methods, and better yet, develop new and better ones.

This review has revealed a surprisingly extensive list of methods which might properly be described as idiographic. These are not isolated trends, as there seems to be a growing interest in idiographic goals and methods across a variety of theoretical orientations. We can find examples of phenomenological, trait, psychodynamic, behavioral, and cognitive theorists all attempting to develop methods and procedures capable of understanding the particularities of individuals and their circumstances. This widespread work on idiographic methods is an exciting development, as it provides a valuable complement to nomothetic work on understanding persons in general and the differential goal of understanding differences between groups of people by sex, race, ethnicity, class, and culture.

Conclusion

No matter how much progress is made at the level of understanding universal processes or the level of understanding group differences, there is much that will remain unknown about particular individuals, as these three levels of analysis are partially independent. Universal and group generalizations can, without doubt, illuminate some facets of individual lives, but there are many other problems in describing, understanding, making predictions about, and intentionally changing the course of individual lives which cannot be accomplished without the use of idiographic methods.

This chapter began by discussing some of the conceptual issues associated with the idiographic-nomothetic debate and placed this debate within the larger issue of the three distinctive levels of analysis in the social sciences. The next section reviewed and responded to a number of common criticisms of the idiographic approach. Finally, it outlined a range of recent developments in idiographic methods, including intra-individual correlational methods, single-case experimental designs, assisted autobiography, and configurational analysis. The following chapter contains a more detailed examination of theory and method in psychobiography, an idiographic method which has received extensive critical attention and is centrally relevant to the study of individual life histories.

NOTES

1. There is a class of borderline statements which contain information about the particular individual in terms of a nomothetic scale or category, such as "John is five feet, eleven inches tall," or "John has brown hair." Such statements occupy an intermediate ground between idiographic and nomothetic forms of analysis, as they contain information about the particular individual expressed solely in nomothetic categories. I have restricted myself in this discussion to types of analysis which more clearly illustrate the idiographic approach.

IO

The Psychobiography Debate

Biographical studies which utilize psychological (often psycho-analytic) theory in interpreting the lives of public or historical figures have become increasingly prominent and increasingly con-troversial in recent years. Advocates of psychobiography see the use of systematic psychology as a significant advance over the commonsense psychology traditionally used in biography. "Viewed in the light of modern depth psychology, the home-spun, commonsense psychological interpretations of past his-torians, even some of the greatest, seem woefully inadequate, not to say naïve" (Langer, 1958, pp. 286–287). Psychological concep-tualizations and assumptions are inevitably embedded in the description and interpretation of lives, and even those categori-cally opposed to systematic psychology are forced to rely on an implicit psychology (Erikson, 1958). The only question, accord-ing to this argument, is not whether to use psychology or not, but whether the biographer should draw upon the discipline of psychology as well as upon commonsense and personal experi-ence.

On the other hand, critics of psychobiography (e.g., Barzun, 1974; Coles, 1975; Stannard, 1980; Stone, 1981) have claimed that the whole enterprise has been "disappointing, partly because of the flimsiness of the evidence of childhood experience, partly be-cause of the speculative nature of the causal links with adult be-havior, partly because of the neglect of the influence of the great processes of historical change in religion, economics, politics, society, and so on" (Stone, 1981, pp. 220–221). In one of the more intemperate critiques of the whole field of psychohistory, including psychobiography, Stannard (1980) charges that "from the earliest endeavors to write psychohistory to those of the present, individual writings of would-be psychohistorians have consistently been characterized by a cavalier atttitude toward fact, a contorted attitude toward logic, an irresponsible attitude toward theory validation, and a myopic attitude toward cultural difference and anachronism" (p. 147).

This chapter attempts to confront the charges of the critics and to take an equally critical look at the claims and methods of practitioners. This examination of foundations and principles in psychobiography should be of use in assessing the field's accomplishments and potentials and also in bringing to light some of the most basic questions about the relationships between evidence, theory, and interpretation encountered in the study of individual life histories.

The next sections of this chapter present a brief historical sketch of work in psychobiography, a sample of three psychobiographical interpretations, and a more systematic definition of the boundaries of the field. Each of the succeeding sections examines a debated issue in the field, including the question of inadequate evidence, postdictive reconstructions, reductionism, the importance of childhood experience for adult behavior, the problem of transhistorical and cross-cultural generality in psychological theory, the place of psychoanalytic theory in psychobiography, nonpsychoanalytic approaches, the training and background of psychobiographers, and finally, ethical issues in the study of living political figures.

Historical Sketch

The psychobiographical enterprise was launched with Freud's *Leonardo da Vinci and a Memory of His Childhood* (1910). A sample of other early psychobiographical (and psychoanalytic) studies includes analyses of Shakespeare as revealed through *Hamlet* (Jones, 1910), the artist Giovanni Segantini (Abraham, 1911), Richard Wagner (Graf, 1911), Amenhotep IV (Abraham, 1912), Martin Luther (Smith, 1913), and Socrates (Karpas, 1915).

A number of these earliest psychobiographical studies are sum-marized in Dooley's "Psychoanalytic Studies of Genius" (1916), and discussed in Barnes (1919) and Fearing (1927). During the 1920's a large number of psychobiographical works were pub-lished, often by those with no formal training in psychoanalysis or psychiatry, with several of the best known (Garraty, 1954) be-ing studies of Margaret Fuller (Anthony, 1920), Samuel Adams (Harlow, 1923), Edgar Allan Poe (Krutch, 1926) and Abraham Lincoln (Clark, 1921, 1933).

This rising tide of psychoanalytic biography led to a number of attacks on the method (e.g., Whilbey, 1924; DeVoto, 1933), but the production of psychobiographies continued through the 1930's. By the end of the decade, there were psychobiographical studies of writers such as Tolstoy, Dostoevsky, Molière, Sand, Goethe, Coleridge, Nietzsche, Poe, and Rousseau and of public figures including Caesar, Lincoln, Napoleon, Darwin, and Alex-ander the Great (Anderson, 1978). "While the father of psycho-analysis, Sigmund Freud, was studying the behavior of Moses, Leonardo da Vinci, and Woodrow Wilson, he himself was under investigation by another psychohistorian. It seemed that by the end of the 1930's almost no one had escaped—even Houdini had been analyzed" (Anderson, 1978, p. 1). In contrast, the 1940's were a relatively slow period for psychological biography, with exceptions such as Guttmacher's (1941) study of George III and Langer's *The Mind of Adolf Hitler,* originally written in 1943 for the Office of Strategic Services but not published until 1972.

The 1950's saw a renewed production of psychobiographies, such as studies of Jonathan Swift and Lewis Carroll (Greenacre, 1955) and Beethoven and his nephew (E. and R. Sterba, 1954). The major turning point, however, in terms of more rigorous and methodologically self-conscious psychobiography was the publication of George and George's *Woodrow Wilson and Colo-nel House: A Personality Study* (1956) and Erikson's *Young Man Luther: A Study in Psychoanalysis and History* (1958). In the 1960's and 1970's there has been an enormous outpouring of psychobiographical analyses of writers, artists, musicians, politi-cians, religious leaders, scientists, and others. (Useful historical reviews are contained in T. Anderson, 1978; Bergmann, 1973; Coles, 1975; Garraty, 1954, 1957; Glad, 1973; and Mack, 1971;

and bibliographies in Cremerius, 1971; deMause, 1975; and Gilmore, 1976, 1979a, 1979b).

Prominent examples of recent psychobiographical works are studies of Henry James (Edel, 1953–72), Isaac Newton (Manuel, 1968), Gandhi (Erikson, 1969), Max Weber (Mitzman, 1969), Emily Dickinson (Cody, 1971), Stalin (Tucker, 1973), James and John Stuart Mill (Mazlish, 1975), Andrew Jackson (Rogin, 1975), T. E. Lawrence (Mack, 1976), Adolf Hitler (Waite, 1977), Beethoven (Solomon, 1977), Samuel Johnson (Bate, 1977), and Richard Nixon (Brodie, 1981); and studies of groups of individuals, such as American presidents (Barber, 1972), revolutionary leaders (Wolfenstein, 1967; Mazlish, 1976), personality theorists (Stolorow and Atwood, 1979), utopians (Manuel and Manuel, 1979) and philosophers (Scharfstein, 1980).

Three Psychobiographical Interpretations

The flavor of the field can be given through a sample of psychobiographical arguments or interpretations. I will briefly present examples drawn from studies of Woodrow Wilson, Emily Dickinson, and Wilhelm Reich. Of necessity, these interpretations are given in barest outline, without the density of detail needed to corroborate or disprove them.

Woodrow Wilson

In three major executive positions—president of Princeton University, Governor of New Jersey, and President of the United States—Woodrow Wilson followed a similar pattern of impressive early accomplishments, followed by a period of controversy, ending in serious setbacks or defeats. The last and most serious of these unnecessary defeats was his failure to obtain Senate ratification of the Versailles Treaty which would have led to participation of the United States in the League of Nations. As noted by Edmund Wilson (1952), "As President of the United States, he repeated after the War his whole tragedy as president of Princeton—with Lodge in the role of West, the League of Nations in the place of the quad system, and the Senate in the place of the Princeton trustees. It is possible to observe in certain lives, where conspicuously superior abilities are united with serious deficiencies, not the progress in a career or vocation that carries the talented man to a solid position or a definite goal, but a curve plotted over and over again and always dropping from some flight of achievement to a steep descent into failure" (p. 322).

How is such a pattern to be explained? George and George's (1964) basic hypothesis, derived from Lasswell (1948), is (as mentioned in Chapter 5) that Wilson's interest in power and his means of exercising it were based on a need to compensate for damaged self-esteem. In the stages of seeking power, he could be flexible and adaptive, but in conflicts which developed in the exercise of power, he often became rigid and self-defeatingly uncompromising. In addition to a personal need for power, Wilson also had a desire for social approval and for feeling virtuous. "His stern Calvinist conscience forbade an unabashed pursuit or use of power for personal gratification. He could express his desire for power only insofar as he convincingly rationalized it in terms of altruistic service, and fused it with laudable social objectives" (George and George, 1964, p. 117).

Once faced with political opposition to a program to which he had committed himself, Wilson painted his own position as the only morally worthy one and refused to compromise. In both the battles at Princeton with Dean Andrew West over the formation of a new graduate school and with the Senate opposition headed by Henry Cabot Lodge over the ratification of the Versailles Treaty, Wilson alienated the moderate elements who could have supported him and drove them into the arms of his opponents. In such situations of conflict, Wilson's desire to achieve a worthwhile political goal "became of less importance than to maintain equilibrium of [his] personality system. He seems to have experienced opposition to his will in such situations as an unbearable threat to his self-esteem. To compromise in these circumstances was to submit to domination in the very sphere of power and political leadership in which he sought to repair his damaged self-esteem. Opposition to his will, therefore, set into motion disruptive anxieties, and brought to the surface long-smouldering aggressive feelings that, as a child, he had not dared to express" (George, 1971, p. 94).

The origins of Wilson's maladaptive behavior in adulthood were traced to his relationships with his father, a severe and demanding Presbyterian minister, Dr. John Ruggles Wilson. Dr. Wilson, a handsome and imposing figure, took an extraordinarily active role in his son's education, not hesitating to use mockery and a caustic wit to force his son to live up to his perfectionist standards in writing and speaking. The child never rebelled or expressed resentment at the harsh treatment he received, and instead became extravagantly devoted to his father, a devotion which lasted a lifetime. The Georges (1964) argue that the angry feelings which Wilson must have felt were too frightening for him to acknowledge, and he reacted against such feelings by continually persuading himself of a surpassing love for his father. This repressed resentment was expressed in atrociously poor performance during the early years of school, and this failure or refusal to learn was an indirect way of expressing his anger toward his father. Wilson had early fears that he was stupid, ugly, worthless, and unlovable, and he felt himself inferior to his father in appearance and accomplishment throughout his life. Perhaps the unappeasable quality of Wilson's needs for affection, power, and achievement could be seen in part as a life-long struggle to disprove his early feelings of inadequacy, and to prove to the world and himself that he was a capable and worthwhile human being.

Emily Dickinson

Emily Dickinson was notorious for seclusiveness in her home town of Amherst, while her poetry was virtually unknown. "As early as her twenty-second year Emily Dickinson was going out of her way to avoid meeting people. A year later she wrote that she was going to church early to avoid having 'to go in after all the people had got there'. By the time she was twenty-eight it was a fixed 'custom' for her to run whenever the doorbell rang. By the age of thirty she was retreating to her room when old friends called and listening to their voices from upstairs. The next year she inaugurated the habit of dressing exclusively in white that she was to maintain for the rest of her life. . . . Eventually she retreated indoors altogether, and for the last fifteen years of her life the neighbors knew she was there by faith alone. . . . On the rare occasions when she consented to visit with old friends, she and the visitor conversed from opposite sides of a door left slightly ajar. She would not allow a physician to examine her during an illness, and he was expected to arrive at his diagnosis from a glimpse of her, fully clothed, as she walked past a doorway" (Cody, 1971, pp. 19–20).

Her seclusiveness has been variously attributed to a frustrated love affair, an effort to conserve energy and have time to write, vengefulness toward her father, or her plain looks. Cody (1971) argues that Emily Dickinson's disturbance can be attributed in part to a troubled relationship with her mother. Her mother is revealed in family correspondence as "an habitually complaining woman, subject to depression and hypochondria. She appears emotionally shallow, self-centered, ineffectual, conventional, timid, submissive, and not very bright" (p. 42). Cody argues that it is likely that Emily Dickinson "experienced what she interpreted as a cruel rejection by her mother. Many of her statements, her choice of certain recurring metaphors and symbols, and the entire course of her life, viewed psychoanalytically, argue for the truth of this assumption. However, there exists no record of any concrete instance in which Mrs. Dickinson took such an attitude toward her daughter. Nevertheless, knowledge gained from the clinical study of patients who bear scars similar to Emily Dickinson's is persuasive evidence for the existence in the poet's life of damaging experiences comparable to theirs" (p. 2). Emily Dickinson once wrote in a letter that if anything upsetting happened to her, she ran home to her brother. "He was an awful Mother, but I liked him better than none" (Cody, 1971, p. 42). The case for the existence of maternal deprivation is based, however, primarily on clinical experience, inferences from psychoanalytic theory, and interpretations of her poetry.

The mother's presumed inadequacies left a painful legacy, but may also have been partly responsible for her daughter's art. The poet frequently identified suffering as the source of her creative life. "Psychological calamities, decades of frustration, isolation, and loneliness all created a void that Emily Dickinson's talent rushed in to fill. Without this void there might well have been no poet. Her afflictions all had their point of origin in the circumstances and personality of Edward Dickinson's [Emily's father] young wife in the early days of her motherhood. To this extent it may be said that Emily Dickinson was able to become a great poet because—not in spite of—her unobtrusive, ungifted, and unstimulating mother" (Cody, 1971, p. 499).

Wilhelm Reich

Certain aspects of the thought of Wilhelm Reich, author of *Character Analysis* (1933), *The Mass Psychology of Fascism* (1933), and *The Function of the Orgasm* (1942), can, it is argued by Stolorow and Atwood (1979), be traced to a traumatic childhood experience. "Our thesis is that Reich's theoretical system reflects and symbolizes a profound personal struggle which is traceable to his childhood experience of his mother's suicide" (Stolorow and Atwood, 1979, p. 111).

Three important themes run through all of Reich's work: "(1) the notion that the expression of sexuality coincides with the expression and functioning of life in general; (2) the notion that the life-sexual functions are being perpetually suppressed and distorted by anti-sexual death forces in the world; and (3) the notion that he, by an inner messianic imperative, be the champion of life and sexuality in their struggle against the forces of death" (Stolorow and Atwood, 1979, pp. 111–112). As a psychotherapist, Reich was concerned with helping patients dissolve the "character armor" or defenses which interfered with the free flow of sexual and life energies. In his political and biological writings, he emphasized a similar theme of supporting these sexual and life energies against oppressive forces.

It seems plausible that these themes running through Reich's work have their origin in a traumatic event that occurred during his fourteenth year. Reich discovered that his mother was having a secret love affair with one of his tutors. He reported this to his jealous and explosively violent father. His mother responded by committing suicide, which seemed to be a direct consequence of his own actions. Stolorow and Atwood (1979) hypothesize that

> the circumstances of her death constituted the nuclear situation around which the structure of his representational world crystallized. . . . If it is assumed that in betraying his mother's unfaithfulness the young Reich was acting out of an identification with his father's authoritarian and sexually restrictive values, then the reasons for his subsequent life of struggle against sexual repression begin to become clear. Since in acting on the basis of a narrow code of sexual morality he was responsible for the death of the one person he loved above all others, an immense burden of pain and guilt must have been generated.

What could be a better way to atone for his fateful act of betrayal than devoting himself to the eradication of all those
values and ways of thinking which had motivated him? This
line of reasoning also sheds light on why he regarded the re-
pression of sexuality as such a vicious and deadly force in human affairs. This was because his own attempt to inhibit his
beloved mother's sexuality led directly to her suicide. . . .
[W]e might interpret his relentless struggle against the death
forces as a sustained attempt to undo his act of betrayal and
thereby magically restore his mother to life [pp. 120–122].

These three examples suggest the kinds of arguments and interpretations offered in psychobiography, and the kinds of analyses which have aroused so much controversy. Can Wilson's
rigid behavior be traced back to unconscious hostility in his
relationship with his father? Is it legitimate to explain Emily
Dickinson's seclusiveness and strange behavior in terms of a reconstruction of her relationship with her mother? Did a single
traumatic event have a life-long impact upon the themes of
Reich's work? After outlining a more systematic definition of
the field of psychobiography, this chapter will examine a number of the specific questions which arise in assessing the validity
of such interpretations.

Definition

As a preliminary distinction, psychohistory can be divided into
two main branches, that of psychobiography, dealing with the
study of individuals, and group psychohistory, dealing with the
psychological characteristics or formative experiences of groups
such as the Nazi youth cohort, American slaves, or Hiroshima
survivors (e.g., Lifton, 1967; Loewenberg, 1971). The following
discussion will occasionally include definitions of psychohistory
in general, which explicitly or implicitly have implications for
the definition of psychobiography.

One apparently sensible approach is to define psychohistory
as the application of psychology to history, with an associated
definition of psychobiography as the use of psychology in biography. One such definition is offered by Anderson (1978): "The
term 'psychohistorian' will be used to include any scholar who
uses psychology in an attempt to understand and explain his-

torical behavior" (p. 2). Although enviably simple, this definition has limitations. Consider the argument of Erikson, Waite,
and others that every biography includes at least the use of an
implicit psychology. Does all biography then become psychobiography? It seems necessary to elaborate this definition so that
it refers to the explicit use of formal or systematic psychological
theory. Thus, the definition could now read: Psychobiography is
the explicit use of formal or systematic psychology in biography.

Many have defined psychohistory as the application of psychoanalytic theory to history and, correspondingly, psychobiography
as the application of psychoanalytic theory to biography. For example, psychobiography is "in other words, the application of
psychoanalytic concepts to biography" (Friedlander, 1978, p. 29).
If this definition is used, how is one to define the application of
other psychological theories to biography? Clearly, this definition
is too restrictive. It seems most sensible to define psychobiography as the use of any explicit or formal psychological theory in
biography, not just the application of psychoanalytic theory.
Works which employ psychoanalytic theory may be described as
psychoanalytic psychobiography, which is a subdivision of psychobiography, along with behavioral psychobiography, or phenomenological psychobiography.

This broader definition of psychobiography and psychohistory
is proposed by a number of writers. For example, Glad (1973)
states, "Psychobiography is, essentially, any life history which
employs an explicit personality theory—that is, a perception that
individual behavior has an internal locus of causation as well as
some degree of structure and organization" (p. 296). Or, Tucker
(1977) says, "What is distinctive of psychobiography as a scholarly enterprise is that the biographer is attempting to make sense
out of the subject's life course, or key phases of it, in terms of a
consciously thought-out psychological interpretation of that subject's personality. . . . It follows that all psychobiographies have
in common a mooring in personality theory, either in one of its
particular forms (Freudian, post-Freudian, or non-Freudian) or
in some eclectic combination of interpretive-theoretical orientations" (p. 606).

These broader definitions in terms of any personality theory
are an improvement, but how are we to characterize a biographical study which makes use of social psychology, developmental

psychology, or some other branch of psychology? Also, how is one to classify a study making use of conceptual frameworks, typologies, data, or methods (such as content analysis, or graphology, or personality assessment procedures) which does not make use of *theory* per se? A case can be made for defining psychobiography not solely as the application of personality theory to biography but also as the application of psychological concepts, data, and methods from any branch of psychology to biography.

In light of these considerations, psychobiography may be defined as the explicit use of systematic or formal psychology in biography. Three aspects of this definition should be noted. First, the field is defined by the use of psychology, which may or may not be psychoanalytic. Second, the use must be explicit or visible, in order to distinguish psychobiography from all those biographies which make implicit use of commonsense psychology. Third, the definition refers not to the application of personality theory but to the use of psychology, which is intended to include within psychobiography those works drawing upon the full range of resources from the field of psychology, including psychological concepts, data, and methods, as well as theory, from developmental, social, and personality psychology. Additional considerations may eventually necessitate the revision of this definition, but it seems adequate for present purposes.

The Question of Inadequate Evidence

The field of psychobiography is marked by considerable controversy over its methods, abuses, and accomplishments. In order to explore the methodological status of the field, a number of these controversies will be examined, beginning with the debate over the quality of evidence. One of the most frequent criticisms is that psychobiographical interpretations are based on inadequate evidence. "The historian's most serious objection to psychohistory is that sweeping declarations about actions or personalities are based on sparse evidence" (T. Anderson, 1978, p. 11). A reviewer of Langer's *The Mind of Adolf Hitler* (1972) charges that "some of the most important conclusions of Langer's book are based on non-existent, unreliable, or misinterpreted evidence" (Gatzke, 1973, p. 400). The issue of inadequate evidence is frequently raised in regard to psychoanalytic biography in the form:

"You can't put the person on the couch." For example, applied psychoanalysis "must proceed without the central instrument for the investigation of the unconscious: free association" (Kohut, 1960, p. 571). "The psychoanalyst (or 'psychohistorian') who wishes to use psychological materials in an effort to obtain a deeper understanding of a historical figure, or in the reconstruction of historical events, is, however, confronted with major problems of evidence. In conducting a psychoanalysis the investigator has only to wait and he is likely, through the processes of free association, interpretation, and working through, to obtain systematic data concerning his patient's past history, motivations, conflicts, and ego strengths. To be sure, resistance and the ego defenses distort, but this very distortion can then be the subject of further analysis and validation. . . . When we try to apply psychological methods to a historical figure, we have no such cooperation and no analogous systematic way to obtain information" (Mack, 1971, p. 153). Or, as expressed by Barzun (1974), everything that the psychohistorian "uses—his 'tools,' his 'method,' his 'data'—is indirect and necessarily scant: the patient is absent, and the clues he may have left to his once living psyche are the product of chance. Diaries, letters, literary work form a random record, in which expressions of mood are more frequent than evidence of actions. 'Dream-material' is extremely rare. Compared to the volume of data elicited under therapy and consciously directed at relevance and completeness by the analyst, this trickle from written remains seems almost negligible" (p. 46). Finally, there is also the criticism that if early childhood experience is particularly influential, this is just the period that the psychohistorian is likely to have the least information about. "Freudian psychology has not been much use to the historian, who is usually unable to penetrate the bedroom, the bathroom or the nursery. If Freud is right, and if these are the places where the action is, there is not much the historian can do about it" (Stone, 1981, p. 53).

There are, in sum, claims of insufficient evidence, of evidence of the wrong kind (not enough free associations or dream reports), and not enough evidence from the right period (i.e., childhood). These are criticisms which need to be taken more seriously than they have been. Both Freud in his study of Leonardo, and Erikson in his analysis of Luther have been severely criticized for developing psychological interpretations from in-adequate data about early experience. In the absence of sufficient historical evidence, it is just not possible to develop credible psychological interpretations of the lives of historical figures.

What are the implications of problems of evidence for the psy-chobiographical enterprise? They do not mean that psychobiog-raphy is impossible, as has sometimes been suggested, but rather that attention is best devoted to historical figures about whom there is sufficient evidence to develop and test psychological ex-planations. Also, in the absence of evidence about childhood experience, some types of early developmental explanations are best avoided, as psychological theory is often not sufficiently de-terminate to permit accurate retrodictions or reconstructions (a problem which will be discussed in the next section). The prob-lems of evidence mean that some types of questions cannot be answered about some individuals, but this in no way impairs the possibility of developing psychological interpretations of the many aspects of behavior and experience of historical individuals for which there is adequate evidence. Third, on a comparative basis, the problems of evidence are not as severe as they may first appear, as there are also a number of evidential advantages that the psychobiographer has over the psychotherapist.

It seems undeniable that the psychobiographer typically has less access to material such as free associations, dreams, and trans-ference reactions than does the psychoanalyst. On the other hand, the psychobiographer has the advantage of having infor-mation about a person who has lived his or her entire life. Pa-tients in psychoanalysis are often relatively young, and may not yet have lived through important life experiences such as the rearing of children, the peak of their career, or the death of their parents. Reactions to these experiences, which may be revelatory of personality, are thus not available for interpretation. But the subject of a psychobiography typically "has lived his entire life and has met death. Not only the development and mid-stages of his life are available for inspection but also its ultimate unfold-ing and final resolution. This means that in discovering the dominant psychological themes of his subject's emotional evolu-tion the psychoanalytic biographer has at his disposal a broader spectrum of behavior through more decades of life than has the analyst with a living patient" (Cody, 1971, p. 5).

Second, the psychobiographer has the advantage of not being limited as the psychoanalyst usually is, to information coming from the subject alone, but may draw heavily on "outside sources" (Hofling, 1976, p. 229). He or she is able to learn how a variety of other informants perceived the situations the subject was in, and their reactions to the individual's personality (Anderson, 1981a). For important public figures confidential information about their lives (including material on their sexual experience, unusual family circumstances, or controversial aspects of their career) is sometimes not released or available until after their death and the death of immediate relatives.

Third, if the subject is a literary or creative person, the psychobiographer has a wealth of creative material, perhaps expressing inner psychological states and conflicts, which may, with caution, be drawn upon in interpretation of the subject's personality. For example, "Emily Dickinson, surely, possessed a greater capacity for the perception and discrimination of psychological processes and a greater ability to find appropriate words to express her inner experiences than any patient who has ever been psychoanalyzed. From this standpoint she is the psychoanalysand par excellence" (Cody, 1971, p. 6). This may put the point a little too strongly, but some creative individuals have been more articulately expressive of their inner states and experiences than the typical therapy patient.

Fourth, there are sometimes substitutes for a person's dreams or free associations (Anderson, 1981a). For example, Davis (1975) analyzes drawings and caricatures made by Theodore Roosevelt in adolescence when he portrayed himself and members of his family turning into animals. Equivalents to free associations have been found in the "language exercises" of archeologist Heinrich Schliemann in which he revealed dreams and unconscious wishes, and in the conversation books written by Beethoven to cope with his deafness (Bergmann, 1973, p. 842).

A fifth advantage is that the evidence used in psychobiography is available to all, so that original interpretations may be critically examined and alternatives may be proposed and tested. In psychotherapy the data are typically not publicly available, which makes it less likely that such a corrective process can take place. In sum, the psychobiographer often has access to information not available to the psychotherapist, such as information about the person's whole life span, from associates of the individual, and from the analysis of expressive or creative activities.

Reconstruction

In response to the paucity of evidence on childhood experience and the importance of such experience within psychoanalytic theory, psychobiographers have sometimes used psychoanalytic theory to reconstruct or postdict what must have happened in childhood. Greenacre (1955), for example, argues that childhood wants can be "reconstructed from known characteristics, problems, and repetitive actions supported by memory traces." Indeed, "the experienced psychoanalyst knows just as definitely as the internist observing later sequelae of tuberculosis . . . that the deformity is the result of specific acts upon the growing organism" (p. 107). Such reconstructions have, however, not gone uncriticized, even when executed with considerable sophistication. Erikson, for example, has been criticized for reconstructing Luther's relationship to his mother on the basis of adult behavior. "In his study of the young Luther, Erikson literally invents little Martin's relation to his mother, using as a basis (as a 'document') the behavior of Luther the man. . . . Erikson does not interpret a repetitive behavior on young Luther's part in terms of an unconscious dynamic; he jumps from a presumed characteristic of the Reformer to the inferential reconstruction of essential data about the latter's family environment" (Friedlander, 1978, p. 27).

The reconstruction of specific life events is not as extreme as the practice of hagiographers, who sometimes reconstructed entire lives if information was unavailable. Agnellus, a Bishop of Ravenna in the ninth century, while completing a series of lives of his predecessors in that position, confessed that "In order that there might not be a break in the series, I have composed the life myself, with the help of God and the prayers of the brethren" (Clifford, 1962, p. x). Some historians are outraged at the more limited psychobiographical practice of reconstructing particular events or relationships and feel that it is no more acceptable than the reconstructive techniques of the bishop. The practice of retrodiction is especially troubling when an earlier event is retrodicted and then is later assumed to have been firmly established. This practice has been roundly criticized both by historians and by some psychoanalysts (e.g., Wyatt, 1956).

Before concluding that retrodiction is never justified in psychobiography, let us consider one of the strongest arguments for reconstruction, and one of its most persuasive examples. "Psychoanalysis is not alone among sciences in providing a means whereby the existence of what is not directly perceptible can be inferred. Thus, the psychoanalytic interpretation of the life of a historical figure is in certain respects comparable to the reassembling of a fossil skeleton. And when the life under consideration has been rent by a psychological cataclysm, the interpretive reconstruction is not unlike the piecing together of the fragments of an aircraft that has exploded in flight.

"In the first instance the paleontologist dovetails the scattered bones according to the laws of comparative anatomy; the progression of vertebrae, for example, have a known and more or less constant relationship to each other throughout the animal kingdom. In the second example, the engineer assembles the shattered metal of the aircraft on a scaffold corresponding to the known dimensions of the type of place to which the wreckage belongs; when all the available pieces are laid out in this way, a sequence of stresses becomes discernible whose concentric waves lead back to and establish the point of origin of the explosion. In either example, what provides the gestalt and guides the interpretation placed on each discrete particle is a body of general knowledge—the laws of bone structure in the one case, the structure or blueprints in the other" (Cody, 1971, pp. 1–2).

As discussed earlier in this chapter, Cody then argues that psychoanalytic theory has discovered conflicts and motives believed to be operative to some degree in all lives, and that when many pieces of evidence are available the theory can sometimes be used to perceive the relationships among the authentic bits of evidence, and to make inferences about the rough structure of missing pieces of evidence. This is equivalent to making plaster bones in reconstructing a fossil skeleton. "One such 'plaster bone' in the present study is the assumption that early in Emily Dickinson's life she experienced what she interpreted as a cruel rejection by her mother. Many of her statements, her choice of certain recurring metaphors and symbols, and the entire course of her life, viewed psychoanalytically, argue for the truth of this assumption" (Cody, 1971, p. 2).

Is such a practice always to be avoided? Perhaps there are a few cases in which extensive evidence is available and in which a clear and well-supported theoretical structure exists which would justify reconstruction of the gross features of an unknown event. Even so, biographical reconstruction is extremely risky, and in most cases unjustified. In light of the uncertainties of developmental theory, the lack of empirical support for psycho-analytic genetic theory, and the multiple possible processes lead-ing to any given outcome, the case for banning reconstruction altogether in psychobiography is a fairly strong one. But if retro-diction is to be practiced at all, it is essential that reconstructions clearly be labelled as such and kept distinct from events for which there is documentary evidence.

Reductionism

Another common charge against psychobiography is that of "re-ductionism." One form of the reductionist critique is that psy-chological factors are overemphasized at the expense of external social and historical factors. "In turning to Freud, historians in-terested in the psychological aspect of their discipline have con-centrated upon the internal biographies of individuals to the almost complete exclusion of the society in which the lives of their subjects take place" (Hundert, 1972, pp. 467–468). Or, "un-like economic, social, political or religious influences, the sub-ject's 'psychology' is considered to be the source. His mental state determines all other variables, and then responds to them" (T. Anderson, 1978, p. 15).

A second version of the reductionist criticism is that psycho-biography focuses excessively on psychopathological processes and gives insufficient attention to normality and creativity. Particu-larly in the early history of psychobiography, works were some-times called "pathographies," thereby "emphasizing the basic concern with abnormality and leading to the conclusion that what psychoanalysis had to offer to an understanding of the lives of great men consisted mainly in a documentation and explica-tion of their foibles and follies" (Meyer, 1972, p. 373).

A third type of reductionism is to explain adult character and behavior exclusively in terms of early childhood experience while neglecting later formative processes and influences. "What is chiefly wrong with the conventional psychoanalytic biography is its crude unilateralism. It suggests a one-to-one relationship, arguing that the protagonist did this or that because of some painful experience in early childhood" (Hughes, 1964, p. 58). Erikson (1969) identified this form of reductionism as "originology," or "the habitual effort to find the 'causes' of a man's whole development in his childhood conflicts" (p. 98). Two other reductive fallacies are " 'the critical period fallacy,' which attempts to build a study of a man's life around a certain 'key' period of development, and 'eventism,' the discovery in some important episode in a man's life of not only the prototype of his behavior but *the* turning point in his life from which all subsequent events and work are derived. Both these oversimplifications lend artistic grace to a biographical study, but also impose unnatural order, shape, and direction to the often rather amorphous nature and fitful course of a human life, even that of a great man" (Mack, 1971, p. 156).

In response to these charges of reductionism, it must be acknowledged that too many psychobiographies have suffered from flaws such as overemphasizing the psychological, the pathological, or the influence of childhood conflicts. A number of contemporary psychobiographers (e.g., Bate, 1977; Mack, 1976; Tucker, 1973) are, however, aware of such dangers, and are avoiding them by integrating the psychological with the social and historical, by analyzing not just pathology but also strengths and adaptive capacities, and by studying formative influences not just in childhood but throughout the life span.

The Relationship of Childhood Experience to Adult Behavior

One of the most complex and difficult issues in the field of psychobiography is that of assessing the influence of childhood experience upon adult character and behavior. In psychoanalytically oriented psychobiographies, aspects of adult behavior are often attributed to circumstances and experiences in childhood. In the worst cases, "hypotheses about early developments are speculatively deduced from adult events and then used to explain those events" (Izenberg, 1975, p. 139). In more fortunate cases, available evidence about childhood experience is interpreted as an important causal determinant of adult personality and behavior. This practice of attributing important causal influence to early experience is consistent with classical psychoanalytic theories of personality development. Freud (1938) stated, for example, that "Analytic experience has convinced us of the complete truth of the assertion so often to be heard that the child is psychologically father to the adult and that the events of his first years are of paramount importance for his whole later life" (p. 187).

This practice of interpreting the whole life in terms of early childhood experience has, however, come under attack from a number of different directions. Historians have challenged the causal interpretations provided for particular cases: "I just do not think that such things as the extermination of six million Jews can be explained by the alleged fact that Hitler's mother was killed by treatment given her by a Jewish doctor in an attempt to cure her cancer of the breast; or that Luther's defiance of the Roman church can be explained by the brutal way he was treated by his father or by his chronic constipation" (Stone, 1981, p. 220). Stone's statement exaggerates the issues, though, as there is an important difference between claiming that childhood experience is *the* cause of later events versus arguing that it is a partial or contributing cause of individual behavior. Even psychoanalytically oriented psychobiographers criticize the practice of positing childhood experience as the only cause of later behavior, as in Erikson's (1969) critique of "originology" and Mack's (1971) critique of the fallacy of attributing all subsequent development to a single important period or event.

From another direction, empirical tests of Freudian theory, reviewed in Kline (1972) and Fisher and Greenberg (1977), raise questions about aspects of Freud's theories of psychosexual development. Although there is some evidence about clusters of traits consistent with Freud's conception of oral character, and substantial evidence about orderliness, obstinacy, and parsimony clustering together as Freud suggested in the anal or obsessive character, the bulk of quantitative empirical studies do not demonstrate connections between character types and specific childhood experiences associated with feeding or toilet-training. Whether more methodologically sophisticated studies in the future will provide more support for these theories is an open question, but at present, a substantial number of studies do not support them and provide little reason for believing them to be valid.

Even if the specific connections between early psychosexual experience and adult character which Freud suggested are not supported, this does not resolve the more general issue of connections between childhood experience and adult behavior. Clinical experience with some clients seems to provide apparently compelling evidence of connections between childhood experience and adult behavior. This may, of course, be no more than a methodological artifact, but it may also be that such clear-cut connections *do* exist for some individuals, even though not for all. Second, more recent developments in psychoanalytic theory, as in the work of Mahler, Winnicott, or Kohut, provide more complex ways of analyzing childhood experience which may provide sounder foundations for connecting childhood experience to adult behavior. Third, the study of childhood experience may be useful in developing interpretations of adult behavior or in forming hypotheses about the meaning of aspects of an individual's adult behavior, even if a causal connection between the two is not explicitly argued.

The study of childhood experience may be of some importance in psychobiography, but perhaps not in the way suggested by classical Freudian theory. There has, in recent years, been a widespread shift in thinking within developmental and personality psychology about the influence of early childhood experience. In contrast to earlier beliefs about the crucial impact of childhood experience upon adult behavior (e.g., Bowlby, 1952; Bloom, 1964; Kelly, 1955), there has been a growing belief that the effects of early deprivation can be substantially modified by later experience and that behavior and personality are shaped and changed throughout the life course (e.g., Brim and Kagan, 1980; Clarke and Clarke, 1976; Mischel, 1968; and Rutter, 1981). The argument is not that early childhood experiences have no effects, but rather that the effects of such experiences are mediated by intervening experiences and contingencies, and personality and behavior are continuously shaped throughout the life cycle.

Early experience, of whatever form, rarely has a direct impact upon adult personality but rather early experience shapes early personality, which influences the kinds of later environments one is likely to encounter, which in turn influences later experience, which affects personality, and so on in an interactive cycle (Wachtel, 1977). The effects of early experiences are mediated through a chain of behavior-determining, person-determining, and situation-determining processes throughout the life course (Runyan, 1978a; Chapter 6). Thus, any given event or experience can have a variety of possible effects and meanings, depending upon initial personality structure, initial environment, and the causal structure of subsequently encountered environments and experiences. Furthermore, the causal structure of the life course is such that there are usually a variety of alternative paths or processes leading to a given outcome.

What are the implications for psychobiography of this transactional view of human development in which personality is modifiable throughout the life span? First, adult personality cannot be attributed directly to specific childhood experiences, and particularly not to specific experiences with breast feeding or toilet training, which empirical evidence indicates are not substantial determinants of adult outcome. Second, if there are alternative paths or processes to a given outcome, then postdiction is, in most instances, to be avoided. Third, if evidence on early experience is available, the effects of such experience ought not be applied directly to adult personality, but rather traced through a sequence of intervening stages and processes. While based in part upon a reconstructed early experience, the following example from Cody's (1971) study of Emily Dickinson illustrates such a sequential-interactional model of analysis in psychobiography: "One sees a circular process inimical to the woman but kindly to the artist; feelings of rejection by the mother lead to hostility and bitter denunciation of the mother and what she represents. As a result, guilt feelings are engendered that in turn evoke a need for punishment that is partly satisfied through self-inflicted social deprivation brought about by means of neurotic symptoms. The ensuing loneliness and frustration then feed the art in ways that have been mentioned. The art in turn, providing its own compensatory and self-reinforcing gratification, demands further self-denial. . . . which is brought about by the perpetuation of the estrangement from and enmity toward mother, religion, God, and society. These hostile rejections in turn evoke more guilt feelings and further suffering and a continuation of the endless cycle" (pp. 498–499).

The study of formative influences throughout the life cycle makes analysis more complicated, but it also has certain advantages for psychobiography in that early childhood experience, for which evidence is frequently unavailable, is no longer so predominantly important. Attention can then be directed to those formative periods and processes for which adequate evidence is more often available. One of the advantages of Eriksonian theory, in which character and identity are importantly shaped at later ages, is that the psychobiographer is more likely to have usable evidence on this period of the subject's life (Stone, 1981, p. 53).

There are, in sum, several serious difficulties with psychobiographical analyses which attribute adult patterns of behavior to particular childhood experiences. Those analyses which do so on the basis of Freudian theories of psychosexual development are problematic because of the bulk of empirical evidence which does not support such theories. On the other hand, the reciprocal-interactive view of development currently advocated in life-span developmental psychology and in personality theory is not far enough advanced to be widely used. What should the psychobiographer do in light of these difficulties? One recommendation is to proceed sparingly with statements attributing adult behavior to childhood experiences, deprivations, or conflicts. In reference to the study of Woodrow Wilson discussed earlier in this chapter, Brodie (1957) states that the authors "are inevitably on weaker ground when they try to explain the genesis of the Wilsonian neurosis than when they describe the manner in which it expressed itself full-blown. . . . It is one thing to observe compulsive behavior and identify it for what it is; it is quite another to find the original causes" (p. 415).

An extensive evaluative review of work in psychobiography and psychohistory by Crosby and Crosby (1981) reaches a similar conclusion about the limitations of explanations in terms of childhood experience. The Crosbys applied a quantitative rating system to 79 articles and books in political psychobiography, and in light of their criteria (e.g. adequacy of evidence, consideration of plausible rival hypotheses, and references to relevant theoretical and empirical literature), those studies focusing on "coherent whole" or pattern explanations of adult behavior were rated more positively than those relying on causal explanations in terms of childhood experience.

Woods (1974) argues that it is not necessary to postulate anything about a subject's childhood in order to do a useful psychoanalytic biography. "Psychoanalytic theory enables the biographer to see, in examining the mature life of a character, behavior that he might not otherwise notice: alteration between active and passive states, how he relates to people, or whether his behavior indicates that he has not relinquished fantasies of omnipotence, whether he is burdened with an unconscious sense of guilt; and to show how these constructs enable us to understand the character more clearly. One does not, in short, have to know the earliest reasons why a character seems incapable of regarding other people except as 'there' to meet his needs, in order to notice that he does relate to people" (p. 729) in such a way.

Psychology can be used for many purposes other than drawing causal connections between childhood experience and adult behavior. It can be useful for identifying patterns in current behavior, for providing concepts and categories for analyzing experience, for suggesting hypotheses about the meaning of circumstances or events for an individual, for providing normative or comparative data about phenomena of interest, for providing methods to use in analyzing biographical evidence, and so on. It may be that the greatest contributions of psychology to biography lie in just such areas, in the conceptualization and interpretation of biographical evidence, without always attempting to relate adult behavior to childhood experience.

Trans-Historical and Cross-Cultural Generality in Psychological Theory

Psychobiographers and psychohistorians are often criticized for applying a parochial psychological theory to individuals of other cultures and historical periods. If psychoanalysis was developed to explain the behavior of neurotic middle- and upper-class Viennese at the turn of the twentieth century, how can it be appropriately used to explain the behavior of those in other cultures and historical periods? The problem was clearly formulated in 1938 by historian Lucien Febvre, "How can we as historians make use of psychology which is the product of observation carried out on twentieth-century man, in order to interpret the actions of the man of the past?" (quoted in Gilmore, 1979b, p. 31). It is alleged that many psychohistorians "begin by postulating that there is a theory of human behavior which transcends history. This claim to possess a scientific system of explanation of human behavior based on proven clinical data, which is of universal validity irrespective of time and place, is wholly unacceptable to the historian since it ignores the critical importance of changing context—religious, moral, cultural, economic, social, and political. It is a claim, moreover, that has recently been rejected by many of the more perceptive members of the psychological profession itself" (Stone, 1981, p. 40).

One final expression of this critique is, "The psychohistorian employs theoretical models and cognitive assumptions created from the material of the present—and then imposes them on the past. In so doing, he or she must assume that in most fundamental ways all people, at all places, at all times, have viewed themselves and the world about them in substantially the same fashion. If man *qua* man were not always essentially the same, the behavior of many past individuals (to say nothing of whole cultures) would be psychoanalytically unintelligible. Their actions and motives would be operating at a level beyond the reach of psychoanalytic concepts and suppositions, which are products of the direct study of primarily urban, post-industrial, literate, twentieth-century, Western individuals—and mostly 'abnormal' and demographically nonrepresentative ones at that" (Stannard, 1980, p. 121). And, "It thus seems clear that even if psychoanalytic theory were an effective technique for understanding the world of the present, it would be a hopeless exercise in intellectual myopia to apply it to the past" (Stannard, 1980, p. 143). "Psychohistory, in a word, is ahistorical. That is its ultimate failing. Perhaps the single most important achievement of modern historical thinking has been the growing recognition on the part of the historian that life in the past was marked by a fundamental social and cognitive differentness from that prevailing in our own time" (Stannard, 1980, p. 151).

What is the validity of such criticisms? First, it must be acknowledged that some of the charges are true, that psychobiographers have, at times, been unaware of cultural and historical differences, which has biased their interpretations. As one example, Langer (1972) is criticized for seeming "largely unaware of the family's social setting or of the customs of the time. It simply will not do to cite Hitler's addressing his father as 'Herr Vater' (Mr. Father) as evidence of paternal tyranny and oppression. Family formality was widespread in nineteenth-century Europe, and did not necessarily indicate either lack of filial affection or the presence of societal authoritarianism" (Orlow, 1974, p. 135). This problem is common to all biographical and historical writing and is not insurmountable; the psychobiographer simply *must* learn about the cultural and historical context of his or her subject.

It can readily be agreed that ethno-centrism and temporo-centrism are to be avoided in interpreting individuals from other cultures and historical periods. Does this, however, cause any insoluble problems for psychobiography? I think not, as there are a variety of effective responses to the problem. As a first step, the psychobiographer must learn enough about the subject's social and historical context to have an adequate frame of reference for interpreting the meaning of specific actions, statements, artistic practices, and so on.

Second, the study of relevant comparison groups and of local contexts within the subject's social and historical world may help in developing understandings of the individual. However, understandings derived from studies of similar groups are not likely to be sufficient either, because we are often most interested in those individuals who stand out significantly from other Renaissance painters, other nineteenth-century writers, or other twentieth-century American politicians. It is also important to conduct idiographic studies of the individual (as discussed in the previous chapter) in order to reveal aspects of his or her personality, situation, and experience that may differentiate him or her from others in the same social and historical context. Finally, if we accept Kluckhohn and Murray's classic statement that persons are in some ways like all others, like some others, and like no others, then it follows that at least some psychological conceptualizations and theories will hold universally (cf. Lonner, 1979; Triandis, 1978), and can be appropriately applied to any psychobiographical subject. The context-boundedness of many psychological theories is not unrecognized by psychologists (e.g., Cronbach, 1975; Gergen, 1973), and it is necessary to examine more closely what aspects of psychological conceptualizations and theories can and cannot be applied across different cultures and historical periods.

In short, errors have sometimes been made in naïvely assuming that psychoanalytic or other psychological theory could automatically be applied to individuals in any cultural or historical setting, but this does not at all mean that psychohistory does not work or cannot work. Rather, psychobiographical interpretation is a complex three-tiered intellectual enterprise which needs to draw not just on those theories which hold universally, but also on group and context-specific generalizations and on idiographic studies of the particular individual.

The Place of Psychoanalytic Theory in Psychobiography

Historically at least, psychoanalytic theory has been of preeminent importance in psychobiography, as the early psychobiographers (e.g., Freud, Sadger, Abraham, Hitschmann) were psychoanalysts and saw the field as applied psychoanalysis. The psychobiographical enterprise is still predominantly psychodynamic, and some still define psychobiography as the application of psychoanalysis to biography. As argued earlier in this chapter, there are compelling reasons for defining the field of psychobiography more widely to include the application of other psychological approaches, with psychoanalytic biography as one important branch of the enterprise.

Even though psychobiography is now often defined more broadly to recognize the contributions of other psychological theories (e.g., Anderson, 1978; Tetlock, Crosby, and Crosby, 1981; Tucker, 1977), many believe that psychoanalysis is still the theory of choice. For example, psychoanalysis is the theory of choice because it is a historical theory of development and "is also concerned with the complexity of emotions and motivations while behavioral psychology is not, making psychoanalysis applicable to a wider range of complex historical phenomena than any other theory" (Loewenberg, 1976, p. 821). Or, "as psychoanalytic personality theory is the most profound, it has in fact become the standard used in the field of biography—no other psychological approach now receives serious consideration from scholars in allied fields" (Gedo, 1972, p. 638).

Particularly for those who see psychoanalysis as the primary foundation of psychobiography, there is a tendency to compare psychobiographical methodology to psychoanalytic treatment, with the implication that the latter is to be approached as closely as possible. The disadvantages of psychohistorical methodology are stated to be that it does not provide free associations, dream material, and transference reactions (e.g., Bergmann, 1973; Gedo, 1972; Mack, 1971). The analytic situation is also seen as providing a check on the correctness of interpretations. "When an interpretation is given to the patient of the basic significance (to him) of some of his thoughts, sensations, emotions, or overt behavior, the patient's reaction to the interpretation usually gives (in time) definite evidence as to both its degree of correctness and its degree of importance" (Hofling, 1976, p. 228).

Although there undoubtedly are advantages in having access to material produced in the analytic hour, and in having the person's reactions to proposed interpretations, it is naïve to approach this situation as a methodological ideal in light of the serious epistemological problems associated with such interviews (Grünbaum, 1979). The errors that individuals commonly make in perceiving and interpreting their own behavior and that of others are extensively documented in recent studies in cognitive psychology and person perception (Nisbett and Ross, 1980; Schneider, Hastorf, and Ellsworth, 1979). For example, "Investigators have found that individuals will enthusiastically accept bogus interpretations as accurate descriptions of their own personalities" (Fisher and Greenberg, 1977, p. 364). After examining such evidence, Crews (1980) concludes that "the situation that produces nearly all psychoanalytic evidence—the clinical interview—is epistemologically contaminated to an extreme degree. It would be hard to find a data-gathering arrangement less conducive to the empirical ideal of neutralizing the investigator's bias" (p. 27). Crews bases his assessment on considerations such as that the materials supposedly uncovered from the patient's unconscious may actually be artifacts of the therapist's suggestions, that there is solid evidence that individuals will accept bogus interpretations as accurate analyses of their own personality, and that other experimental evidence indicates that individuals are often unable to accurately identify through introspection the causes of their own thoughts and feelings.

Although Crews' summary may be seen as unduly harsh, the point is that the psychoanalytic interview has significant methodological problems of its own. Such considerations force us, I believe, to a shift in perspective. Rather than taking the therapeutic situation as a methodological ideal to be approached as closely as possible, the clinical encounter needs to be placed into a larger epistemological context and to be seen as one among many research methods, each with its own strengths and weaknesses. The adequacy of psychohistorical methods cannot be assessed by simply comparing them to psychoanalytic clinical procedures. As noted earlier in the chapter, psychobiographical methods have a number of advantages over the clinical interview, as well as limitations of their own.

In addition to questions about psychoanalytic methods of data collection, questions have also been raised about the adequacy of psychoanalytic theory as a foundation for psychohistory, most noticeably by Stannard (1980). His claim that good psychohistory is impossible is based on the argument that psychoanalytic theory itself is fundamentally defective. Stannard argues that not only are individual psychohistorical works flawed, but that "the best possible psychohistory would still be bad history because of the limitations imposed by the weaknesses of the underlying theoretical structure" (p. 21). He says that psychoanalytic theory provides the strongest foundation for psychohistory, and then argues that psychoanalytic theory is so defective that psychohistorical work should be abandoned. He believes that psychoanalytic theory "suffers from problems of illogic, experimental nonconfirmation, and cultural parochialism" (p. 30), and he quotes approvingly Medawar's statement that, "psychoanalytic theory is the most stupendous intellectual confidence trick of the twentieth century and a terminal product as well—something akin to a dinosaur or zeppelin in the history of ideas, a vast structure of radically unsound design and with no posterity" (Medawar, 1975,

p. 17). After reviewing selected aspects of psychoanalytic theory, Stannard concludes that "psychohistory does not work and cannot work. The time has come to face the fact that, behind all its rhetorical posturing, the psychoanalytic approach to history is—irremediably—one of logical perversity, scientific unsoundness, and cultural naïveté. The time has come, in short, to move on" (p. 156).

As pointed out by reviewers (e.g., Adelson, 1981; Basch, 1980; Crosby, 1980), there are many things wrong with Stannard's assessment of psychoanalytic theory and the field of psychohistory. For one thing, to say that psychohistory is necessarily psychoanalytic history is incorrect. Second, his review of the evidence in relation to psychoanalytic theory is one-sided and polemical. Third, the identification of examples of cultural parochialism or historical naïveté does not mean that such problems have not been adequately handled by some practicing psychohistorians, much less that they never could be. Finally, problems with some aspects of psychoanalytic theory, acknowledged even by many psychoanalysts, does not mean that all of the theory can be rejected. In sum, the assumption that psychohistory necessarily rests on psychoanalytic theory is unjustified; Stannard does not explain away or deal with the more successful examples of psychobiographical analysis (e.g., Bate, 1977; Cody, 1971; George and George, 1956; Solomon, 1977; Tucker, 1973); and the evidence supporting psychoanalytic theory is both more complex and more positive (cf. Fisher and Greenberg, 1977; Kline, 1972) than revealed by Stannard's tendentious review.

One of the mysteries of the field is why, if psychoanalytic theory is as defective as some believe, is it so widely employed in psychobiographical works? A number of possible explanations come to mind. First, perhaps psychoanalytic theory has a special relevance to the kinds of explanatory or interpretive problems encountered in psychobiography in that it seems effective in explaining just those kinds of odd or unusual patterns of behavior that the psychobiographer feels are most in need of explanation.

Second, perhaps psychoanalytically oriented theorists are able, or willing, to speculate from the kinds of fragments of evidence available about historical figures, while adherents of other theoretical orientations are unable or unwilling to do so.

Third, perhaps the explanation lies in *how* psychoanalytic

theory is used. It may be that psychoanalysis provides a set of conceptual tools that can be used in a flexible and partially idiographic way; they are flexible enough to be used to construct interpretations of a wide range of particular patterns of individual behavior. This characteristic of the theoretical system may be a liability for some theory-testing purposes (Popper, 1962), but a virtue for interpretive purposes. The theory identifies a large number of mechanisms and processes, which can then be used in constructing interpretations of the particular patterns found within the individual case.

A fourth possibility is that psychobiographers who believe that psychoanalysis has been helpful in their interpretive tasks have been mistaken in some way. While having the subjective experience of gaining insight, they may actually have been led into errors or false interpretations. Perhaps psychoanalytic theory satisfies a human need to find pattern or meaning, but such patterns can be found in biographical material even where none actually exist, or at least not the ones suggested by the theory.

Finally, perhaps psychodynamic theory is profoundly true in some ways, not necessarily all of it, but at least parts of it. Perhaps working intensively with biographical data leads writers to find that psychoanalytic theory repeatedly proves itself more illuminating or more useful than any other body of psychological theory, just as many clinicians find it useful in clinical situations. While some aspects of psychoanalytic theory, such as a belief in the paramount importance of early psychosexual experience, should in my opinion probably be revised or abandoned, other aspects of the theory, such as the concept of unconscious motives and conflicts, the notion of identification, and the operation of defense mechanisms may prove of enduring utility for psychobiographers. Psychoanalytic theory also has the heuristic value of leading investigators to explore a range of hypotheses that might not otherwise have occurred to them.

My reading of the psychobiographical literature suggests that, in spite of the errors sometimes arising from doctrinaire application of psychoanalytic theory, its many positive contributions indicate that it has a role of fundamental importance in psychobiography. The challenge is to use psychoanalytic theory selectively, to avoid those aspects of it which accumulating evidence suggests are incorrect, and to self-critically consider its implications while developing and evaluating interpretations of the available biographical evidence.

Nonpsychoanalytic Approaches

What are the possibilities for nonpsychoanalytic work in psychobiography? To some, it seems that "the psychoanalytic basis of psychohistory has become something of an orthodoxy, a limiting, constraining orientation that chokes off creative dissent" (Strozier, 1979, p. 5), and that other approaches need to be explored. In principle, it seems that psychobiography could well draw not solely from psychoanalytic theory, but also from other personality theories, from social and cognitive psychology, and from developmental psychology. What though, has actually been done in using nonpsychoanalytic contributions from these other areas of psychology?

Personality Psychology

The field of personality psychology can be seen as being organized around several major theoretical orientations: the psychodynamic, behavioral or social learning, trait-factor and psychometric, and phenomenological or humanistic. This survey will concentrate on nonpsychoanalytic approaches and will not discuss the many contributions of psychoanalytic theory, and its more recent developments in ego psychology, object relations theory, and self-psychology, which have been reviewed elsewhere (Loewenberg, 1982; Mack, 1971; Strozier, 1980), nor the related psychodynamic systems of Jung and Adler, which have also been used in psychobiography (e.g., Ansbacher, 1966; Brink, 1975; Progoff, 1966; Ward, 1961).

Since behavioral or learning theory is a general theory of human behavior, it could, in principle, provide a foundation for psychobiographical interpretation. What, in fact, has been done with it? In the clinical literature, perhaps the most well-known example of a learning theory interpretation of historical material is that of Wolpe and Rachman's (1960) reinterpretation of the case of Little Hans. As discussed in Chapter 8, Wolpe and Rachman severely criticized Freud's Oedipal interpretation of the causes of Little Hans' fear of horses, and argued that his phobia was caused not by a displaced fear of his father, but rather by a learning process in which the neutral stimuli of horses had been paired with fear-producing situations, leading to a conditioned fear of horses.

A second example of a behavioral approach to psychobiography is provided by a recent article on "Ben Franklin the Proto-behaviorist . . ." (Mountjoy and Sundberg, 1981). The authors argue that Benjamin Franklin's efforts to arrive at moral perfection can be seen as an early example of behavioral self-management. Franklin made a list of 13 virtues, including temperance, frugality, industry, chastity, and humility, and attempted to make his practice of each of these virtues habitual. He drew up a chart on which he recorded on a daily basis his failure to practice any of the 13 virtues. For a week at a time he would concentrate on practicing one of the virtues, and then, once the practice of that virtue became more habitual, he would move ahead to concentrate on the next virtue on the list. Described in behavioral terms, he identified response classes that he wanted to change, recorded a baseline of the frequency of different classes of behavior, recorded data on his performance at the end of each day, and was reinforced by seeing the frequency of undesirable behaviors decrease over time as he repeatedly worked his way through the chart.

Probably the most extensively developed behavioral interpretation of a life history is contained in the two volumes of B. F. Skinner's autobiography, *Particulars of My Life* (1976) and *The Shaping of a Behaviorist* (1979). Skinner states that, "Whether from narcissism or scientific curiosity, I have been as much interested in myself as in rats and pigeons. I have applied the same formulation, I have looked for the same kinds of causal relations, and I have manipulated behavior in the same way and sometimes with comparable success" (Skinner, 1967, p. 407). A goal of his autobiography is to provide a case history of human behavior analyzed from an operant point of view. His analytic strategy is to describe "how my environment changed and how these changes affected me" (APA Monitor, 1977, p. 6). The focus is on changes in the external environment and their effect on his overt behavior, without referring to inner experiences or feelings.

One of the more dramatic examples is his description of the end of a love relationship. The woman, Neda, told him at dinner that they should break it off, as she was going back to a former fiancée. "It was a reasonable decision, but it hit me very hard. As we walked back to her apartment from the subway, I found myself moving very slowly. It was not a pose; I simply could not move faster. For a week I was in almost physical pain, and one day I bent a wire in the shape of an N, heated it in a Bunsen burner, and branded my left arm" (Skinner, 1979, p. 137). This dramatic description of environmental events and his behavioral response is not accompanied by a description of his thoughts and feelings about the incident. Skinner's work illustrates that a behavioral approach to psychobiography is possible, although there may be disagreement about whether this approach illuminates or obscures our understanding of a life.

The possibilities for applying trait-factor and psychometric approaches to the lives of historical figures are suggested by the work of Kenneth Craik in applying standard personality assessment procedures such as the adjective check list, trait-rating scales, and Q-sort personality descriptions to figures such as Adolf Hitler, Woodrow Wilson, and other American Presidents (Historical Figures Assessment Collaborative, 1977). Techniques of intra-individual correlational analysis developed by Raymond Cattell have been applied to individual clinical cases (e.g., Cattell, 1966; Bath, Daly, and Nesselroade, 1976; Luborsky and Mintz, 1972), and might in some instances be applicable to historical figures. It could be argued, however, that such approaches are concerned primarily with describing the personalities of individuals, which is one facet of biography, but do not provide a foundation for interpreting or explaining an entire life history.

Another influential theoretical orientation in personality psychology is that of phenomenological-existential or humanistic psychology, represented by the works of Abraham Maslow, Carl Rogers, Charlotte Bühler, and Rollo May. How extensively has humanistic psychology been used in psychobiography? As one example, Carl Rogers (1980) reinterpreted the case of Ellen West (originally described by Binswanger, 1958), a young woman with anorexia nervosa who eventually committed suicide. A second example is a study of Clarence Darrow presented in terms of Charlotte Bühler's theory of stages of goal seeking (Horner, 1968). A third example is a book by Nancy Clinch, *The Kennedy Neurosis* (1973), which claims to rely in part on humanistic psychology, although the book has often been criticized as a psychological hatchet job.

The most extensive use of existential theory in psychobiography is contained in the work of Sartre, with his biographical studies of Baudelaire (1950), Genet (1952), and Flaubert (1981). In his magnum opus on Flaubert, Sartre (1981) says the question he wants to address is, "What at this point in time, can we know about a man? It seemed to me that this question could only be answered by studying a specific case. What do we know, for example, about Gustave Flaubert?" (p. ix). This complex book might best be described, though, as an example of an eclectic work, part biography, part novel, part philosophy, drawing upon psychoanalysis, Marxism, and Sartre's own version of existentialism (Barnes, 1981).

Social Psychology

The field of social psychology tends to be organized around the study of particular kinds of events or processes, such as person perception, interpersonal attraction, persuasion and influence, obedience to authority, prejudice and discrimination, socialization, self-concept and self-esteem, attitude change, and so on. In principle, research and theory on any of these specific processes could be drawn upon in interpreting related events in a psychobiography. For example, research on obedience to authority (Milgram, 1974) could be used in analyzing the behavior of Lt. Calley during the My Lai massacre in Viet Nam, or the behavior of Adolf Eichmann and other Nazis during World War II, or research on group influences on judgment and decision-making used in studying the decisions of President Kennedy in planning the Bay of Pigs invasion (Janis, 1972).

One increasingly influential part of social psychology is concerned with processes of social cognition, or the cognitive processes by which individuals perceive, interpret, and attribute causes to the behavior of others. Research on social cognition and the common biases in everyday cognitive processes (Nisbett and Ross, 1980) may well be drawn upon in studying the attitudes, belief systems, and decision-making processes of individual historical figures, issues of particular importance in the lives of political leaders. An extensive review of the use of theories of social perception and cognition in studying political leaders is provided in Jervis's *Perception and Misperception in International Politics* (1976) and Janis and Mann's *Decision-Making* (1977). In short, social psychology and cognitive psychology seem to have significant promise in psychobiography, not as a foundation or organizing principle for the study of an entire life, but rather as a resource to draw upon in understanding particular events or processes.

Developmental Psychology

Developmental psychology, which is concerned with the description and explanation of changes in behavior and psychological structures, would seem to have a special relevance for psychobiography. The field of developmental psychology can be seen as being organized around (1) major theoretical orientations, such as the Piagetian-cognitive, psychodynamic, or behavioral, (2) the growth of particular systems, such as motor behavior, sensory processes, linguistic ability, or personality, (3) particular classes or types of behavior, such as aggression, altruism, or creativity, (4) particular periods or stages of the life cycle, e.g. infancy, childhood, adolescence, or (5) as in adult developmental psychology, organized around particular events or transitions, such as leaving home, becoming a parent, or getting divorced.

Each of these components of the field of developmental psychology could at times be used in psychobiography. Since major theoretical orientations were discussed in the section on personality, they will not be mentioned here except to note the use of some aspects of Piagetian concepts in Gruber's (1981) study of intellectual growth and change in the career of Charles Darwin. Studies of the development of particular classes of behavior, or of particular life transitions (such as choosing a marriage partner, establishing a career, retirement, or grieving at the loss of a spouse) could be drawn upon as needed for analyzing specific psychobiographical events.

Within developmental psychology, some of the most relevant theory may come from work in adult developmental psychology and life-span developmental psychology. One theoretical framework which appears particularly promising for psychobiographical purposes is presented in Daniel Levinson's *The Seasons of a Man's Life* (1978; also, Levinson, 1981). Levinson argues that the course of adult development can be understood not as the development of personality, but rather as the development or evolution of the life structure, with life structure defined as the pattern or fit between self and world in areas such as occupation, relationships, and leisure activities. In every period of adulthood, a man must make certain key choices, form a structure around them, and pursue his goals and values within this structure. Adult life alternates between a sequence of stable or structure-building periods, and transitional or structure-changing periods, in which individuals assess and re-evaluate their existing life structure, and may make new choices in regard to career, marriage, family, or other aspects of life.

Two components of the life structure which Levinson discusses are that of "The Dream," and mentor relationships. The Dream is an imagined vision of oneself in the world that generates excitement and vitality. The mentor, typically a person of greater experience and seniority, serves to facilitate realization of the life dream by serving as teacher, model, guide, and sponsor. One of Levinson's students has drawn upon this framework to examine two important mentoring relationships in the career of Willy Brandt before he became Chancellor of West Germany (Kellerman, 1978).

A more comprehensive application of Levinson's theory is in a recent study of C. G. Jung by Staude (1981). Staude looks at Jung's relationship to Freud as an example of a mentor relationship, and analyzes Jung's midlife transition in terms of Levinson's conception of a structure-changing period. After considerable success in the tasks of early adulthood, as indicated by scientific accomplishments, a happy marriage and family life, a successful private practice, and international recognition in the psychoanalytic movement, Jung entered a period of profound questioning of his previous life structure. With the advent of this midlife re-examination, Jung saw "his early adult life structure crumble and fall apart before his eyes" (Staude, 1981, p. 47), and was forced to forge a new life structure which took greater account of his mystical and archetypical inner experience.

Additional Examples

While the focus of this discussion is on the use of nonpsychoanalytic psychology in psychobiography, it should also be noted that interpretive biographies can draw on nonpsychological theories as well. One example is Wolfenstein's *The Victims of Democracy: Malcolm X and the Black Revolution* (1981), which draws on Marxist as well as Freudian interpretive principles.

This Marxist and psychoanalytic approach can be illustrated by an interpretation of the experience which formed Malcolm X's first vivid memory. Malcolm's father was a Baptist minister and an organizer for Marcus Garvey's Universal Negro Improvement Association (U.N.I.A.). In 1929, when Malcolm was four years old, the family was living in Lansing, Michigan, where his father had been harrassed by the Black Legion, a local variant of the Ku Klux Klan. Malcolm's earliest vivid memory is waking up in the night to find the house in flames and his father shooting at two white men who had set the fire and were running away. Earlier, while his mother was pregnant with him, the Ku Klux Klan had come to their house one night and threatened her to get out of town because the white people were not going to stand for her husband's preaching of Garvey's back-to-Africa message. In Wolfenstein's analysis, the fire-setting in Lansing needs to be seen not as an isolated event but as part of a continuing battle between the Garveyites and members of the Ku Klux Klan. Thus, interpretation of the event follows a two-pronged strategy. From a social-historical perspective, the nightmare event is seen as part of a larger historical conflict and as "resulting from the conflicting interests of two national racial movements, organizationally embodied in the UNIA and the KKK and mediated through the activity of Earl Little and the Black Legionnaires" (Wolfenstein, 1981, p. 55). The rise and fall of Garvey's U.N.I.A. and the Ku Klux Klan are in turn explained in terms of the economy, particularly the changes in labor supply and demand in the 1920's. "The mutual animosity of the UNIA and the KKK, which at one historical moment was materialized in the attack upon and unsuccessful defense of the Little home, can now be seen as resulting ultimately from the conflict of class interests in American society" (Wolfenstein, 1981, p. 70).

Second, the nightmare event also needs to be explained in terms of its personal meaning for Malcolm X. Part of Wolfenstein's argument is that the legionnaires who set fire to Malcolm's house were the first "white devils" of his life, and that a groundwork had been established in his character "for seeing the white man as a powerful and evil force that black people had every reason to fear and hate" (p. 88). Wolfenstein's book suggests some of the possibilities of supplementing a psychodynamic analysis with a social and economic interpretation of an individual life.

In addition to the studies mentioned above, there are a number of other psychobiographical works which are at least partially nonpsychoanalytic, such as

1. Barber's (1972) four-fold typological analysis of presidential personalities
2. Studies of medical or biological pathology in political leaders (L'Etang, 1970), and a medical-psychological study of King George III (Macalpine and Hunter, 1969)
3. An application of Tomkin's theory of affect and motivation to the lives of four American abolitionists (1965)
4. An application of Tomkin's script theory to an adult woman (Carlson, 1981)
5. Existential, learning, and structural analyses of *Letters from Jenny* (Allport, 1965)
6. A study of Winston Churchill which draws upon Sheldon's theory of somatotypes, Jungian psychology, and descriptive psychiatry, as well as psychoanalysis (Storr, 1968), and
7. A variety of forms of content analysis applied to biography, such as "personal structure analysis" (Baldwin, 1942), application of the computerized "General Inquirer" system to personal documents (Paige, 1966), a set of content analytic and observational techniques for assessing the personalities of political leaders (Hermann, 1977), and a content analytic study by Sears et al. (1978) of longitudinal changes in indications of separation anxiety in Mark Twain's novels and letters.

Further examples are contained in an issue of *The Psychohistory Review* on "Non-Psychoanalytic Ventures in Psychohistory," with two bibliographies on this topic by Gilmore (1979a, 1979b), although most of the examples are more broadly psychohistorical rather than specifically psychobiographical.

In conclusion, what do nonpsychoanalytic approaches have to contribute to psychobiography? Work in nonpsychoanalytic psychobiography does exist, but it is scattered and disorganized, appearing in discrete bits and pieces, and has not developed anything like the cumulative tradition of work in psychoanalytic psychobiography. Nonpsychoanalytic approaches have not yet matched psychoanalytic ones in either quantity or quality. At present, there does not seem to be any serious contender on the horizon, threatening to challenge the position of psychoanalysis as the dominant theoretical orientation in the field.

The *possibilities* for using particular theories and bodies of research from nonpsychoanalytic psychology seem substantial, although relatively underdeveloped. One optimistic view of the future of nonpsychoanalytic approaches is that, "A likely prospect would see the emergence of academic psychology as the central treasury upon which thoughtful researchers and an intelligent public would draw" (Schoenwald, 1973, p. 17). To date, however, this promise is largely unfulfilled. Academic psychology can be extremely valuable in shedding light on particular processes, classes of behavior, and life transitions, and can provide a useful corrective to excesses and errors in psychodynamic interpretations. It remains to be seen, though, if adherents of nonpsychoanalytic approaches can be equally or more effective in interpreting lives than the best practitioners of psychodynamic psychobiography.

Training

There are a number of additional issues about psychobiography which might be discussed, such as problems of interpretations not supported by sufficient evidence (as in the question of why Van Gogh cut off his ear, examined in Chapter 3), or the relationship of the author to the biographical subject, discussed from the psychoanalytic point of view as the issue of countertransference. The last two issues to be discussed here, however, are those of the appropriate training and disciplinary background of psychobiographers and the ethical issues involved in the study of living subjects. One doctrinaire position on the training of psychobiographers is enunciated by Hitschman (1956): "Let me repeat again that only an analyst is competent and qualified to write the biographies of great men" (p. 269). More commonly (e.g., Friedlander, 1978; Gatzke, 1973; Hofling, 1976), it is recognized that both psychiatrists or psychologists and historians have deficiencies in their training, as expertise in both areas is required. "In view of the arduous nature of the disciplines, it is not surprising that there have been very few writers of psycho-history who have been well trained in both historiography and psychoanalysis or dynamic psychiatry" (Hofling, 1976, p. 234). The psychiatrist is usually untrained in history, and thus is prone to errors such as inadequate attention to primary source material, insufficient awareness of historical and cultural differences, and misinterpretation of the subject's social-historical context. On the other hand, the professional historian typically has a limited knowledge of psychoanalytic and psychological theory, a lack of firsthand clinical experience, and a tendency to rely on lay psychology which may or may not be supported by systematic research. The solution usually recommended is to have individuals get systematic training in both historiography and psychoanalysis or psychology, or to develop collaborative working relationships between historians and psychiatrists or psychologists. "It is conceivable that some day there may be scholars equally well versed in both disciplines, history and psychology, to write acceptable psychohistory. . . . Such persons will be hard to find. Until then, Professor Langer's suggestion of collaboration between scholars from both disciplines remains the most promising approach if psychohistory is to take its place as a respectable field of scholarship" (Gatzke, 1973, p. 401).

The problem of training is, however, often even more complex than this. Is it possible to do an adequate biography of Einstein or Newton without a knowledge of physics, of Henry James or Virginia Woolf without a knowledge of literature, of Mozart or Beethoven without a knowledge of music? Such an important part of creative people's lives is often intertwined with their work, their career, their professional associations and accomplishments, that a biographer has to have, or be willing to acquire, detailed knowledge of this world of work. In psycho-biography as well as in general biography, "It is necessary to master the field of the subject's activity in order to achieve biographic success" (Gedo, 1972, p. 646). Without this extensive background knowledge, the biography may be mercilessly attacked as naïve or uninformed by experts in that field.

The interest in a musician, scientist, or writer is often strongest among those within that field, and members of the profession may be most likely to undertake studies of prominent individuals within the field. In order to produce a competent biography, the amount of knowledge and expertise about the subject's professional world may approach the amount of knowledge needed about psychology or the techniques of biography. If this is so, it would help to explain why biography is practiced by so many different groups and why it has remained such a fragmented and loosely organized field throughout its history.

To summarize, the problem of training is not fully resolved through getting training in historiography and psychoanalysis. Ideally, psychobiography rests not just on the two legs of historiography and psychoanalysis, but also on knowledge of the subject's professional field, knowledge of general psychology, and some measure of literary skill. This range of requirements may help to explain why it is so difficult to produce a psychobiography which satisfies all interested parties, and why a gem such as Bate's *Samuel Johnson* (1977) is to be so highly prized for its expertise in historical inquiry, familiarity with Johnson's literary world and work, grasp of psychological theory, and grace in exposition.

Ethical Issues

The psychobiographical enterprise raises a number of difficult ethical issues about the invasion of privacy and about potential embarrassment or harm to the subject, and the individual's relatives and associates. These issues are particularly acute in psychobiographical studies of living political figures (e.g., Chesen, 1973; Clinch, 1973; Mazlish, 1972) and have led some to conclude that the field should be limited to subjects in the past. A summary of these arguments is that "for one thing, the data necessary for a 'psychohistorical' study of a living political leader is usually lacking—the autobiographies are not yet all written, the memoirs not yet all published, the archives not yet opened. For another, even if considerable information is available its use is almost certain to constitute an obnoxious invasion of privacy. A further impediment is that the scholar, being human and a member of his society, is likely to be caught up in the passions of his time. His own political values may becloud that objectivity which is an absolute requisite to any serious psychoanalytic inquiry" (George and George, 1973, p. 94).

The dangers and abuses of psychological studies of living

figures can be most vividly illustrated by a poll conducted by *Fact* magazine in 1964 to assess Barry Goldwater's psychological qualifications to be President, published under the title, "The Unconscious of a Conservative: A Special Issue on the Mind of Barry Goldwater." *Fact* sent a questionnaire to "all of the nation's 12,356 psychiatrists," asking "Do you believe Barry Goldwater is psychologically fit to serve as President of the United States?" Four-fifths of the psychiatrists did not reply, but of the 2,417 who did reply, slightly less than one-half (1,189) said he was not psychologically fit to be President, slightly more than one-quarter (657) said that he was fit, and the remainder (571) said they did not know enough about Goldwater to answer the question.

A sample of the negative comments were "I believe Goldwater has the same pathological make-up as Hitler, Castro, Stalin and other known schizophrenic leaders" (p. 26). "I know nothing about Senator Goldwater except his public utterances, but their often ill-considered, impulsive quality is, in my mind, sufficient to disqualify him from the Presidency" (p. 31). "Senator Goldwater seems to represent a relatively common type of personality disorder of an infantile narcissistic variety, prone to function in tyrannical dictatorial ways and to be susceptible to breakdowns because of immaturity" (p. 55).

On the other hand, a number of respondents commented favorably on Goldwater. "I not only believe Barry Goldwater is psychologically fit to serve as President of the United States, but I believe he is a very mature person" (p. 31). "Compared to Harry Truman and John Kennedy, Barry Goldwater is a psychological 'superman' in my opinion" (p. 29). "I think Barry Goldwater is intellectually honest, reliable, consistent, and emotionally mature" (p. 62). Several compared him with Lincoln, for example, "If psychiatry had been as popular a hundred years ago as it is today, Abraham Lincoln would have been subjected to the same question you now raise re Goldwater. Lincoln doubtless would have been seen by many of my group as unfit to serve due to his having suffered a psychiatric illness previously. It would have been a tragedy to have thus prevented him from becoming President" (p. 52).

Some suggested that a proper analysis required firsthand interviewing. "Your questionnaire reflects naïveté about what a psychiatrist can or cannot do. One cannot make a meaningful appraisal of a public figure one has not personally interviewed. . . . However, if you can arrange for B. G. to see me in my office and he signs a release, I will be glad to forward my observations" (p. 36). Or, "Please arrange an appointment for Senator Goldwater with our office at his convenience and mine. At that time I will be pleased to do a psychological evaluation as this is the only way a PROPER evaluation can be done" (p. 46).

Others argued that the public deserved to receive more information about Goldwater's two alleged earlier breakdowns in order to better assess his psychological fitness. "The public deserves full details of the two 'nervous breakdowns'. Eminent psychiatrists should have an opportunity to evaluate these episodes. The full facts of Eisenhower's heart attacks and Johnson's were made known. It is even much more important that the facts about Goldwater's mental illness be fully disclosed" (p. 47). "In recent years the American voter has demanded and received many details about the illnesses of Presidents Eisenhower, Kennedy, and Johnson and has taken these factors into consideration in determining his choice at the polls. In like manner, I believe such information should also be made available about Senator Goldwater's illness(es). I am not requesting data about the most intimate details of his life—anyone, no matter how central he may be in the public eye, has a right to certain privacies—but it is reasonable, in my opinion, for us to ask for answers to the following questions: What was the exact nature of Goldwater's 'breakdowns'? Was he hospitalized, and if so, was it voluntarily or by commitment? What treatment did he receive? What has been the course of his recovery?" (p. 32).

Finally, a few attacked the morality of the whole undertaking. "What type of yellow rag are you operating? I have never in my life witnessed such a shabby attempt to smear a political candidate. I would suggest that you change the name of your magazine to 'Fancy,' or better, 'Smear'! (p. 50). "Your 'survey' raises doubts in my mind as to your psychological fitness to publish any national magazine, especially one named 'FACT' " (p. 52).

These quotations suggest the lack of consensus in long-distance diagnoses, the ideological influences on psychiatric assessment, and the heated emotions aroused by such psychiatric judgments. (It should be noted that Goldwater successfully pursued a libel suit against *Fact* magazine and eventually collected $75,000 (Rogow, 1970, p. 128).) These quotations also raise the important issues of whether psychological assessments can be made without direct contact and whether the public has a right to know about the psychiatric history of political candidates. This kind of fiasco led some to a general opposition to psycho-biographical studies of prominent individuals. "Unless a person spent a good deal of time on a psychotherapist's couch, the argument went, the psychotherapist was in no position to draw inferences about his personality. And if the person *did* spend time on the therapist's couch, professional ethics would prevent the therapist from publishing any identifiable information about him" (Elms, 1976, pp. 89–90). This would have the effect of barring the public from reading any psychological study of any political leader.

From a scholarly standpoint, the *Fact* poll employed about the worst method imaginable, of asking for psychiatric judgments based on neither personal contact nor systematic study of historical evidence. Before the results of the poll were published, the medical director of the American Psychiatric Association wrote *Fact* magazine that a medical opinion depended upon a thorough clinical examination of the patient and that the Association would "take all possible measures" to disavow the validity of the survey (American Psychiatric Association, 1976, p. 1). Politically, the business of assessing the psychological status of political candidates is a dangerous one to be involved with. In a later effort by Mazlish to secure funding for a psychohistorical study of the winner of the U.S. Presidential election in 1968, the foundations, not unexpectedly, replied that the project looked interesting, "but it was politically inadvisable for those particular foundations to help finance such a study" (Mazlish, 1973, p. vii).

The ethical, political, and intellectual concerns raised by the *Fact* survey and by later psychobiographical studies of active politicians (e.g., Chesen, 1973; Clinch, 1973; Mazlish, 1972) led the American Psychiatric Association to appoint a Task Force on Psychohistory, which was charged with developing ethical and scholarly guidelines for psychohistorical studies, particularly for psychobiographies and psychiatric profiles. The Task Force concluded that there seemed to be few ethical problems in the psychobiographical study of deceased subjects, particularly if there were no surviving relatives, but that for living subjects who did not provide informed consent, there seemed to be generally compelling ethical reasons for not proceeding. "As to the basic question of whether it is ethical for a psychiatrist to write and publish a psychohistory, psychobiography, or psycho-profile of a living person, it is difficult for the Task Force to perceive how this could be done ethically without the written, informed, and freely given consent of the subject or subjects for personal interviews and publication" (American Psychiatric Association, 1976, p. 13). The exceptions that the Task Force identified were those such as Langer's study of Adolf Hitler written for the Office of Strategic Services in 1943 (Langer, 1972), and psychiatric profiles of criminals (e.g., the Boston Strangler) at large in the community.

In a separately published article, the chairman of the Task Force, Charles K. Hofling (1976), proposed yet stricter ethical constraints on the practice of psychohistory. He proposes, "It shall be unethical for a psychiatrist to publish a psychohistorical study of a living person (including psychobiography and psychiatric profiling) without first obtaining his written, informed, and freely given consent for (1) personal interviews and (2) publication. In this context, 'informed consent' means consent after full disclosure to the subject by the psychiatrist of the way in which the material is to be used and published" (p. 233). He tentatively proposed that "it shall be unethical to publish a psychohistorical study involving analysis of a recently deceased person without the written, informed, freely-given consent of the next-of-kin, who might otherwise suffer undue embarrassment and an undesired invasion of their privacy in respect to their relationship to the deceased person" (p. 233); and finally, "It shall be unethical for a psychiatrist, acting in his professional capacity, to produce a psychiatric profile of a fellow-citizen whose identity is known to him without the consent of his subject" (p. 234). The clause "whose identity is known to him" is designed to make it acceptable to produce psychological profiles of unidentified criminals, as in the search for a "mad bomber." Both Hofling and the American Psychiatric Association Task Force state that the problems of doing psychobiographical studies of living figures are more acute for psychiatrists than for historians or journalists because the psychiatrist is in a special position to discern things not apparent to the subject or to untrained observers, and because the status of the psychiatrist leads his or her reports to have greater authority than might be claimed or warranted.

Hofling and the Task Force on Psychohistory also distinguish between psychological analyses of fellow citizens and citizens of other countries. One of the dangers of analyzing a living political figure in one's own country is the possibility that "a psychological vulnerability, hitherto unrecognized by the subject and perhaps not within his ability to modify voluntarily, would, if discovered and mentioned in the published analysis, place the subject, and therefore the Nation, at a disadvantage in negotiating with foreign powers" (American Psychiatric Association, 1976, p. 10). The Task Force suggests that it would be ethically acceptable to produce "for the confidential use of government officials psychobiographies or profiles of significant international figures whose personality formation needs to be understood to carry out national policy more effectively" (p. 12). This would presumably include a study such as the study of Khrushchev made by the C.I.A. in 1960 (Wedge, 1968).

Another controversial example, not explicitly discussed by Hofling or the Task Force, is the psychiatric profile of Daniel Ellsberg produced by the C.I.A. in 1971 in response to his leaking of the Pentagon papers (*The Boston Globe*, July 19, 1974, p. 16). From the guidelines as specified, it seems that this practice would not be prohibited by the Task Force which concludes that it is not necessarily unethical to produce confidential profiles of individuals in the service of the national interest (with national interest presumably defined by the President or other government officials). The Ellsberg profile would be deemed unethical by Hofling, who holds that, with the exception of certain criminal cases, it should be deemed unethical to produce psychobiographies of living fellow citizens without their consent.

On the issue of political candidates and officeholders in one's own nation, the A.P.A. Task Force and Hofling hold that it is unethical to publish psychobiographical studies of such persons without their consent. The counterargument is that citizens implicitly make psychological assessments in deciding which political candidates to support, and they need to make such judgments in order to anticipate the person's performance in office. Since the decisions and actions of American Presidents have such extensive repercussions upon the lives of human beings within and outside the country, don't citizens have a right or even a responsibility to understand such people and their likely behavior in office as well as possible before placing them in a position of such power? If citizens have such a responsibility, should they rely for their assessments on the intuitive judgments of journalists and media people or should they also have access to the most professional personality assessments possible?

One effort along these lines is Barber's *The Presidential Character: Predicting Performance in the White House* (1972, 1977). Barber argues that a vote for a presidential candidate is, in effect, a prediction that one candidate is likely to perform more satisfactorily in office than another. Since Presidential behavior is influenced not only by the political environment but also by the individual's personality, an understanding of individual character can be of substantial value in making an informed decision among alternative candidates. Barber assesses Presidents in terms of their character, world view, and style of working. Character is analyzed in terms of a four-fold typology of active-positive, active-negative, passive-positive, and passive-negative patterns. The merits of this particular typological approach have been debated (George, 1974; Qualls, 1977; Barber, 1977), but such discussion can lead to refinements and improvements in the enterprise.

There will inevitably be different professional opinions, but as in the political process as a whole, such differences can and should be subject to debate and discussion. In the complex process of assessing political candidates and leaders, is it possible to defend the position that all views and opinions should be considered except those of the professional psychobiographer? A formal psychological screening of political candidates seems out of the question, but a systematic analysis of available biographical and psychological information seems a potentially worthwhile contribution to the political debate. What would be an appropriate scope for such analyses? To guard against unwarranted invasions of privacy, one possibility would be to base psychological analyses on the individual's public political behavior, excluding material on childhood or intimate personal life. A concern is that psychobiographical analyses could be embarrassing or damaging to politicians. "Many able political leaders would doubtless shrink from seeking public office because they would be unwilling to run themselves and their families through such a gantlet" (George and George, 1973, p. 98). On the other hand, financial disclosure statements have similarly been defined as an invasion of privacy, but in many cases, the public interest has been seen as outweighing this risk of personal embarrassment.

A second concern not often expressed is that studying active political leaders could lead to political repercussions unfavorable to psychohistorians or psychobiographers. The issues in this situation are most complex, as the rights of individual politicians and their families need to be balanced against the responsibilities of an informed citizenry. A conclusion on these issues may be premature, but it seems that the argument supporting psychobiographical studies of living political figures is somewhat stronger than was implied by the A.P.A. Task Force. Any resolution of the ethical issues in psychobiography will require consideration of a wide range of examples, such as the Goldwater affair, the war-time study of Hitler, the C.I.A. profile of Ellsberg, Barber's efforts to predict the behavior of presidential candidates, profiles of unidentified criminals, and studies of foreign political leaders; and might well profit from a consideration of the ethical dilemmas involved in a number of adjacent fields such as biography, journalistic profiling, history, psychotherapeutic practice, and social scientific research.

Conclusion

What does the future hold for psychobiography? In terms of specifics such as theories and methods used, subjects chosen, the quantity and quality of future work, and particular interpretations offered, it is difficult to speculate with much confidence. I do, however, feel convinced that psychobiography has an enduring place within the intellectual firmament. Psychology has, at its best, proved so useful that many biographers, historians, and political scientists would be unwilling to do without it and return to the alternative of relying on lay beliefs alone as a foundation for interpretive work in biography. A number of reductionistic interpretive errors have been identified and are being avoided by more knowledgeable practitioners as the sophistication of the genre increases.

This chapter has reviewed a variety of opinions about psychobiography and examined arguments and examples related to issues such as the problem of inadequate evidence, historical reconstruction, reductionism, the importance of childhood experience, the issue of cross-cultural and trans-historical generality in psychological theory, the place of psychoanalytic and non-psychoanalytic approaches in psychobiography, and issues in training and ethics. The diverse evaluations of psychobiography can be understood in part by considering the backgrounds and training of individual commentators. For example, historians tend to be particularly sensitive to historiographic errors such as relying on faulty sources, working with inadequate evidence, or insensitivity to trans-historical and cross-cultural differences. Psychiatrists and psychoanalysts are often concerned with methodological deviations from traditional clinical practice, such as not having access to free associations and dream reports, or not having the subject's responses to interpretations.

The variety of assessments can be further illuminated through considering the trajectory or temporal course of these opinions, and the context of examples, arguments, and colleague's opinions within which these assessments were formed, maintained, or changed. Such assessments are not set in concrete, either historically or within the lives of single individuals. Fritz Wittels, for example, published a psychobiographical study of Sigmund Freud in 1923 which was sharply critical of aspects of Freud's theory and personality. Interspersed with many favorable comments, Wittels stated that "Freud has an overwhelmingly high opinion of himself—the Jehovah complex; that he is a despot who will not tolerate deviations from his system; that he brings his disciples into hypnotic dependence upon him; that he repels his friends and especially if they are men of importance themselves; that he rarely abandons errors which are obviously such. . . ." (Wittels, 1933, p. 362). In his "Revision of a Biography," Wittels (1933) writes that it is embarrassing to him that these criticisms have become widely known, since "I have, in the ten years that have elapsed since the appearance of the book, changed my opinion considerably concerning psychoanalysis and its founder, and therefore can no longer stand sponsor for the errors and misrepresentations which I have come to recognize as such" (Wittels, 1933, p. 361). Wittels knew and worked with Freud from 1905 to 1910, but had a "personal difference" with him in 1910 which led to their split. After publishing the biography in 1923, Freud "drew me back to his school and gave me the opportunity to relearn and to see for myself whether my opinion of his personality and his teaching was correct or not" (Wittels, 1933, p. 362). After this experience, Wittels retracted many of his criticisms of Freud and of psychoanalysis. Additional exposure does not, however, always have similar results as evidenced by the experience of Frederick Crews, who moved from using psychoanalytic theory in his study of Hawthorne (1966), to defending its interpretive utility within a more limited domain (Crews, 1975), to a scathing critique of the entire structure of psychoanalytic theory and interpretation (Crews, 1980).

The course of opinions about psychobiography is influenced not only by disciplinary background but by such factors as the quality of examples read, evaluative criteria used, and arguments encountered. This discussion will have achieved its objectives if it encourages readers to reexamine their own thoughts and opinions about psychobiography in light of a more extensive body of examples, arguments, and counterarguments, leading to a more informed and more differentiated assessment of the enterprise and its possibilities.

I I

Conclusion

This book has attempted to identify and explore a number of basic methodological and conceptual problems encountered in the study of individual life histories. Individual chapters have examined problems in evaluating alternative interpretations and alternative accounts of lives, in conceptualizing the life course, and in critically examining the case study, idiographic, and psychobiographical methods used in the study of lives. These issues have widespread significance, as the understanding of individual lives is an important task within psychology, sociology, anthropology, history, and political science, as well as within the clinical professions. This conclusion provides an opportunity to bring together several of the general themes raised in individual chapters and to consider the kinds of progress which have been made and can continue to be made in the study of life histories.

The first and perhaps most basic issue is that of the place of the study of individual lives within the social sciences. It is often suggested that studies of individual life histories are useful primarily as a source of hypotheses, which must then be investigated with more rigorous statistical and experimental studies. In contrast, this book has argued that it is necessary to consider three different levels of generality in the social sciences: the universal, the group, and the individual. The goals of social scientific inquiry include discovering what is true of persons-in-general, of groups of persons, and of individuals. It is a serious mistake to assume that resolving problems at the universal or group level will necessarily resolve problems at the individual level of analysis. Although advances at one level can sometimes have implications at the other levels, the three levels of analysis are partially autonomous, and there is a need to develop methods and procedures appropriate for each level of inquiry, including that of the in-depth study of particular individuals.

One of the more pervasive issues, encountered repeatedly in discussions in earlier chapters on alternative biographical accounts, alternative explanations in psychobiography, the case study method, and idiographic methods, is the problem of developing appropriate criteria and procedures for evaluating studies of individual lives. Far too frequently, work in this area is judged on criteria or standards derived from other domains, such as a psychometric criterion of "reliability" or an experimental criterion of efficacy in ruling out alternative causal hypotheses.

The application of inappropriate evaluative criteria has had damaging consequences in several ways, both in leading to disparagement of the study of individual lives and its neglect in favor of larger-scale quantitative and experimental studies, and in a failure to develop and apply those criteria and procedures which can lead to meaningful improvements in life history studies. Progress in the study of life histories requires the use of evaluative criteria which are relevant to its primary functions of presenting, organizing, and interpreting information about the course of experience in a single life. It is essential to move away from the attitude that case studies of individual lives can be used to prove anything or can be interpreted just as effectively with one theory as any other, and to move instead toward appropriately rigorous standards and criteria for the study of individual cases. A valuable development along these lines is suggested by the quasi-judicial approach (Bromley, 1977) in which evidence, inferences, and arguments are subjected to critical assessment by those holding opposing points of view. Rigorous use of the case study method requires that studies of individual lives be assessed not only on the internal criteria of coherence and interest but also on the external criteria of correspondence with the full range of available facts, their ability to stand up under tests of attempted falsification, and plausibility when weighed against alternative accounts and interpretations.

Inappropriate criteria for evaluating life history studies have sometimes come from inside the enterprise as well as from without. The field of life history studies is probably harmed more than helped by making exaggerated claims for it, such as that personal life-records provide "the *perfect* type of sociological material" (Thomas and Znaniecki, 1927, Vol. II, p. 1833), or that the life history is "the basic criterion against which all other methods should be tested" (Allport, 1961, p. 410). It is simply unconvincing to argue that the study of individual life histories is, in any absolute sense, better than experimental or statistical methods, as each approach is optimally useful for somewhat different goals and purposes. Correlational methods are best suited for studying co-variations among variables in the natural environment, while experimental methods are best suited for the testing of hypotheses about causal relationships. For these important purposes, these methods are substantially superior to life history studies. On the other hand, detailed studies of individual life histories are far more useful than experimental or correlational studies for tasks such as delineating the particulars of persons and their circumstances; conveying what individuals said, thought, felt, and did; representing the subjective meanings of actions and events; and developing context-specific or idiographic interpretations and explanations of individual behavior. The real contributions of life history studies are needlessly obscured by making exaggerated and indefensible claims for them.

Progress in the study of life histories can be seen in a number of different areas. Advances have been made in clarifying appropriate criteria to use in assessing alternative biographical accounts and alternative explanations, and in understanding how rational considerations interact with social factors in shaping the course of explanatory endeavors. In conceptualizing the life course, progress has been made in moving away from an oversimplified conception of character being permanently determined in childhood and moving toward analyses of the reciprocal influences of persons and their social-historical environments throughout the life course, resulting in a more complex understanding of the variety of possible connections between child-hood experience and adult behavior.

More rigorous standards and procedures for case studies have been developed, as illustrated in Bromley's (1977) quasi-judicial approach to case studies or Horowitz's (1979) sequential procedures for observation, formulation, discussion, re-observation, and re-formulation of clinical transactions. Methods for idiographic analysis have been expanded to include intra-individual correlational methods, idiographic measurement strategies, single-case experimental designs, narrative methods, the assisted autobiography, and configurational analysis. Finally, progress in psychobiography has been marked by a greater awareness of common methodological pitfalls, and by more sophisticated interpretations which avoid the reductionistic errors of considering the psychological at the expense of the social and historical, the pathological at the expense of the adaptive, and infantile determinants at the expense of life-long formative processes. Perhaps the most persuasive testimony to advances in the study of life histories is provided by the increasing number of insightful and intelligent psychobiographies, such as those of Henry James (Edel, 1953–72), Woodrow Wilson (George and George, 1964), Stalin (Tucker, 1973), T. E. Lawrence (Mack, 1976), Samuel Johnson (Bate, 1977), Hitler (Waite, 1977), and Beethoven (Solomon, 1977).

This review of progress is not at all to imply that there is nothing more to be done. On the contrary, there are a great many important problems in theory and method which remain unresolved, problems arising both within the field and in its relationships with other disciplines. Two limitations of the present work suggest directions for further inquiry. First, this book has focused primarily on qualitative, descriptive, and interpretive approaches to the study of life histories, which although important, are not the whole story. More also needs to be done with psychometric, quantitative, and statistical approaches to the study of lives. Second, my background in personality and clinical psychology has led to a relatively heavy emphasis on psychological issues in the study of life histories. There is, obviously, much more that can and should be done in the study of life histories by those with primary training and expertise in sociology, anthropology, history, and philosophy as well, contributing to greater illumination of the social, cultural, historical, and philosophical aspects of the enterprise.

Finally, in a view to the future, progress in the social and human sciences should be measured not solely by the development of more elaborate experimental and statistical procedures and the creation of increasingly comprehensive theories, but also by the development of more rigorous and insightful case studies and psychobiographies, and by advances in our understanding of individual lives.

References

Aaron, D. (Ed.). *Studies in biography*. Cambridge, Mass.: Harvard University Press, 1978.

Abraham, K. Giovanni Segantini: A psychoanalytical study (1911). In *Clinical Papers and Essays*. New York: Basic Books, 1955.

Abraham, K. Amenhotep IV (Ikhnaton): A psychoanalytic contribution to the understanding of his personality and the monotheistic cult of Aton. (Originally in *Imago*, 1912.) *Psychoanalytic Quarterly*, 1935, *4*, 537–569.

Adelson, J. Review of D. Stannard, *Shrinking history: On Freud and the failure of psychohistory*. *The American Spectator*, Jan. 1981, 31–33.

Ajzen, I. Intuitive theories of events and the effects of base-rate information on prediction. *Journal of Personality and Social Psychology*, 1977, *35*, 303–314.

Alfert, E. An idiographic analysis of personality differences between reactors to a vicariously experienced threat and reactors to a direct threat. *Journal of Experimental Research in Personality*, 1967, *2*, 200–207.

Alker, H. A. Is personality situationally specific or intrapsychically consistent? *Journal of Personality*, 1972, *40*, 1–16.

Allport, G. W. *Personality: A psychological interpretation*. New York: Holt, 1937.

Allport, G. W. *The use of personal documents in psychological science*. New York: Social Science Research Council, 1942.

Allport, G. W. *Pattern and growth in personality*. New York: Holt, Rinehart and Winston, 1961.

Allport, G. W. The general and the unique in psychological science. *Journal of Personality*, 1962, *30*, 405–422.

Allport, G. W. *Letters from Jenny.* New York: Harcourt, Brace and World, 1965.

Allport, G. W. Gordon W. Allport. In E. Boring & G. Lindzey (Eds.), *A history of psychology in autobiography* (Vol. 5). New York: Appleton-Century-Crofts, 1967.

Allport, G. W. & Vernon, P. E. *Studies in expressive movement.* New York: Macmillan, 1933.

Allport, G. W., Vernon, P. E., & Lindzey, G. *A study of values,* 3rd ed. Boston: Houghton Mifflin, 1960.

Altick, R. D. *Lives and letters: A history of literary biography in England and America.* New York: Knopf, 1965.

American Psychiatric Association, Report of the Task Force on Psychohistory. *The psychiatrist as psychohistorian.* Washington, D.C.: American Psychiatric Association, 1976.

Anderson, C. C. *Critical quests of Jesus.* Grand Rapids, Mich.: Eerdmans, 1969.

Anderson, H. (Ed.). *Jesus.* Englewood Cliffs, N.J.: Prentice-Hall, 1967.

Anderson, J. W. The methodology of psychological biography. *Journal of Interdisciplinary History,* 1981, *11,* 455–475. (a)

Anderson, J. W. Psychobiographical methodology: The case of William James. In L. Wheeler (Ed.), *Review of Personality and Social Psychology* (Vol. 2). Beverly Hills, Calif.: Sage, 1981. (b)

Anderson, T. H. Becoming sane with psychohistory. *The Historian,* 1978, *41,* 1–20.

Angell, R. A critical review of the development of the personal document method in sociology 1920–1940. In L. Gottschalk, C. Kluckhohn, & R. Angell, *The use of personal documents in history, anthropology and sociology.* New York: Social Science Research Council, 1945.

Angle, P. M. (Ed.). *A shelf of Lincoln books.* New Brunswick, N.J.: Rutgers University Press, 1947.

Ansbacher, H., et al. Lee Harvey Oswald: An Adlerian interpretation. *Psychoanalytic Review,* 1966, *53,* 55–68.

Anthony, K. *Margaret Fuller: A psychological biography.* New York: Harcourt, Brace, 1920.

Arendt, H. *Eichmann in Jerusalem: A report on the banality of evil,* rev. ed. New York: Penguin, 1964.

Argyle, M. & Little, B. Do personality traits apply to social behavior? *Journal for the Theory of Social Behavior,* 1972, 2, 1–35.

Arnold, M. (Ed.). *Steve Biko: Black Consciousness in South Africa.* New York: Vintage Books, 1978.

Aron, R. Relativism in history. In H. Meyerhoff (Ed.), *The philosophy of history in our time: An anthology*. New York: Doubleday Anchor, 1959.

Arthur, A. Z. A decision-making approach to psychological assessment in the clinic. *Journal of Consulting Psychology*, 1966, *30*, 435–438.

Atkinson, R. F. *Knowledge and explanation in history*. Ithaca, N.Y.: Cornell University Press, 1978.

Back, K. W. (Ed.). *Life course: Integrative theories and exemplary populations*. Boulder, Colo.: Westview Press, 1980.

Baldwin, A. L. Personal structure analysis: A statistical method for investigation of the single personality. *Journal of Abnormal and Social Psychology*, 1942, *37*, 163–183.

Baldwin, B. Personality dynamics: Ideographic (sic) and nomothetic data in the classroom. *Counselor Education & Supervision*, 1972, *12*, 75–78.

Baltes, P. B., Reese, H. W., & Lipsitt, L. P. Life-span developmental psychology. *Annual Review of Psychology*, 1980, *31*, 65–110.

Baltes, P. B. & Schaie, K. W. (Eds.), *Life-span developmental psychology: Personality and socialization*. New York: Academic Press, 1973.

Baltes, P. B. (Ed.). *Life-span development and behavior* (Vol. 1). New York: Academic Press, 1978.

Baltes, P. B. & Brim, O. G., Jr. (Eds.). *Life-span development and behavior* (Vol. 2). New York: Academic Press, 1979.

Bandura, A. *Social learning theory*. Englewood Cliffs, N.J.: Prentice-Hall, 1977.

Barber, J. D. *The presidential character: Predicting performance in the White House*. Englewood Cliffs, N.J.: Prentice-Hall, 1972; 2nd ed., 1977.

Barber, J. D. Comment: Qualls's nonsensical analysis of nonexistent works. *American Political Science Review*, 1977, *71*, 212–225.

Barnes, H. *Sartre and Flaubert*. Chicago: University of Chicago Press, 1981.

Barnes, H. E. Psychology and history: Some reasons for predicting their more active cooperation in the future. *American Journal of Psychology*, 1919, *30*, 337–376.

Barzun, J. *Clio and the doctors: Psycho-history, quanto-history and history*. Chicago: The University of Chicago Press, 1974.

Basch, M. F. Comment on Stannard's *Shrinking History*. *The Psychohistory Review*, 1980, *9*, 136–144.

Bate, W. J. *Samuel Johnson*. New York: Harcourt Brace Jovanovich, 1977.

Bath, K. E., Daly, D. L., & Nesselroade, J. R. Replicability of factors derived from individual p-technique analyses. *Multivariate Behavioral Research*, 1976, *11*, 147–156.

Beck, S. J. The science of personality: Nomothetic or idiographic? *Psychological Review*, 1953, *60*, 353–359.

Becker, H. *Outsiders: Studies in the sociology of deviance*. New York: Free Press, 1963.

Becker, H. Introduction. In C. Shaw, *The jack-roller*. Chicago: University of Chicago Press, 1966.

Bell, Q. *Virginia Woolf: A biography*. New York: Harcourt Brace Jovanovich, 1972.

Bem, D. & Allen, A. On predicting some of the people some of the time: The search for cross-situational consistencies in behavior. *Psychological Review*, 1974, *81*, 506–520.

Bentley, G. E. *Shakespeare: A biographical handbook*. New Haven: Yale University Press, 1961.

Berger, P. L. & Luckman, T. *The social construction of reality: A treatise in the sociology of knowledge*. New York: Anchor Books, 1966.

Bergin, A. & Garfield, S. (Eds.). *Handbook of psychotherapy and behavior change: An empirical analysis*. New York: Wiley, 1971.

Bergmann, M. S. Limitations of method in psychoanalytic biography: A historical inquiry. *Journal of the American Psychoanalytic Association*, 1973, *21*, 833–850.

Bertaux, D. (Ed.). *Biography and society: The life history approach in the social sciences*. Beverly Hills, Calif.: Sage, 1981.

Binswanger, L. The case of Ellen West. In May, R., Angel, E., & Ellenberger, H. F. (Eds.), *Existence*. New York: Basic Books, 1958.

Birren, J. E. & Schaie, K. W. (Eds.). *Handbook of the psychology of aging*. New York: Reinhold-Van Nostrand, 1977.

Blalock, H. *Causal inferences in nonexperimental research*. New York: Norton, 1964.

Blau, P. M. & Duncan, O. D. *The American occupational structure*. New York: Wiley, 1967.

Block, J. *The Q-sort method in personality assessment and psychiatric research*. Springfield, Ill.: Charles C. Thomas, 1961.

Block, J. *Lives through time*. Berkeley, Calif.: Bancroft Books, 1971.

Block, J. Advancing the psychology of personality: Paradigmatic shift or improving the quality of research? In D. Magnusson & N. Endler (Eds.), *Personality at the crossroads*. Hillsdale, N.J.: Erlbaum, 1977.

Bloom, B. *Stability and change in human characteristics*. New York: Wiley, 1964.

Blumer, H. *An appraisal of Thomas and Znaniecki's The Polish Peasant in Europe and America.* New York: Social Science Research Council, 1939.

Bolgar, H. The case study method. In B. Wolman (Ed.), *Handbook of Clinical Psychology,* New York: McGraw-Hill, 1965.

Bowen, C. D. *Biography: The craft and the calling.* Boston: Little, Brown, 1969.

Bower, G. H. Experiments on story comprehension and recall. *Discourse Processes,* 1978, *1,* 211–231.

Bowers, K. Situationism in psychology: An analysis and a critique. *Psychological Review,* 1973, *80,* 307–336.

Bowlby, J. *Maternal care and mental health.* Geneva, Switzerland: World Health Organization, 1952.

Brecher, E. M. *Licit and illicit drugs.* Boston: Little, Brown, 1972.

Brekstad, A. Factors influencing the reliability of anamnestic recall. *Child Development,* 1966, *37,* 603–612.

Brim, O. G., Jr. & Kagan, J. (Eds.). *Constancy and change in human development.* Cambridge, Mass.: Harvard University Press, 1980.

Brim, O. G., Jr. & Wheeler, S. *Socialization after childhood.* New York: Wiley, 1966.

Brink, T. L. The case of Hitler: An Adlerian perspective on psychohistory. *Journal of Individual Psychology,* 1975, *31,* 23–31.

Brodie, B. A psychoanalytic intrepretation of Woodrow Wilson. *World Politics,* 1957, *9,* 413–422.

Brodie, F. *Richard Nixon: The shaping of his character,* New York: Norton, 1981.

Bromley, D. B. *Personality description in ordinary language.* New York: Wiley, 1977.

Bronfenbrenner, U. & Mahoney, M. *Influences on human development,* 2nd ed., Hinsdale, Ill.: Dryden, 1975.

Broverman, D. M. Cognitive style and intra-individual variation in abilities. *Journal of Personality,* 1960, *28,* 240–256.

Broverman, D. M. Normative and ipsative measurement in psychology. *Psychological Review,* 1962, *69,* 295–305.

Bühler, C. *Der menschliche Lebenslauf als psychologisches Problem* (The human course of life as a psychological problem). Leipzig: Hirzel, 1933.

Bühler, C. & Massarik, F. (Eds.). *The course of human life.* New York: Springer, 1968.

Burton, A. & Harris, R. (Eds.). *Clinical studies of personality* (Vol. 1). New York: Harper & Row, 1955.

Butterfield, S. *Black autobiography in America*. Amherst: University of Massachusetts Press, 1974.

Calder, R. *Medicine and man*. New York: Signet, 1958.

Campbell, D. T. "Degrees of freedom" and the case study. *Comparative Political Studies*, 1975, *8*, 178–193.

Campbell, D. T. & Stanley, J. C. *Experimental and quasi-experimental designs for research*. Chicago: Rand McNally, 1966.

Carlsmith, J. M., Ellsworth, P. C., & Aronson, E. *Methods of research in social psychology*. Reading, Mass.: Addison-Wesley, 1976.

Carlson, R. Where is the person in personality research? *Psychological Bulletin*, 1971, *75*, 203–219.

Carlson, R. Studies in script theory: I. Adult analogs of a childhood nuclear scene. *Journal of Personality and Social Psychology*, 1981, *40*, 501–510.

Cartwright, D. & French, J. R. P., Jr. The reliability of life-history studies. *Character & Personality*, 1939, *8*, 110–119.

Cattell, R. B. *The description and measurement of personality*. Yonkers-on-Hudson, N.Y.: World Book, 1946.

Cattell, R. B. (Ed.). *Handbook of multivariate experimental psychology*. Chicago: Rand McNally, 1966.

Chassan, J. B. *Research design in clinical psychology and psychiatry*. New York: Appleton-Century-Crofts, 1967. Second edition, revised and enlarged, New York: Irvington, 1979.

Chatman, S. *Story and discourse: Narrative structure in fiction and film*. Ithaca, N.Y.: Cornell University Press, 1978.

Chein, I., Gerard, D., Lee, R., & Rosenfeld, E. *The road to H: Narcotics, delinquency, and social policy*. New York: Basic Books, 1964.

Chesen, E. *President Nixon's psychiatric profile*. New York: Peter H. Wyden, 1973.

Cheshire, N. M. *The nature of psychodynamic interpretation*. London: Wiley, 1975.

Cheshire, N. M. A big hand for Little Hans. *Bulletin of the British Psychological Society*, 1979, *32*, 320–323.

Clark, L. P. Unconscious motives underlying the personalities of great statesmen. I. A psychologic study of Abraham Lincoln. *Psychoanalytic Review*, 1923, *10*, 56–69.

Clark, L. P. *Lincoln: A psychobiography*. New York: Scribner's, 1933.

Clarke, A. M. & Clarke, A. D. B. (Eds.). *Early experience: Myth and evidence*. New York: Free Press, 1976.

Clausen, J. Drug addiction. In R. Merton & R. Nisbet (Eds.), *Contemporary social problems*, 2nd ed. New York: Harcourt, Brace & World, 1966.

Clausen, J. (Ed.). *Socialization and society*. Boston: Little, Brown, 1968.

Clausen, J. The life course of individuals. In M. Riley et al. (Eds.), *Aging and society* (Vol. 3). New York: Russell Sage, 1972.

Clifford, J. L. (Ed.). *Biography as an art*. New York: Oxford University Press, 1962.

Clifford, J. L. *From puzzles to portraits: Problems of a literary biographer*. Chapel Hill: University of North Carolina Press, 1970.

Clinch, N. G. *The Kennedy neurosis*. New York: Grosset and Dunlap, 1973.

Cody, J. *After great pain: The inner life of Emily Dickinson*. Cambridge, Mass.: Harvard University Press, 1971.

Cohler, B. J. Personal narrative and life-course. In P. Baltes & O. G. Brim, Jr. (Eds.), *Life-span development and behavior* (Vol. 4). New York: Academic Press, 1982.

Coles, R. On psychohistory. In *The Mind's Fate*. Boston: Little, Brown and Co., 1975.

Collingwood, R. G. *The idea of history*. New York: Oxford University Press, 1946.

Conrad, H. S. The validity of personality ratings of preschool children. *Journal of Educational Psychology*, 1932, *23*, 671–680.

Conway, A. V. Little Hans: Misrepresentation of the evidence? *Bulletin of the British Psychological Society*, 1978, *31*, 285–287.

Cook, T. D. & Campbell, D. T. *Quasi-experimentation*. Chicago: Rand McNally, 1979.

Cooley, T. *Educated lives: The rise of modern autobiography in America*. Columbus: Ohio State University Press, 1976.

Cremerius, J. (Ed.). *Neurose und genialität: Psychoanalytische biographien*. Frankfurt am Main: S. Fischer, 1971.

Crews, F. *Sins of the fathers: Hawthorne's psychological themes*. New York: Oxford University Press, 1966.

Crews, F. *Out of my system: Psychoanalysis, ideology, and critical method*. New York: Oxford University Press, 1975.

Crews, F. Analysis terminable. *Commentary*, 1980, *70*, 25–34.

Cronbach, L. Beyond the two disciplines of scientific psychology. *American Psychologist*, 1975, *30*, 116–127.

Crosby, F. Evaluating psychohistorical explanations. *Psychohistory Review*, 1979, *7*(4), 6–16.

Crosby, F. & Crosby, T. L. Psychobiography and psychohistory. In S. Long (Ed.), *Handbook of political behavior* (Vol. 1). New York: Plenum, 1981.

Crosby, T. L. Comment on Stannard's *Shrinking History*. *Psychohistory Review*, 1980, *9*, 145–150.

Dailey, C. A. The practical utility of the clinical report. *Journal of Consulting Psychology*, 1953, *17*, 297–302.

Dailey, C. A. *The assessment of lives*. San Francisco: Jossey-Bass, 1971.

Danto, A. C. *Analytical philosophy of history*. London: Cambridge University Press, 1965.

Datan, N. & Ginsberg, L. H. (Eds.). *Life-span developmental psychology: Normative life crises*. New York: Academic Press, 1975.

Davidson, P. O. & Costello, C. G. *N = 1: Experimental studies of single cases*. New York: Van Nostrand-Reinhold, 1969.

Davis, G. The early years of Theodore Roosevelt: A study in character formation. *History of Childhood Quarterly*, 1975, *II*, 461–492.

Delehaye, H. *The legends of the saints* (1907). Reprinted by University of Notre Dame Press, 1961.

DeMause, L. (Ed.). *A bibliography of psychohistory*. New York: Garland, 1975.

Denzin, N. K. *The research act*. Chicago: Aldine, 1970.

Denzin, N. K. *The research act*. 2nd edition, New York: McGraw-Hill, 1978.

DeVoto, B. The skeptical biographer. *Harper's Magazine*, 1933, *166*, 181–192.

De Waele, J.-P. *La méthode des cas programmés*. Bruxelles: Dessart, 1971.

De Waele, J.-P. & Harré, R. Autobiography as a psychological method. In G. P. Ginsburg (Ed.), *Emerging strategies in social psychological research*. New York: Wiley, 1979.

Dewald, P. A. *The psychoanalytic process: A case illustration*. New York: Basic Books, 1972.

Dollard, J. *Criteria for the life history*. New Haven: Yale University Press, 1935.

Dooley, L. Psychoanalytic studies of genius. *American Journal of Psychology*, 1916, 27, 363–416.

Dray, W. H. *Laws and explanation in history*. Oxford: Oxford University Press, 1957.

Dray, W. H. The historian's problem of selection. In E. Nagel, P. Suppes & A. Tarski (Eds.), *Logic, methodology, and philosophy of science*. Stanford: Stanford University Press, 1962.

Dray, W. H. *Philosophy of history*. Englewood Cliffs, N.J.: Prentice-Hall, 1964.

Dray, W. H. On the nature of narrative in historiography. *History and Theory*, 1971, X, 153–171.

DuBois, C. A. *The people of Alor*. Minneapolis: University of Minnesota Press, 1944.

Dukes, W. F. N = 1. *Psychological Bulletin,* 1965, *64,* 75–79.

Duncan, O. D. *Introduction to structural equation models.* New York: Academic Press, 1975.

Duvall, H., Locke, B., & Brill, L. Follow-up study of narcotic drug addicts five years after hospitalization. *Public Health Reports,* 1963, *78,* 185–193.

Dyk, W. *Son of Old Man Hat: A Navaho autobiography recorded by Walter Dyk.* New York: Harcourt, 1938.

Easterlin, R. A. *Birth and fortune: The impact of numbers on personal welfare.* New York: Basic Books, 1980.

Edel, L. *Henry James,* 5 vols. Philadelphia: Lippincott, 1953–72.

Edel, L. *Literary biography.* Bloomington: Indiana University Press, 1959.

Eichorn, D., Clausen, J., Haan, N., Honzik, M., & Mussen, P. (Eds.). *Present and past in middle life.* New York: Academic Press, 1981.

Ekehammar, B. Interactionism in personality from a historical perspective. *Psychological Bulletin,* 1974, *81,* 1026–1048.

Elder, G. H., Jr. *Children of the Great Depression.* Chicago: University of Chicago Press, 1974.

Elder, G. H., Jr. Age differentiation and the life course. *Annual review of sociology* (Vol. 1). Palo Alto, Calif.: Annual Reviews, 1975.

Elder, G. H., Jr. Family history and the life course. *Journal of Family History,* 1977, *2,* 279–304.

Elder, G. H., Jr. History and the family: The discovery of complexity. *Journal of Marriage and the Family,* 1981, *43,* 489–519. (a)

Elder, G. H., Jr. History and the life course. In D. Bertaux (Ed.), *Biography and society.* Beverly Hills, Calif.: Sage, 1981. (b)

Elms, A. C. *Personality in politics.* New York: Harcourt Brace Jovanovich, 1976.

Elstein, A. S., Shulman, L. S., & Sprafka, S. A. *Medical problem-solving: An analysis of clinical reasoning.* Cambridge, Mass.: Harvard University Press, 1978.

Emmerich, W. Personality development and concepts of structure. *Child Development,* 1968, *39,* 671–690.

Endler, N. & Magnusson, D. (Eds.). *Interactional psychology and personality.* Washington, D.C.: Hemisphere, 1976.

Erikson, E. H. *Young man Luther.* New York: Norton, 1958.

Erikson, E. H. *Childhood and society* (2nd ed.). New York: Norton, 1963.

Erikson, E. H. *Gandhi's truth.* New York: Norton, 1969.

Erikson, E. H. *Life history and the historical moment.* New York: Norton, 1975.

Etiemble, R. *Le mythe de Rimbaud.* Paris: Gallimard, 1961.

Eysenck, H. J. The science of personality: Nomothetic! *Psychological Review,* 1954, *61,* 339–342.

Eysenck, H. J. (Ed.). *Case studies in behaviour therapy.* London: Routledge & Kegan Paul, 1976.

Fact magazine. The unconscious of a conservative: A special issue on the mind of Barry Goldwater. *Fact,* 1964, *1*(5), 1–64.

Falk, J. L. Issues distinguishing idiographic from nomothetic approaches to personality theory. *Psychological Review,* 1956, *63,* 53–62.

Fearing, F. Psychological studies of historical personalities. *Psychological Bulletin,* 1927, *24,* 521–539.

Featherman, D. L. & Hauser, R. M. *Opportunity and change.* New York: Academic Press, 1978.

Feldman, H. Ideological supports to becoming and remaining a heroin addict. *Journal of Health and Social Behavior,* 1968, *9,* 131–139.

Fisher, S. & Greenberg, R. P. *The scientific credibility of Freud's theories and therapy.* New York: Basic Books, 1977.

Frank, G. Finding the common denominator: A phenomenological critique of life history method. *Ethos,* 1979, *7*(1), 68–94.

Freeman, J. M. *Untouchable: An Indian life history.* Stanford: Stanford University Press, 1979.

Freud, S. Analysis of a phobia in a five-year-old boy (1909). In S. Freud. *The sexual enlightenment of children.* New York: Collier Books, 1963. (a)

Freud, S. *Leonardo da Vinci and a memory of his childhood* (1910). *Standard Edition, 12:* 3–82. London: Hogarth Press, 1957.

Freud, S. Psychoanalytic notes upon an autobiographical account of a case of paranoia (dementia paranoides) (1911). In S. Freud, *Three case histories.* New York: Collier Books, 1963. (b)

Freud, S. *An outline of psychoanalysis* (1938). *Standard Edition, 23:* 141–207. London: Hogarth Press, 1969.

Freud, S. *Three Case Histories.* New York: Collier Books, 1963. (b)

Friedlander, S. *History and psychoanalysis* (1975). English translation, 1978. New York: Holmes & Meier, 1978.

Gallie, W. B. *Philosophy and the historical understanding.* New York: Schocken, 1964.

Gambrill, E. D. *Behavior modification: Handbook of assessment, intervention, and evaluation.* San Francisco: Jossey-Bass, 1977.

Garraty, J. A. The interrelations of psychology and biography. *Psychological Bulletin,* 1954, *51,* 569–582.

Garraty, J. A. Gordon Allport's rules for the preparation of life histories and case studies. *Biography,* 1981, *4,* 283–292.

Garraty, J. A. *The nature of biography.* New York: Vintage Books, 1957.

Gatzke, H. W. Hitler and psychohistory. *American Historical Review,* 1973, *78,* 394–401.

Gedo, J. E. The methodology of psychoanalytic biography. *Journal of the American Psychoanalytic Association,* 1972, *20,* 638–649.

George, A. L. Some uses of dynamic psychology in political biography. In F. L. Greenstein & M. Lerner (Eds.), *A source book for the study of personality and politics.* Chicago: Markham, 1971.

George, A. L. Assessing presidential character. *World Politics,* 1974, *26,* 234–282.

George, A. L. & George, J. L. *Woodrow Wilson and Colonel House: A personality study* (1956). New York: Dover, 1964.

George, A. L. & George, J. L. Psycho-McCarthyism. *Psychology Today,* 1973, *7*(1), 94–98.

George, J. L. & George, A. L. *Woodrow Wilson and Colonel House:* A reply to Weinstein, Anderson and Link. *Political Science Quarterly,* 1981–82, *96,* 641–665.

Gergen, K. J. Social psychology as history. *Journal of Personality and Social Psychology,* 1973, *26,* 309–320.

Gergen, K. J. Stability, change, and chance in understanding human development. In N. Datan & H. Reese (Eds.), *Life-span developmental psychology: Dialectical perspectives on experimental research.* New York: Academic Press, 1977.

Gilmore, W. The methodology of psychohistory: An annotated bibliography. *The Psychohistory Review,* 1976, *5*(2), 4–33.

Gilmore, W. Paths recently crossed: Alternatives to psychoanalytic psychohistory. *The Psychohistory Review,* 1979, *7*(3), 43–49. (a).

Gilmore, W. Paths recently crossed: Alternatives to psychoanalytic psychohistory (continued). *The Psychohistory Review,* 1979, *7*(4), 26–42. (b).

Gittings, R. *The nature of biography.* Seattle: University of Washington Press, 1978.

Glad, B. Contributions of psychobiography. In J. Knutson (Ed.), *Handbook of political psychology.* San Francisco: Jossey-Bass, 1973.

Goldberg, L. Simple models or simple processes? Some research on clinical judgments. *American Psychologist,* 1968, *23,* 483–496.

Golding, S. Flies in the ointment: Methodological problems in the analysis of the percentage of variance due to persons and situations. *Psychological Bulletin,* 1975, *82,* 278–288.

Goode, E. The major drugs of use among adolescents and young adults. In E. Harms (Ed.), *Drugs and youth: The challenge of today.* Elmsford, N.Y.: Pergamon, 1973.

Goodman, N. *Fact, fiction, and forecast,* 3rd ed. Indianapolis: Bobbs-Merrill, 1973.

Gordon, M. (Ed.). *The American family in social-historical perspective*, 2nd ed. New York: St. Martin's Press, 1978.

Gottschalk, L. Categories of historiographical generalization. In L. Gottschalk (Ed.), *Generalization in the writing of history*. Chicago: University of Chicago Press, 1963.

Gottschalk, L., Kluckhohn, D., & Angell, R. *The use of personal documents in history, anthropology and sociology*. New York: Social Science Research Council, 1945.

Gough, H. G. Clinical versus statistical prediction in psychology. In L. Postman (Ed.), *Psychology in the making*. New York: Knopf, 1962.

Gould, R. L. *Transformations: Growth and change in adult life*. New York: Simon and Schuster, 1978.

Goulet, L. R. & Baltes, P. B. (Eds.). *Life-span developmental psychology: Research and theory*. New York: Academic Press, 1970.

Graf, M. Richard Wagner in the "Flying Dutchman." A contribution to the psychology of artistic creation (English translation). *Schriften zur angenwandten Seelunkunde*. 1911, *IX*, 45 pages.

Greenacre, P. *Swift and Carroll: A psychoanalytic study of two lives*. New York: International Universities Press, 1955.

Greenstein, F. *Personality and politics: Problems of evidence, inference, and conceptualization*, new ed. New York: Norton, 1975. (a)

Greenstein, F. Personality and politics. In F. Greenstein & N. Polsby (Eds.), *The handbook of political science* (Vol. 2). Reading, Mass.: Addison-Wesley, 1975. (b)

Greenwald, H. (Ed.). *Great cases in psychoanalysis*. New York: Ballantine Books, 1959.

Gruber, H. E. *Darwin on man: A psychological study of scientific creativity*, 2nd ed. Chicago: University of Chicago Press, 1981.

Grünbaum, A. Epistemological liabilities of the clinical appraisal of psychoanalytic theory. In *Psychoanalysis and Contemporary Thought*, 1979, *2*, 451–526.

Guttmacher, M. G. *America's last king: An interpretation of the madness of George III*. New York: Scribner's, 1941.

Haan, N. *Coping and defending: Processes of self-environment organization*. New York: Academic Press, 1977.

Hall, C. S. & Lindzey, G. *Theories of Personality*, 3rd ed. New York: Wiley, 1978.

Hareven, T. K. (Ed.). *Transitions: The family and the life course in historical perspective*. New York: Academic Press, 1978.

Harlow, R. V. *Samuel Adams*. New York: Holt, 1923.

Hausner, G. *Justice in Jerusalem*. New York: Holocaust Library, 1966.

Hempel, C. G. *Aspects of scientific explanation*. New York: Free Press, 1965.

Hempel, C. G. *Philosophy of natural science*. Englewood Cliffs, N.J.: Prentice-Hall, 1966.

Herbst, P. G. *Behavioural worlds: The study of single cases*. London: Tavistock Publications, 1970.

Hermann, M. G. (Ed.). *A psychological examination of political leaders*. New York: Free Press, 1977.

Herndon, W. H. & Weik, J. W. *Herndon's Lincoln: The true story of a great life*, 3 vols. Chicago and New York: Belford, Clarke & Co., 1889.

Hersen, M. & Barlow, D. H. *Single case experimental designs*. New York: Pergamon Press, 1976.

Hexter, J. H. *The history primer*. New York: Basic Books, 1971.

Hirsch, E. D., Jr. *Validity in interpretation*. New Haven, Conn.: Yale University Press, 1967.

Hirsch, W. *Conclusions of a psychiatrist*. New York, 1912.

Historical Figures Assessment Collaborative. Assessing historical figures: The use of observer-based personality descriptions. *Historical Methods Newsletter*, 1977, *10*(2), 66–76.

Hitschmann, E. Some psycho-analytic aspects of biography. *The International Journal of Psycho-Analysis*. 1956, *37*, 265–269.

Hofling, C. K. Current problems in psychohistory. *Comprehensive Psychiatry*, 1976, *17*(1), 227–239.

Hogan, D. P. The variable order of events in the life course. *American Sociological Review*, 1978, *43*, 573–586.

Hogan, D. P. *Transitions and social change: The early lives of American men*. New York: Academic Press, 1981.

Hogan, R. *Personality theory: The personological tradition*. Englewood Cliffs, N.J.: Prentice-Hall, 1976.

Holt, R. R. Individuality and generalization in the psychology of personality. *Journal of Personality*, 1962, *30*, 377–404.

Holt, R. R. *Methods in clinical psychology, Vol. 2: Prediction and research*. New York: Plenum, 1978.

Hook, S. *The hero in history*. Boston: Beacon, 1955. (Originally published 1943.)

Hook, S. (Ed.). *Philosophy and history*. New York: New York University Press, 1963.

Horner, A. The evolution of goals in the life of Clarence Darrow. In C. Bühler & F. Massarik (Eds.), *The course of human life*. New York: Springer, 1968.

Horowitz, M. J. *States of mind: Analysis of change in psychotherapy.* New York: Plenum Medical, 1979.

Hughes, H. S. *History as art and as science.* New York: Harper Torchbooks, 1964.

Hundert, E. J. History, psychology, and the study of deviant behavior. *Journal of Interdisciplinary History,* 1972, *2*(4), 453–472.

Hunt, G. & Odoroff, M. Follow-up study of narcotic drug addiction after hospitalization. *Public Health Reports,* 1962, 77, 41–54.

Izenberg, G. Psychohistory and intellectual history. *History and Theory,* 1975, *14,* 139–155.

Janis, I. L. *Victims of groupthink.* Boston: Houghton Mifflin, 1972.

Janis, I. L. & Mann, L. *Decision making.* New York: Free Press, 1977.

Jayaratne, S. & Levy, R. L. *Empirical clinical practice.* New York: Columbia University Press, 1979.

Jervis, R. *Perception and misperception in international politics.* Princeton: Princeton University Press, 1976.

Johnson, E. *One mighty torrent: The drama of biography.* New York: Macmillan, 1937.

Jones, E. The Oedipus complex as an explanation of Hamlet's mystery: A study in motive. *American Journal of Psychology,* 1910, *21,* 72–113.

Jones, E. E., et al. *Attribution: Perceiving the causes of behavior.* Morristown, N.J.: General Learning Press, 1971.

Jones, M. C., Bayley, N., Macfarlane, J., & Honzik, M. (Eds.). *The course of human development.* New York: Wiley, 1971.

Judson, H. F. *Heroin addiction: What Americans can learn from the English experience.* New York: Vintage, 1974.

Kanzer, M. & Glenn, J. (Eds.). *Freud and his patients.* New York: Aronson, 1980.

Karpas, M. J. Socrates in the light of modern psychopathology. *Journal of Abnormal Psychology,* 1915, *10,* 185–200.

Kazdin, A. E. *Research design in clinical psychology.* New York: Harper & Row, 1980.

Kellerman, B. Mentoring in political life: The case of Willy Brandt. *American Political Science Review,* 1978, *72,* 422–433.

Kelly, E. L. Consistency of the adult personality. *American Psychologist,* 1955, *10,* 659–681.

Kelly, G. A. *The psychology of personal constructs.* New York: Norton, 1955.

Kendall, P. M. *The art of biography.* New York: Norton, 1965.

Kenrick, D. T. & Stringfield, D. O. Personality traits and the eye of the beholder: Crossing some traditional philosophical boundaries in the search for consistency in all of the people. *Psychological Review*, 1980, *87*, 88–104.

Kilpatrick, F. P. & Cantril, H. Self-anchoring scale: A measure of the individual's unique reality world. *Journal of Individual Psychology*, 1960, *16*, 158–170.

Kitchener, R. F. Epigenesis: The role of biological models in developmental psychology. *Human Development*, 1978, *21*, 141–160.

Klein, D. F. & Davis, J. M. *Diagnosis and drug treatment of psychiatric disorders*. Baltimore, Md.: Williams & Wilkins, 1969.

Kline, P. *Fact and fantasy in Freudian theory*. London: Methuen, 1972.

Kluckhohn, C. The personal document in anthropological science. In L. Gottschalk et al. *The use of personal documents in history, anthropology, and sociology*. New York: Social Science Research Council, 1945.

Kluckhohn, C. & Murray, H. A. Personality formation: The determinants. In C. Kluckhohn, H. Murray, & D. Schneider (Eds.), *Personality in nature, society and culture*. New York: Knopf, 1953.

Kohlberg, L. Stage and sequence: The cognitive-developmental approach to socialization. In D. Goslin (Ed.), *Handbook of socialization theory and research*. Chicago: Rand McNally, 1969.

Kohut, H. Beyond the bounds of the basic rule. *Journal of the American Psychoanalytic Association*, 1960, *8*, 567–586.

Kratochwill, T. R. (Ed.). *Single subject research*. New York: Academic Press, 1978.

Krech, D. Discussion: Theory and reduction. *Psychological Review*, 1955, *62*, 229–231.

Krutch, J. W. *Edgar Allan Poe*. New York: Knopf, 1926.

Kuhn, T. S. *The structure of scientific revolutions*, 2nd ed. Chicago: University of Chicago Press, 1970.

Kurtines, W., Hogan, R., & Weiss, D. Personality dynamics of heroin use. *Journal of Abnormal Psychology*, 1975, *84*, 87–89.

Lamiell, J. T. Toward an idiothetic psychology of personality. *American Psychologist*, 1981, *36*, 276–289.

Langer, Walter C. *The Mind of Adolf Hitler*. New York: Basic Books, 1972.

Langer, William L. The next assignment. *American Historical Review*, 1958, *63*(2), 283–304.

Langness, L. L. *The life history in anthropological science*. New York: Holt, Rinehart & Winston, 1965.

Langness, L. L. & Frank, G. *Lives: An anthropological approach to biography*. Novato, Calif.: Chandler & Sharp Publishers, 1981.

Lasswell, H. D. *Power and personality*. New York: Norton, 1948.

Laudan, L. *Progress and its problems*. Berkeley: University of California Press, 1977.

Lazarus, R. & Launier, R. Stress-related transactions between person and environment. In L. Pervin & M. Lewis (Eds.), *Internal and external determinants of behavior*. New York: Plenum, 1978.

Leighton, A. & Leighton, D. *Gregorio The Hand-Trembler: A psychobiological study of a Navaho Indian*. Papers of the Peabody Museum, Harvard University, *40*, 1949.

Leitenberg, H. The use of single-case methodology in psychotherapy research. *Journal of Abnormal Psychology*, 1973, *82*, 87–101.

Lemert, E. A. *Social pathology*. New York: McGraw-Hill, 1951.

Leon, G. R. *Case histories of deviant behavior*, 2nd ed. Boston: Allyn and Bacon, 1977.

L'Etang, H. *The pathology of leadership*. New York: Hawthorn, 1970.

LeVine, R. A. Adulthood among the Gusii of Kenya. In N. J. Smelser & E. H. Erikson (Eds.), *Themes of work and love in adulthood*. Cambridge, Mass.: Harvard University Press, 1980.

Levinson, D. J. Exploration in biography: Evolution of the individual life structure in adulthood. In A. Rabin et al. (Eds.), *Further explorations in personality*. New York: Wiley, 1981.

Levinson, D. J., Darrow, C., Klein, E., Levinson, M., & McKee, B. *The seasons of a man's life*. New York: Knopf, 1978.

Levy, L. *Conceptions of personality*. New York: Random House, 1970.

Lewin, K. *Field theory in social science*. New York: Harper Torchbooks, 1951.

Lewis, O. *The children of Sanchez: Autobiography of a Mexican family*. New York: Random House, 1961.

Lewis, O., Lewis, R. M., & Rigdon, S. *Four men*. Urbana: University of Illinois Press, 1977. (a)

Lewis, O., Lewis, R. M., & Rigdon, S. *Four women*. Urbana: University of Illinois Press, 1977. (b)

Liebert, R. M. & Spiegler, M. D. *Personality: Strategies and issues*. Homewood, Ill.: Dorsey Press, 1978.

Lifton, R. J. & Olson, E. (Eds.). *Explorations in psychohistory*. New York: Simon and Schuster, 1974.

Lifton, R. J. *Death in life: Survivors of Hiroshima*. New York: Random House, 1967.

Light, D. *Becoming psychiatrists*. New York: Norton, 1980.

Lindesmith, A. *Opiate addiction*. Bloomington, Ind.: Principia, 1947.

Lindner, R. *The fifty-minute hour*. New York: Bantam, 1954.

Loevinger, J. *Ego development*. San Francisco: Jossey-Bass, 1976.

Loewenberg, P. Review of S. Friedlander, *Historie et psychoanalyse*

(History and psychoanalysis). *American Historical Review*, 1976, *81*(4), 821–822.

Loewenberg, P. The psychohistorical origins of the Nazi youth cohort. *American Historical Review*, 1971, *76*, 1457–1502.

Loewenberg, P. Psychoanalytic models of history: Freud and after. Paper presented at the conference on "History and Psychology," Stanford University, May 7–9, 1982.

Lonner, W. The search for psychological universals. In H. C. Triandis & W. W. Lambert (Eds.), *The Handbook of cross-cultural psychology* (Vol. 1). Boston: Allyn and Bacon, 1979.

Lowenthal, M., Thurnher, M., & Chiriboga, D. *Four stages of life.* San Francisco: Jossey-Bass, 1975.

Lubin, A. J. *Stranger on the earth: A psychological biography of Vincent Van Gogh.* New York: Holt, Rinehart & Winston, 1972.

Luborsky, L. & Mintz, J. The contribution of P-technique to personality, psychotherapy, and psychosomatic research. In R. M. Dreger (Ed.), *Multivariate personality research: Contributions to the understanding of personality in honor of Raymond B. Cattell.* Baton Rouge, La.: Claitor's Publishing Division, 1972.

Lundberg, G. A. Case work and the statistical method. *Social Forces*, 1926, *5*, 61–65.

Maas, H. S. & Kuypers, J. A. *From thirty to seventy.* San Francisco: Jossey-Bass, 1974.

Macalpine, I. & Hunter, R. *George III and the mad business.* New York: Pantheon, 1969.

McAuliffe, W. & Gordon, R. A test of Lindesmith's theory of addiction: The frequency of euphoria among long-term addicts. *American Journal of Sociology*, 1974, *79*, 795–840.

McCord, J. A thirty-year follow-up of treatment effects. *American Psychologist*, 1978, *33*, 284–289.

McGlothlin, W. Drug use and abuse. *Annual Review of Psychology*, 1975, *26*, 45–64.

Mack, J. E. Psychoanalysis and historical biography. *Journal of the American Psychoanalytic Association*, 1971, *19*, 143–179.

Mack, J. E. *A prince of our disorder: The life of T. E. Lawrence.* Boston: Little, Brown, 1976.

Magnusson, D. & Endler, N. *Personality at the crossroads: Current issues in interactional psychology.* Hillsdale, N.J.: Erlbaum, 1977.

Mandelbaum, D. G. The study of life history: Gandhi. *Current Anthropology*, 1973, *14*(3), 177–206.

Mandelbaum, M. *The anatomy of historical knowledge.* Baltimore: The Johns Hopkins University Press, 1977.

Manuel, F. E. *A portrait of Isaac Newton*. Cambridge, Mass.: Harvard University Press, 1968.

Manuel, F. E. & Manuel, F. P. *Utopian thought in the Western World*. Cambridge, Mass.: Harvard University Press, 1979.

Marceil, J. C. Implicit dimensions of idiography and nomothesis: A reformulation. *American Psychologist*, 1977, *32*, 1046–1055.

Marti-Ibanez, F. *Centaur: Essays on the history of medical ideas*. New York: M. D. Publications, 1958.

Martin, A. R. Adapting psychoanalytic procedure to the uniqueness of the individual. *The American Journal of Psychoanalysis*, 1978, *38*, 99–110.

Mazlish, B. *In search of Nixon: A psychohistorical inquiry* (1972). Baltimore: Penguin Books, 1973.

Mazlish, B. *James and John Stuart Mill: Father and son in the nineteenth century*. New York: Basic Books, 1975.

Mazlish, B. *The revolutionary ascetic: Evolution of a political type*. New York: Basic Books, 1976.

Mazlish, B. (Ed.). *Psychoanalysis and history,* rev. ed. New York: Grosset & Dunlap, 1971.

Mazlish, B. Clio on the couch: Prolegomena to psychohistory. *Encounter,* 1968, *31*, 46–64.

Medawar, P. B. Victims of psychiatry. *New York Review of Books,* January 23, 1975, 21.

Mednick, S. A. & Baert, A. E. (Eds.). *Prospective longitudinal research: An empirical basis for the primary prevention of psychosocial disorders*. Oxford: Oxford University Press, 1981.

Meehl, P. E. *Clinical versus statistical prediction*. Minneapolis: University of Minnesota Press, 1954.

Meehl, P. E. Seer over sign: The first good example. *Journal of Experimental Research in Personality*, 1965, *1*, 27–32.

Meehl, P. E. Why I do not attend case conferences. In P. E. Meehl, *Psychodiagnosis: Selected papers*. Minneapolis: University of Minnesota Press, 1973.

Meier-Graeffe, J. *Vincent Van Gogh: A biographical study*. (J. Holroyd-Reece, Trans.). New York: Blue Ribbon Books, 1933.

Merton, R. *Social theory and social structure*. New York: Free Press, 1968 ed.

Metcalfe, M. Demonstration of a psychosomatic relationship. *British Journal of Medical Psychology*, 1956, *29*, 63–66.

Meyer, B. C. Some reflections on the contribution of psychoanalysis to biography. In R. Holt & E. Peterfreund (Eds.), *Psychoanalysis and contemporary science* (Vol. 1). New York: International Universities Press, 1972.

Miers, E. *Lincoln day by day: A chronology*, 3 vols. Washington, D.C.: Lincoln Sesquicentennial Commission, 1960.

Milgram, S. *Obedience to authority*. New York: Harper & Row, 1974.

Mink, L. O. History and fiction as modes of comprehension. *New Literary History*, 1969–70, *1*, 541–558.

Mischel, W. *Personality and assessment*. New York: Wiley, 1968.

Mischel, W. Toward a cognitive social learning reconceptualization of personality. *Psychological Review*, 1973, *80*, 252–283.

Mitzman, A. *The iron cage: An historical interpretation of Max Weber*. New York: Grosset & Dunlap, 1969.

Momigliano, A. *The development of Greek biography*. Cambridge, Mass.: Harvard University Press, 1971.

Monroe, R. R. The episodic psychoses of Vincent Van Gogh. *Journal of Nervous and Mental Disease*, 1978, *166*, 480–488.

Moos, R. *The human context: Environmental determinants of behavior*. New York: Wiley-Interscience, 1976.

Morris, J. N. *Versions of the self: Studies in English autobiography from John Bunyan to John Stuart Mill*. New York: Basic Books, 1966.

Mortimer, J. T. & Simmons, R. Adult socialization. *Annual Review of Sociology*, 1978, *4*, 421–454.

Mountjoy, P. T. & Sundberg, M. L. Ben Franklin the protobehaviorist I: Self-management of behavior. *The Psychological Record*, 1981, *31*, 13–24.

Murray, H. A., et al. *Explorations in personality*. New York: Oxford University Press, 1938.

Murray, H. A., et al. *Assessment of men*. New York: Rinehart, 1948.

Murray, H. A. Introduction. In A. Burton & R. Harris (Eds.), *Clinical studies of personality* (Vol. I). New York: Harper & Row, 1955.

Murray, H. A. Preparations for the scaffold of a comprehensive system. In S. Koch (Ed.), *Psychology: A study of a science* (Vol. 3). New York: McGraw-Hill, 1959.

Murray, H. A. *Endeavors in psychology: Selections from the personology of Henry A. Murray*. Edited by E. S. Shneidman. New York: Harper & Row, 1981.

Nagel, E. *The structure of science*. New York: Harcourt, Brace & World, 1961.

Nagera, H. *Vincent Van Gogh: A psychological study*. London: Allen & Unwin, 1967.

Nash, R. H. *Ideas of history. Vol. two: The critical philosophy of history*. New York: Dutton, 1969.

Nesselroade, J. R. & Baltes, P. B. (Eds.). *Longitudinal research in the study of behavior and development*. New York: Academic Press, 1979.

Nesselroade, J. R. & Baltes, P. B. Adolescent personality development and historical change: 1970–1972. *Monographs of the Society for Research in Child Development,* 1974, *39* (1, Serial No. 154).

Nesselroade, J. R. & Reese, H. W. (Eds.). *Life-span developmental psychology: Methodological issues.* New York: Academic Press, 1973.

Neu, J. *Emotion, thought & therapy.* Berkeley: University of California Press, 1977.

Neufeld, R. W. J. *Clinical quantitative methods.* New York: Grune and Stratton, 1977.

Neugarten, B. L. (Ed.). *Middle age and aging.* Chicago: University of Chicago Press, 1968.

Neugarten, B. L. & Datan, N. Sociological perspectives on the life cycle. In P. Baltes & K. Schaie (Eds.), *Life-span developmental psychology: Personality and socialization.* New York: Academic Press, 1973.

Nicolay, J. G. & Hay, J. *Abraham Lincoln: A history,* 10 vols. New York: The Century Co., 1890.

Nicolson, H. *The development of English biography.* London: Hogarth Press, 1928.

Niederland, W. G. *The Schreber case.* New York: Quadrangle, 1974.

Nisbett, R. E. & Borgida, E. Attribution and the psychology of prediction. *Journal of Personality and Social Psychology,* 1975, *32,* 932–943.

Nisbett, R. E. & Ross, L. *Human inference: Strategies and shortcomings of social judgment.* Englewood Cliffs, N.J.: Prentice-Hall, 1980.

Nisbett, R. E. & Wilson, T. D. Telling more than we can know: Verbal reports on mental processes. *Psychological Review,* 1977, *84,* 231–259.

Nunnally, J. C. An investigation of some propositions of self-conception: The case of Miss Sun. *Journal of Abnormal and Social Psychology,* 1955, *50,* 87–92.

Nunnally, J. C. *Psychometric theory,* 2nd ed. New York: McGraw-Hill, 1978.

OSS Assessment Staff. *Assessment of men.* New York: Rinehart & Co., 1948.

Olweus, D. A critical analysis of the "modern" interactionist position. In D. Magnusson & N. Endler (Eds.), *Personality at the crossroads.* Hillsdale, N.J.: Erlbaum, 1977.

O'Neill, E. H. *A history of American biography 1800–1935.* New York: A. S. Barnes & Co., 1935.

Orlow, D. The significance of time and place in psychohistory. *Journal of Interdisciplinary History,* 1974, *1,* 131–138.

Overton, W. & Reese, H. Models of development: Methodological implications. In J. Nesselroade & H. Reese (Eds.), *Life span developmental psychology: Methodological issues*. New York: Academic Press, 1973.

Pachter, M. (Ed.). *Telling lives: The biographer's art*. Washington, D.C.: New Republic Books, 1979.

Pagels, E. *The gnostic gospels*. New York: Random House, 1979.

Paige, J. M. Letters from Jenny: An approach to the clinical analysis of personality structure by computer. In P. Stone (Ed.), *The general inquirer: A computer approach to content analysis*. Cambridge, Mass.: M.I.T. Press, 1966.

Pascal, R. *Design and truth in autobiography*. Cambridge, Mass.: Harvard University Press, 1960.

Paul, S. *Begegnungen. Zur Geschichte personlicher Dokumente in Ethnologie, Soziologie, Psychologie* (Encounters. Contribution to the history of personal documents in ethnology, sociology, psychology), 2 vols. Hohenschaftlarn, Austria: Klaus Renner Verlag, 1979.

Payne, R. *The life and death of Lenin*. New York: Simon and Schuster, 1964.

Perry, R. B. *The thought and character of William James*. Boston: Little, Brown, 1936.

Pervin, L. Some perspectives on the dichotomy between internal and external determinants of behavior. In L. Pervin and M. Lewis (Eds.), *Internal and external determinants of behavior*. New York: Plenum, 1978.

Peterson, D. *The clinical study of social behavior*. New York: Appleton-Century-Crofts, 1968.

Peterson, D. A functional approach to the study of person-person interactions. In D. Magnusson & N. Endler (Eds.), *Personality at the crossroads*. Hillsdale, N.J.: Erlbaum, 1977.

Peterson, M. D. *The Jefferson image in the American mind*. New York: Oxford University Press, 1960.

Platt, J. & Labate, C. *Heroin addiction: Theory, research, and treatment*. New York: Wiley, 1976.

Plutarch. *The lives of the noble Grecians and Romans*. Clough translation. New York: Modern Library, 1864.

Polansky, N. A. How shall a life-history be written? *Character and Personality*, 1941, *9*, 188–207.

Popper, K. R. *Conjectures and refutations*. New York: Basic Books, 1972.

Pressey, S. & Kuhlen, R. *Psychological development through the life span*. New York: Harper and Brothers, 1957.

Progoff, I. The psychology of Lee Harvey Oswald: A Jungian approach. *Journal of Individual Psychology*, 1966, *23*, 37–47.

Pye, L. Letter to the editor. *Psychohistory Review*, 1979, *8*(3), 50–53.

Qualls, J. H. Barber's typological analysis of political leaders. *American Political Science Review*, 1977, *71*, 182–211.

Radin, P. (Ed.). *Crashing Thunder: The autobiography of an American Indian*. New York: Appleton, 1926.

Raush, H. Interaction sequences. *Journal of Personality and Social Psychology*, 1965, *2*, 487–499.

Raush, H., et al. *Communication, conflict and marriage: Explorations in the theory and study of intimate relationships*. San Francisco: Jossey-Bass, 1974.

Reich, W. *Character analysis* (1933a). New York: Noonday Press, 1949.

Reich, W. *The mass psychology of fascism* (1933b). New York: Farrar, Straus and Giroux, 1973.

Reich, W. *The function of the orgasm* (1942). New York: World Publishing Co., 1971.

Reinert, G. Prolegomena to a history of life-span developmental psychology. In P. Baltes (Ed.), *Life-span development and behavior* (Vol. 1). New York: Academic Press, 1979.

Reith, G., Crockett, D., & Craig, K. Personality characteristics in heroin addicts and non-addicted prisoners using the Edwards Personal Preference Schedule. *International Journal of the Addictions*, 1975, *10*, 97–112.

Rewald, J. *Post-impressionism from Van Gogh to Gauguin*. New York: Museum of Modern Art, 1956.

Ricks, D. F. Life history research in psychopathology: Retrospect and prospect. In M. Roff and D. F. Ricks (Eds.), *Life history research in psychopathology* (Vol. 1). Minneapolis: University of Minnesota Press, 1970.

Ricks, D. F., Thomas, A., & Roff, M. (Eds.). *Life history research in psychopathology* (Vol. 3). Minneapolis: University of Minnesota Press, 1974.

Ricks, D. F. Supershrink: Methods of a therapist judged successful on the basis of adult outcomes of adolescent patients. In D. F. Ricks et al. (Eds.), *Life history research in psychopathology* (Vol. 3). Minneapolis: University of Minnesota Press, 1974.

Ricoeur, P. The question of proof in Freud's psychoanalytic writings. *Journal of the American Psychoanalytic Association*, 1977, *25*, 835–872.

Riegel, K. F. Adult life crises: A dialectic interpretation of development.

In N. Datan & L. Ginsberg (Eds.), *Life-span developmental psychology: Normative life crises.* New York: Academic Press, 1975.

Riley, M. W. (Ed.). *Aging from birth to death.* Boulder, Colo.: Westview, 1979.

Riley, M. W., Johnson, W., & Foner, A. (Eds.). *Aging and society, Vol 3: A sociology of age stratification.* New York: Russell Sage Foundation, 1972.

Roff, M. & Ricks, D. (Eds.). *Life history research in psychopathology* (Vol. 1). Minneapolis: University of Minnesota Press, 1970.

Roff, M., Robins, L., & Pollack, M. (Eds.). *Life history research in psychopathology* (Vol. 2). Minneapolis: University of Minnesota Press, 1972.

Rogers, C. R. Ellen West—and loneliness. In C. R. Rogers, *A way of being.* Boston: Houghton Mifflin, 1980.

Rogin, M. P. *Fathers and children: Andrew Jackson and the subjugation of the American Indian.* New York: Knopf, 1975.

Rogow, A. A. *The psychiatrists.* New York: Putnam's, 1970.

Rosaldo, R. The story of Tukbaw: "They listen as he orates." In F. Reynolds & D. Capps, *The biographical process: Studies in the history and psychology of religion.* The Hague: Mouton, 1976.

Rosaldo, R. *Ilongot headhunting, 1883 to 1974: A study in society and history.* Stanford: Stanford University Press, 1980.

Rosenberg, S. & Jones, R. A method for investigating and representing a person's implicit theory of personality: Theodore Dreiser's view of people. *Journal of Personality and Social Psychology,* 1972, *22,* 372–386.

Rosenzweig, S. The place of the individual and of idiodynamics in psychology: A dialogue. *Journal of Individual Psychology,* 1958, *14,* 3–21.

Ross, L. The intuitive psychologist and his shortcomings: Distortions in the attribution process. In L. Berkowitz (Ed.), *Advances in experimental social psychology* (Vol. 10). New York: Academic Press, 1977.

Runyan, W. M. How should treatment recommendations be made? Three studies in the logical and empirical bases of clinical decision making. *Journal of Consulting and Clinical Psychology,* 1977, *45,* 552–558.

Runyan, W. M. The life course as a theoretical orientation: Sequences of person-situation interaction. *Journal of Personality,* 1978, *46,* 569–593. (a)

Runyan, W. M. Review of D. B. Bromley, *Personality description in ordinary language.* In *Journal of Personality Assessment,* 1978, *42,* 547–549. (b)

Runyan, W. M. Alternative accounts of lives: An argument for epistemological relativism. *Biography,* 1980, *3,* 209–224. (a)

Runyan, W. M. A stage-state analysis of the life course. *Journal of Personality and Social Psychology,* 1980, *38,* 951–962. (b)

Runyan, W. M. Why did Van Gogh cut off his ear? The problem of alternative explanations in psychobiography. *Journal of Personality and Social Psychology,* 1981, *40,* 1070–1077.

Runyan, W. M. In defense of the case study method. *American Journal of Orthopsychiatry,* 1982, *52,* 440–446. (a)

Runyan, W. M. The psychobiography debate: An analytical review. In L. Wheeler (Ed.), *Review of Personality and Social Psychology* (Vol. 3). Beverly Hills, Calif.: Sage, 1982. (b)

Rutter, M. *Maternal deprivation reassessed,* 2nd ed. New York: Penguin, 1981.

Saks, M. J. *Jury verdicts: The role of group size and social decision rule.* Lexington, Mass.: Lexington Books, 1977.

Sarason, S. B. *Work, aging, and social change.* New York: Free Press, 1977.

Sargent, H., et al. *Prediction in psychotherapy research.* New York: International Universities Press, 1968.

Sartre, J. P. *Baudelaire.* New York: New Directions, 1950.

Sartre, J. P. *Saint Genet.* New York: New American Library, 1952.

Sartre, J. P. *The family idiot: Gustave Flaubert, 1821–1857.* (Vol. 1) (tr. C. Cosman). Chicago: University of Chicago Press, 1981.

Sawyer, J. Measurement *and* prediction, clinical *and* statistical. *Psychological Bulletin,* 1966, *66,* 178–200.

Schank, R. & Abelson, R. *Scripts, plans, goals and understanding: An inquiry into human knowledge structures.* Hillsdale, N.J.: LEA, 1977.

Scharfstein, B. *The philosophers: Their lives and the nature of their thought.* New York: Oxford University Press, 1980.

Schatzman, M. *Soul murder.* New York: Random House, 1973.

Schneider, D. E. *The psychoanalyst and the artist.* New York: International Universities Press, 1950.

Schneider, D. J. Implicit personality theory: A review. *Psychological Bulletin,* 1973, *79,* 294–309.

Schneider, D. J., Hastorf, A. H., & Ellsworth, P. C. *Person Perception,* 2nd ed. Reading, Mass.: Addison-Wesley, 1979.

Schnier, J. The blazing sun: A psychoanalytic approach to Van Gogh. *American Imago,* 1950, *7,* 143–162.

Schoenbaum, S. *Shakespeare's lives.* New York: Oxford University Press, 1970.

Schoenwald, R. L. Using psychology in history: A review essay. *Historical Methods Newsletter,* 1973, 7(1), 9–24.

Scholes, R. & Kellogg, R. *The nature of narrative.* New York: Oxford University Press, 1966.

Schutz, A. *Collected papers, Vol. 1: The problem of social reality.* The Hague: Martinus Nijhoff, 1962.

Schweitzer, A. *The quest of the historical Jesus.* (Trans. W. Montgomery). New York: Macmillan, 1910.

Schweitzer, A. *The psychiatric study of Jesus: Exposition and criticism* (1913). Boston: Beacon Press, 1948.

Sears, R. R., Lapidus, D. & Cozzens, C. Content analysis of Mark Twain's novels and letters as a biographical method. *Poetics,* 1978, 7, 155–175.

Seeman, W. & Galanter, E. Objectivity in systematic and "idiodynamic" psychology. *Psychological Review,* 1952, 59, 285–289.

Shapiro, M. B. The single case in fundamental clinical psychological research. *British Journal of Medical Psychology,* 1961, 34, 255–262.

Shapiro, M. B. The single case in clinical psychological research. *Journal of General Psychology,* 1966, 74, 3–23.

Shaw, B. Life history writing in anthropology: A methodological review. *Mankind,* 1980, 12, 226–233.

Shaw, C. R. *The jack-roller: A delinquent boy's own story.* Chicago: University of Chicago Press, 1930.

Shaw, C. R. *The natural history of a delinquent career.* Chicago: University of Chicago Press, 1931.

Shaw, C. R. *Brothers in crime.* Chicago: University of Chicago Press, 1936.

Sheppard, C., Ricca, E., Fracchia, J., & Merlis, S. Personality characteristics of urban and suburban heroin abusers: More data and another reply to Sutker and Allain (1973). *Psychological Reports,* 1973, 33, 999–1008.

Sherwood, M. *The logic of explanation in psychoanalysis.* New York: Academic Press, 1969.

Shorter, E. *The making of the modern family.* New York: Basic Books, 1975.

Sigerist, H. E. *The great doctors: A biographical history of medicine.* Garden City, N.Y.: Doubleday, 1958.

Silverman, M. A. A fresh look at the case of Little Hans. In M. Kanzer & J. Glenn (Eds.), *Freud and his patients.* New York: Aronson, 1980.

Simmons, L. W. *Sun Chief: The autobiography of a Hopi Indian*. New Haven: Yale University Press, 1942.

Simonton, D. K. Sociocultural context of individual creativity: A trans-historical time-series analysis. *Journal of Personality and Social Psychology*, 1975, *32*, 1119–1133.

Simonton, D. K. Biographical determinants of achieved eminence: A multivariate approach to the Cox data. *Journal of Personality and Social Psychology*, 1976, *33*, 218–226.

Simonton, D. K. Creative productivity, age, and stress: A biographical time-series analysis of 10 classical composers. *Journal of Personality and Social Psychology*, 1977, *35*, 791–804.

Simonton, D. K. The library laboratory: Archival data in personality and social psychology. In L. Wheeler (Ed.), *Review of Personality and Social Psychology* (Vol. 2). Beverly Hills, Calif.: Sage, 1981.

Skaggs, E. B. Personalistic psychology as science. *Psychological Review*, 1945, *52*, 234–238.

Skinner, B. F. *Science and human behavior*. New York: Macmillan, 1953.

Skinner, B. F. B. F. Skinner (autobiography). In E. G. Boring & G. Lindzey (Eds.), *A history of psychology in autobiography* (Vol. 5). New York: Appleton-Century-Crofts, 1967.

Skinner, B. F. *Particulars of my life*. New York: Knopf, 1976.

Skinner, B. F. *The shaping of a behaviorist*. New York: Knopf, 1979.

Slovic, P. & Lichtenstein, S. Comparison of Bayesian and regression approaches to the study of information processing in judgment. *Organizational Behavior and Human Performance*, 1971, *6*, 649–744.

Smelser, N. J. & Erikson, E. H. (Eds.). *Themes of work and love in adulthood*. Cambridge, Mass.: Harvard University Press, 1980.

Smith, P. Luther's early development in the light of psycho-analysis. *American Journal of Psychology*, 1913, *24*, 360–377.

Snyder, C. R. & Fromkin, H. L. *Uniqueness: The human pursuit of difference*. New York: Plenum, 1980.

Solomon, M. *Beethoven*. New York: Schirmer Books, 1977.

Spence, D. P. Clinical interpretation: Some comments on the nature of evidence. In T. Shapiro (Ed.), *Psychoanalysis and contemporary science* (Vol. V). New York: International Universities Press, 1976.

Stanfield, J. *An essay on the study and composition of biography*. Sunderland, England: Garbutt, 1813.

Stannard, D. E. *Shrinking history: On Freud and the failure of psychohistory*. New York: Oxford University Press, 1980.

Staude, J.-R. *The adult development of C. G. Jung*. Boston: Routledge & Kegan Paul, 1981.

versity of Chicago

A psychoanalytic
1954.
bjectivity in per-

ge & Kegan Paul,

evised: A critical

he Psychohistory

tion. In A. Gold-
rk: International

research. Beverly

e psychoanalytic

Urbana: Univer-

addicts: A per-
32, 243–246.
liffs, N.J.: Pren-

sychobiography.

ographers. Free-

in Europe and
on: Richard C.
7.
d: Oxford Uni-

models of social
9, 29–44.
structure. Lin-

nstructive role
for his society.
rd. Princeton:

Tralbaut, M. E. *Vincent Van*

Triandis, H. C. Some univ
   Social Psychology Bull

Tucker, R. C. *Stalin as rev*
   and personality. New

Tucker, R. C. The Georges'
   biography. *American*
   618.

Tversky, A. & Kahneman, D
   and biases. *Science*, 19

Tyler, L. E. *Individuality:*
   the psychological deve
   Jossey-Bass, 1978.

Ullmann, L. P. & Krasner,
   New York: Holt, Rine

Untermeyer, L. *Makers of* t
   Schuster, 1955.

U.S. House of Representati
   Assassinations. *The Fi*
   tam, 1979.

Vaillant, G. E. *Adaptation to*

Vernon, P. E. The matching
   sonality. *Psychological*

Vernon, P. E. *Personality ass*
   1964.

Vinovskis, M. A. From hous
   havioral Scientist, 197

Wachtel, P. Psychodynamics
   perimeter: An inqui
   nal of Abnormal Psyc

Wachtel, P. Interaction cyc
   situation issue. In D.
   at the crossroads, Hill

Waite, R. G. L. *The psycho*
   Books, 1977.

Walsh, W. H. *Philosophy*
   York: Harper Torchb

Ward, T. *The capsule of*
   Dickinson. Cambridg

Watson, L. C. Understandi
   Hermeneutical and p
   4, 95–131.

Stephenson, W. *The study of behavior*. Chicago: University of Chicago Press, 1953.

Sterba, E. & Sterba, R. *Beethoven and his nephew: A psychoanalytic study of their relationship*. New York: Pantheon, 1954.

Stolorow, R. D. & Atwood, G. E. *Faces in a cloud: Subjectivity in personality theory*. New York: Aronson, 1979.

Stone, L. *The past and the present*. Boston: Routledge & Kegan Paul, 1981.

Storr, A. The man. In A. J. P. Taylor (Ed.), *Churchill revised: A critical assessment*. New York: Dial Press, 1968.

Strozier, C. B. Communications from the editor. *The Psychohistory Review*, 1979, 7(3), 5.

Strozier, C. B. Heinz Kohut and the historical imagination. In A. Goldberg (Ed.), *Advances in self psychology*. New York: International Universities Press, 1980.

Struening, E. & Guttentag, M. *Handbook of evaluation research*. Beverly Hills, Calif.: Sage, 1975.

Sulloway, F. J. *Freud, biologist of the mind: Beyond the psychoanalytic legend*. New York: Basic Books, 1979.

Suppe, F. *The structure of scientific theories* (2nd ed.). Urbana: University of Illinois, 1977.

Sutker, P. & Allain, A. Incarcerated and street heroin addicts: A personality comparison. *Psychological Reports*, 1973, *32*, 243–246.

Tallent, N. *Psychological report writing*. Englewood Cliffs, N.J.: Prentice-Hall, 1976.

Tetlock, P. E., Crosby, F., & Crosby, T. L. Political psychobiography. *Micropolitics*, 1981, *1*, 191–213.

Thomas, B. P. *Portrait for posterity: Lincoln and his biographers*. Freeport, N.Y.: Books for Libraries Press, 1947.

Thomas, W. I. & Znaniecki, F. *The Polish peasant in Europe and America*. (Originally, 5 volumes, 1918–1920, Boston: Richard C. Badger). New York: Knopf (2-volume edition), 1927.

Thompson, P. *The voice of the past: Oral history*. Oxford: Oxford University Press, 1978.

Tibbitt, J. E. A sociological comparison of stochastic models of social mobility. *Sociological Review Monographs*, 1973, *19*, 29–44.

Toliver, H. *Animate illusions: Explorations of narrative structure*. Lincoln: University of Nebraska Press, 1974.

Tomkins, S. S. The psychology of commitment: The constructive role of violence and suffering for the individual and for his society. In M. Duberman (Ed.), *The antislavery vanguard*. Princeton: Princeton University Press, 1965.

Tralbaut, M. E. *Vincent Van Gogh*. New York: Macmillan, 1969.

Triandis, H. C. Some universals of social behavior. *Personality and Social Psychology Bulletin*, 1978, *4*, 1–16.

Tucker, R. C. *Stalin as revolutionary 1879–1929: A study in history and personality*. New York: Norton, 1973.

Tucker, R. C. The Georges' Wilson reexamined: An essay on psychobiography. *American Political Science Review*, 1977, *71*, 606–618.

Tversky, A. & Kahneman, D. Judgment under uncertainty: Heuristics and biases. *Science*, 1974, *184*, 1124–1131.

Tyler, L. E. *Individuality: Human possibilities and personal choice in the psychological development of men and women*. San Francisco: Jossey-Bass, 1978.

Ullmann, L. P. & Krasner, L. *Case studies in behavior modification*. New York: Holt, Rinehart & Winston, 1965.

Untermeyer, L. *Makers of the modern world*. New York: Simon and Schuster, 1955.

U.S. House of Representatives, Report of the Select Committee on Assassinations. *The Final Assassinations Report*. New York: Bantam, 1979.

Vaillant, G. E. *Adaptation to life*. Boston: Little, Brown, 1977.

Vernon, P. E. The matching method applied to investigations of personality. *Psychological Bulletin*, 1936, *33*, 149–177.

Vernon, P. E. *Personality assessment: A critical survey*. New York: Wiley, 1964.

Vinovskis, M. A. From household size to the life course. *American Behavioral Scientist*, 1977, *21*, 263–287.

Wachtel, P. Psychodynamics, behavior therapy, and the implacable experimenter: An inquiry into the consistency of personality. *Journal of Abnormal Psychology*, 1973, *82*, 323–334.

Wachtel, P. Interaction cycles, unconscious processes, and the person-situation issue. In D. Magnusson & N. Endler (Eds.), *Personality at the crossroads*, Hillsdale, N.J.: Erlbaum, 1977.

Waite, R. G. L. *The psychopathic God: Adolf Hitler*. New York: Basic Books, 1977.

Walsh, W. H. *Philosophy of history: An introduction*, rev. ed. New York: Harper Torchbooks, 1967.

Ward, T. *The capsule of the mind: Chapters in the life of Emily Dickinson*. Cambridge, Mass.: Harvard University Press, 1961.

Watson, L. C. Understanding a life history as a subjective document: Hermeneutical and phenomenological perspectives. *Ethos*. 1976, *4*, 95–131.

Wedding, D. & Corsini, R. J. (Eds.). *Great cases in psychotherapy*. Itasca, Ill.: Peacock, 1979.

Wedge, B. Khrushchev at a distance—A study of public personality. *Transaction*, 1968, *5*(10), 24–29.

Weinstein, E., Anderson, J., & Link, A. Woodrow Wilson's political personality: A reappraisal. *Political Science Quarterly*, 1978, *93*, 585–598.

Wells, H. G. *Experiment in autobiography*. New York: Macmillan, 1934.

Westerman Holstijn, A. J. The psychological development of Vincent Van Gogh. *American Imago*, 1951, *8*, 239–273.

Wheelright, P. (Ed.). *Aristotle*. New York: Odyssey, 1951.

Whilbey, C. The indiscretions of biography. *English Review*, 1924, *39*, 769–772.

White, M. *Foundations of historical knowledge*. New York: Harper Torchbooks, 1965.

White, R. W. *Lives in progress*. New York: Holt, Rinehart & Winston, 1952; 2nd ed., 1966; 3rd ed., 1975.

White, R. W. (Ed.). *The study of lives*. New York: Atherton, 1966.

White, R. W. *The enterprise of living*. New York: Holt, Rinehart & Winston, 1972.

Wiggins, J. S. *Personality and prediction: Principles of personality assessment*. Reading, Mass.: Addison-Wesley, 1973.

Wilson, E. Woodrow Wilson at Princeton. In *Shores of light*. New York: Farrar, Straus and Young, 1952.

Windelband, W. *Geschichte und Naturwissenschaft*, 3rd ed. Strassburg: Heitz, 1904.

Winer, B. J. *Statistical principles in experimental design* (2nd ed.). New York: McGraw-Hill, 1971.

Wittels, F. *Sigmund Freud: His personality, his teaching, and his school* (1923). New York: Dodd, Mead, 1924.

Wittels, F. Revision of a biography. *The Psychoanalytic Review*, 1933, *20*(4), 361–374.

Wolfenstein, E. V. *The revolutionary personality: Lenin, Trotsky, Gandhi*. Princeton: Princeton University Press, 1967.

Wolfenstein, E. V. *The victims of democracy: Malcolm X and the Black revolution*. Berkeley: University of California Press, 1981.

Wolpe, J. & Rachman, S. Psychoanalytic "evidence": A critique based on Freud's case of Little Hans. *Journal of Nervous and Mental Disease*, 1960, *131*, 135–148.

Wolstein, B. Toward a conception of unique individuality. *Contemporary Psychoanalysis*, 1975, *11*, 146–160.

Woods, D. *Biko*. New York: Vintage, 1978.

Woods, J. M. Some considerations on psycho-history. *The Historian*, 1974, *6*(4), 722–735.

Wrightsman, L. S. Personal documents as data in conceptualizing adult personality development. *Personality and Social Psychology Bulletin*, 1981, 7, 367–385.

Wyatt, F. Psychoanalytic biography. (A review of P. Greenacre, *Swift and Carroll*). *Contemporary Psychology*, 1956, *1*, 105–107.

Yarrow, M., Campbell, J., & Burton, J. Recollections of childhood: A study of the retrospective method. *Monographs of the Society for Research in Child Development*, 1970, *35*: 5.

Yinger, J. M. *Toward a field theory of behavior*. New York: McGraw-Hill, 1965.

Young, K. *Personality and problems of adjustment*. New York: Appleton-Century-Crofts, 1952.

Index

The Author

William McKinley Runyan is Assistant Professor in the School of Social Welfare, and Assistant Research Psychologist at the Institute of Personality Assessment and Research, both at the University of California, Berkeley. He received his Ph.D. in Clinical Psychology and Public Practice from Harvard University in 1975, and was a post-doctoral fellow at the Institute of Human Development at the University of California, Berkeley.